The Rise of Global Corporate Social Responsibility

Combining insights from international relations theory with institutional approaches from organization theory and public policy, this book provides a complete explanation for the adoption of corporate social responsibility (CSR), showing how global norms influenced CSR adoption in the mining industry. Global normative developments have clearly had an important influence on major mining companies: by the mid-2000s, the majority had adopted sustainable development as a normative frame for their CSR policies and practices. However, there is significant variation between firms in terms of the timing, degree of commitment, and the willingness to assume a leadership role in promoting global standards for the mining industry. The author finds that attributes internal to the firm, including the critical role of leadership, and the way in which management responds to the institutional context and operational challenges faced in different countries are important influences on CSR adoption and important factors explaining variation.

HEVINA S. DASHWOOD is Associate Professor of Political Science at Brock University, Canada. Her broad research and teaching interests encompass international political economy, the role of non-state actors in global governance, international public policy, and Canadian foreign policy. Professor Dashwood is the author of numerous journal articles and book chapters on corporate social responsibility (CSR) in the mining sector, and has conducted case-study research on Canadian mining companies' CSR in Africa and Latin America.

Business and Public Policy

Series Editor:

ASEEM PRAKASH, University of Washington

Series Board:

Vinod K. Aggarwal, University of California, Berkeley
Tanja A. Börzel, Freie Universität Berlin
David Coen, University College London
Peter Gourevitch, University of California, San Diego
Neil Gunningham, The Australian National University
Witold J. Henisz, University of Pennsylvania
Adrienne Héritier, European University Institute
Chung-in Moon, Yonsei University
Sarah A. Soule, Stanford University
David Vogel, University of California, Berkeley

This series aims to play a pioneering role in shaping the emerging field of business and public policy. *Business and Public Policy* focuses on two central questions. First, how does public policy influence business strategy, operations, organization, and governance, and with what consequences for both business and society? Second, how do businesses themselves influence policy institutions, policy processes, and other policy actors, and with what outcomes?

Other books in the series:

TIMOTHY WERNER, *Public Forces and Private Politics in American Big Business*

The Rise of Global Corporate Social Responsibility

Mining and the Spread of Global Norms

HEVINA S. DASHWOOD
Brock University, Canada

CAMBRIDGE
UNIVERSITY PRESS

CAMBRIDGE UNIVERSITY PRESS
Cambridge, New York, Melbourne, Madrid, Cape Town,
Singapore, São Paulo, Delhi, Mexico City

Cambridge University Press
The Edinburgh Building, Cambridge CB2 8RU, UK

Published in the United States of America by Cambridge University Press, New York

www.cambridge.org
Information on this title: www.cambridge.org/9781107015531

First published 2012

Printed and Bound in Great Britain by the MPG Books Group

A catalog record for this publication is available from the British Library

Library of Congress Cataloging in Publication data
Dashwood, Hevina S. (Hevina Smith), 1960–
The rise of global corporate social responsibility: mining and the spread of global norms /
Hevina S. Dashwood.
pages   cm. – (Business and public policy)
ISBN 978-1-107-01553-1 (hardback)
1. Mineral industries – Management – Moral and ethical aspects.   2. Social
responsibility of business.   3. Corporate governance.   I. Title.
HD9506.A2.D37   2012
622.068'4–dc23
2012007516

ISBN 978-1-107-01553-1 Hardback

To my parents, J. Noreen and James W. Smith

Contents

Figures

Tables

Preface

The research and writing of this book has been a long journey that began in the early 2000s. The question I wanted to explore was to what extent emerging global corporate social responsibility (CSR) "norms" (standards) influenced the policies and practices of major mining companies. With support from the Social Sciences and Humanities Research Council of Canada (SSHRC) in the form of a Standard Research Grant, I commenced research hoping to find answers within my field of international relations. It did not take me long to realize that the international relations literature could provide only a partial answer to my research question. Global CSR norms are important, as evidenced in the uptake of sustainable development norms by mining companies, but the explanation for CSR adoption requires a multidisciplinary approach. Preliminary interviews with company officials revealed that operational challenges in the countries in which they had operations were a major influence on the adoption of CSR policies and specific practices.

The significance of institutional context led me to adopt a three-level institutional approach, drawing from rational choice institutionalism, historical institutionalism and the "new" institutionalism in organization theory. Together with the global governance and constructivist literature in international relations theory, I was able to develop a more complete explanation of CSR adoption on the part of major mining companies. A major contribution of this study is that it builds bridges between different methodological and theoretical approaches, and crucial debates on the role of norms/interests and agency/structure in shaping action.

I owe a huge intellectual debt to Aseem Prakash, editor of the series in which this book is published, who provided exceptional direction and guidance. He drew my attention to the promise of institutional analysis and provided invaluable insight into how to execute this project. Aseem has been a major source of support in encouraging me to publish my research in various scholarly outlets, and in overseeing the completion of this book. I would also like to thank the two anonymous reviewers, whose careful reading of the manuscript and constructive comments allowed me to further refine the theoretical and methodological approach. I am grateful to John Haslam and Carrie Parkinson for their patient oversight in moving the manuscript forward.

This study involved case-study research of three major Canadian mining companies, Noranda, Placer Dome and Barrick Gold. I am very grateful to the people from these companies who gave so generously of their time. It can often be challenging for social scientists to gain access to busy people in major companies, even more so since they are not always prepared to divulge pertinent information. In this respect, I was very fortunate to have the full support of all three companies. I would like to thank my "key informants" from Noranda and Placer Dome who, even though they are all retired, kindly met and/or talked with me multiple times over a good many years. These include Dr. Frank Frantisak and David Rodier (Noranda) and James Cooney (Placer Dome). Many other company officials within those companies kindly provided their time, as did officials at Barrick Gold. With their help, I have been able to systematically examine the variation in CSR adoption among major mining companies, constituting an important empirical contribution.

Many others provided helpful input on this book. I am grateful to Virginia Haufler, who very generously provided theoretical guidance at an early stage of this book's development. Tony Porter, Fred Bird, Rosalyn Warner, Steve Bernstein, Mary Louise McAllister, Wes Cragg, Fred Eidlin, and Kernaghan Webb also provided useful insights on various aspects of the book. Through research collaboration with Bill Puplampu, I have gained insights on CSR in the developing country context. I would like to thank my colleagues at Brock University, Dan Madar, who pointed me to some very useful data sources, and Livianna Tossutti, who provided excellent guidance on research methods. A number of graduate students at Brock University provided superb research assistance, including Calum McNeil, Katie Winstanley, Isaac Odoom, Jeff Cornelissen, Nathan Andrews, and Denis Dogah. I also benefited greatly from the research assistance of Chris Hann (BA, Brock University), who helped with some critically important data compilation.

This book may well not have been written without the love and support of my family. My husband, Geoff, provided unwavering support over the years. My two sons, James and John, in addition to putting up with a sometimes distracted mother, also provided invaluable IT support. They instructed me to acknowledge our springer spaniel, Cedric, who kept me company during the many lonely hours of writing. Finally, I am grateful for the support and encouragement of my parents, J. Noreen and James W. Smith, throughout my academic career. It is to them that this book is dedicated.

1 | Introduction

Over the past two decades, private companies have made increasing efforts at the global level to promote corporate social responsibility (CSR) in the environmental, labor, and human rights realms. This book traces private sector initiatives at the global, or international, level to promote social and environmental standards applicable to the mining sector. In light of the fact that private corporations are not subjects of international environmental and human rights treaties, the numerous voluntary or quasi-voluntary initiatives undertaken by the private sector, alone or together with states and non-governmental organizations (NGOs) at the global level, assume a degree of importance in the global push to promote CSR. This book asks how and to what extent emerging global CSR norms (collectively held understandings of appropriate behavior) have an impact on the policies and practices of mining multinationals.

For the past decade or two, mining companies have been struggling to improve the bad reputation they acquired through the environmental devastation and social disruption associated with their operations. The mining industry has left a legacy of polluted water through acid-rock drainage, toxic waste associated with metals processing, airborne pollution associated with smelting processes, and the massive displacement of earth in the case of open-pit mining (Diamond 2005: 441–85; Miranda et al. 2003). Social dislocation associated with mining, brought to the world's attention by the media and NGOs, has further worked to damage the reputation of the mining industry as a whole.

An exploration of the influence of global CSR norms on mining companies is theoretically interesting, because for mining companies to voluntarily seek to improve their environmental and social performance is contrary to what might be expected of them. The very severe and long-lasting nature of pollution problems associated with mining increases the financial burden of environmental responsibility, which would lead one to expect that mining executives would be reactive and defensive about their policies and practices. As such, a focus on the mining sector represents a "hard" case for theorizing on CSR. In the early 1990s, most mining companies remained content to treat environmental impacts as an externality and lacked a sense of responsibility towards the communities in which they operated. By the end of the 1990s, mining companies were much more attuned to their environmental and social responsibilities, and some mining companies took on a leading role in promoting global CSR norms relevant to the mining sector. How can these developments best be explained?

This book takes up the challenge raised by Campbell (2006) to come to a better theoretical understanding of the conditions under which firms are likely to behave in a socially responsible manner. This book contributes to the broad research agenda on CSR by employing a three-level institutional analysis, drawing on insights from rational choice institutionalism (which emphasizes instrumental motives), institutionalism in organization theory (which emphasizes cognitive processes and the normative environment), and historical institutionalism, to explain why firms adopt CSR policies, and the extent of their commitment to them. Furthermore, this book expands on the research agenda on CSR, by incorporating global normative dynamics into the analysis, and linking global developments with internal processes at the level of the firm.

A commonly held assumption is that profit maximizing firms are not swayed by normative considerations, but are motivated strictly by interests that can be defined in cost-benefit terms. Rational choice literature expects that a firm is primarily motivated by maximization of profit and shareholder value. Stakeholder theory extends the range of actors to which firms are considered responsible, but sees this as driven by the strategic rational choice to achieve organizational value-maximizing goals and improved profitability. Normative behavior is seen to be the preserve of NGOs, because firms are considered self-interested (instrumental) actors, while NGOs are portrayed as disinterested entities acting on principled beliefs (Keck and Sikkink 1998). This book argues that firms are responsive to normative shifts within the larger society for both strategic and normative reasons, and can themselves play a role in the dissemination of norms through collaborative efforts at industry self-regulation (Sell and Prakash 2004). As such, the argument is consistent with research that points to the interplay between strategic and norms-driven motives in explaining firm behavior (Cashore 2002; Cashore et al. 2004; Flohr et al. 2010; Prakash 2000; Sell and Prakash 2004; Suchman 1995).

At the time research was commenced for this book in the early 2000s, there was a huge interest in CSR, and a large body of literature had emerged on the role of NGOs in disseminating norms at the global level (for a review, see Price 2003). Within the Political Science discipline and social sciences more broadly, there was little in the way of conceptual tools or theoretical frameworks for analyzing the impact of global CSR norms on companies. Within the business literature, much had been written about the various drivers (such as pending regulation) influencing companies' CSR policies, but little attention had been paid to the role of emerging global CSR norms, or how they are diffused. In a special issue of *Corporate Governance*, the lack of research that can account for the relationship between business and global societal forces is lamented (2008). This book helps to fill that gap, by joining theories from International Relations scholarship with theories from the management and public policy literatures as a step towards developing a shared paradigmatic understanding of dynamic global political processes, and the place of global corporations within them.

Notwithstanding the profusion of literature on CSR over the past two decades (for a literature review, see Margolis and Walsh 2003; Orlitzky et al. 2003), research and theory building on why and under what conditions companies behave in socially responsible ways is underdeveloped (Buhner et al. 1998; Campbell 2006; Gunningham et al. 2003). After considerable attention in the 1970s from a critical political economy perspective, the international relations literature is only just reawakening to the role and importance of multinationals in global governance processes (see, for example, Bernstein and Cashore 2007; Grande and Pauly 2005; Keohane 2008; May 2006; Ruggie 2004).[1] The decision to focus on the mining sector was influenced by relatively recent efforts on the part of mining executives to develop global CSR standards applicable to mining, and the lack of research analyzing what is driving these efforts and their impact. Furthermore, there is a lack of balanced empirical studies on how and why individual mining

---

[1] Some would refer to the recognition of the role of multinationals in global governance as a "re-awakening," echoing earlier works in the 1970s on "transnational relations." (See Keohane 2008.)

companies have responded to global developments through their CSR policies and practices. This book is timely in that it meets an identified theoretical need to embrace multidisciplinary approaches to better understand the relationship of business to a globalized society. It fills an empirical gap with respect to the influence of global developments on the mining sector, the response of mining companies to those influences, and their role in disseminating global CSR norms.

The changing global context

The dissemination of global norms of corporate social responsibility is best conceptualized as a dynamic process, where multinationals are playing a central role, often in conjunction with NGOs and states. Firms need to be recognized as political actors in their own right, through their agenda, norms, and rule-setting behavior (Fuchs 2007; Haufler 2001). This study is broadly situated in the global governance literature that recognizes the importance of understanding the wide range of global actors who are active agents, or "governors," seeking to establish new structures and rules in order to solve problems that cannot be addressed through unilateral action (Avant et al. 2010).

Mining companies such as Noranda and Placer Dome were active at the global level, working through industry associations and international organizations to promote standards of behavior applicable to the mining sector. The most salient example of this is the creation in 1991 of the International Council on Metals and the Environment (ICME) and in 2001 of the ICME's successor organization, the International Council on Mining and Metals (ICMM). Through these efforts, global norms have not simply filtered down, but have also been shaped by companies themselves, in an interactive or dynamic process.

The role of private actors and norms in global governance reflects the growing complexity of global political and economic governance. The provision of public goods is no longer the preserve solely of governments, and private actors, such as NGOs and multinationals, are involved in global governance processes (Bernstein and Pauly 2007; Grande and Pauly 2005; Peters et al. 2009; Ruggie 2004; Schaferhoff et al. 2009). For example, mining industry representatives have participated in global public policy decision-making through the United Nations Environment Program (UNEP) and the World Bank, and have attended important global conferences, such as the 2002 World Summit on Sustainable Development in Johannesburg (UN 2002).

At the broadest level, the devolution of state authority to the local and global levels, and the emergence of private authority in some issue areas, created the political space for non-state actors, including NGOs and multinationals, to participate in governance at both the global and national levels (Hall and Biersteker 2002; Levy and Prakash 2003). This has resulted in more complex, multi-layered governance processes, involving a range of stakeholders (Bernstein and Coleman 2009; Lipschutz 2000; O'Brien et al. 2000; Scholte 2000).

The international relations literature which best captures these dynamics is the constructivist and global governance literature (for example, Ruggie 1998; Wendt 1992, 1999). Until recently, studies employing constructivist approaches have focused primarily on states and NGOs (Florini 2000; Keck and Sikkink 1998; Risse et al. 1999). Recent contributions to the literature on global governance have advanced understanding of the sorts of activities firms are engaged in at the global level (Fuchs 2007), and provided a more nuanced appreciation of the differentiated power position and preferences of firms across issues and sectors (Levy and Prakash 2003). Firms employ similar strategies to NGOs to set agendas and shape the discourse on issues of concern to them (Fuchs 2007; Sell and Prakash 2004). Firms are agents of norms dissemination, as much as they are influenced by norms at both the national and global levels (Dashwood 2007a, 2011; Flohr et al. 2010).

The devolution of the political authority of the state in some areas, and the development of new domains of governance involving multinational corporations, has now attracted scholarly attention in the global governance literature (Keohane 2008; Kollman 2008; Pattberg 2005; Ruggie 2004). Different forms of global governance structures involving multinationals and the promotion of CSR have developed. For example, governance systems involving companies and NGOs, but excluding states, have emerged that ensure compliance with environmental standards in sectors such as forestry (Bernstein 2006; Bernstein and Cashore 2007; Cashore 2002; Cashore et al. 2004; Falkner 2003). There is a growing literature on the potential for private governance in areas of "limited statehood," where CSR practiced by international business provides a "functional equivalent" to the governance normally provided by governments (Borzel and Risse 2010; Haufler 2010).

The emergence of private regimes, and the concept of private authority, is central to capturing the impact of emerging global norms of corporate social responsibility, as well as the role of multinationals in disseminating global CSR norms (Buthe 2010; Cutler 2003; Cutler et al. 1999; Hall and Biersteker 2002). Private authority is defined as non-state actors who "perform the role of authorship over some important issue or domain" (Hall and Biersteker 2002: 4). This literature is concerned with strictly private governance initiatives, either on the part of companies acting on their own, or collaborating to develop a common set of standards, but nevertheless operating within the context of a state-based international system.

Building on the concept of private authority is Ruggie's notion of a "reconstituted global public domain," which is being shaped by the interaction between civil society actors and multinational corporations, alongside states (Ruggie 2004, 2002; but see Cutler 2006). The point is not so much that there has been a shift in authority away from the state to the private sector, or that the state is in retreat (Strange 1996), but that the private sector has created a new transnational space (Ruggie 2004: 503). The provision of global public goods is no longer (if it ever was) the exclusive domain of the sovereign state and the interstate order. The state still has a role to play, as this new global public domain is conceived as "an increasingly institutionalized transnational arena of discourse, contestation, and action concerning the production of global public goods, involving private as well as public actors" (ibid.: 504).

Avant et al. (2010) demonstrate that the literature on global governance must account not only for the variation in types of global actors, but also the variation in actual governance that takes place. Global governance is best understood as a political process where variables such as power, access, mobilization, and leadership influence outcomes, such as the mechanisms chosen for resolving a problem (Avant et al. 2010: 7). Although multinationals are often considered to be all-powerful, it is important to distinguish between material sources of power, and discursive sources of power (Levy and Prakash 2003: 144–5). Mining companies had lost ground to environmental NGOs in setting the global agenda and framing debates. The leadership provided by a small number of mining companies was critical in efforts to reposition the global mining industry to align it more closely with shifting societal values. In so doing, leading mining companies set in motion a process that resulted in a transformation in how the industry addresses its environmental and social responsibilities.

The role of mining multinationals in global governance encapsulates elements of private authority. Many mining companies developed their own codes of conduct, and worked together to develop private governance structures through the ICME and then the ICMM. Mining companies have also sought extensive multistakeholder consultations with NGOs (and other interested parties) as part of the process that led to the creation of the ICMM. NGOs are regularly consulted as the ICMM develops voluntary standards to enhance the environmental and social performance of the mining sector. At the same time, the ICMM and individual mining companies have participated alongside states in international organizations to develop CSR standards relevant to mining. The most pertinent example of this is the World Bank's Extractive Industry Review (EIR), which entailed extensive consultations between the Bank, NGOs, and mining and oil and gas companies. These developments suggest that a hybrid public/private governance process is taking place at the global (and domestic) levels, where private sector norms are shaping the delivery of public goods (Clapp 1998).

Global norms and mining

Notwithstanding the huge interest in CSR, research and theory building on why and how companies embrace beyond-compliance measures is underdeveloped (Gunningham et al. 2003: 39). In the absence of a critical mass of empirical studies upon which theory could be developed, available theoretical tools for explaining the central research question of this book were found wanting. In particular, the existing theoretical literature proved ill-suited to explain three important findings that emerged from the research. The first is that most large mining multinationals came to adopt the norm of sustainable development as a means to frame their CSR policies, pointing to the impact of global CSR norms on these companies. The second finding is that senior management in the companies studied viewed the experience of mining in the countries where they had operations to be the single most important influence on their CSR policies, pointing to the importance of institutional context. Third, some mining multinationals have taken on leadership roles in disseminating CSR norms globally, pointing to the need to account for companies as actors in their own right, and the variation in timing in terms of the uptake of CSR norms.

Leading mining companies launched a major stakeholder consultation initiative (Global Mining Initiative) and worked through the ICME, and later the ICMM, to promote the concept of sustainable development. By the early 2000s, most major mining companies had converged around the norm of sustainable development, and by the late 2000s, a growing number of junior mining companies had accepted the normative validity of sustainable development. Of the companies surveyed in KPMG's *Global Mining Reporting Survey* (2006), 59% published a separate sustainability-related report in 2006, compared with 44% in 2003.[2] This trend also parallels developments in industry as a whole. The KPMG *International Survey of Corporate Responsibility Reporting* 2005, found a dramatic upward trend in the number of companies that had adopted sustainable development strategies, as reflected in reporting on social, environmental, and economic issues (KPMG 2005).

One could conclude that macro-level, or systemic, factors were therefore key to the explanation of why, starting in the late 1990s, mining multinationals came to adopt CSR policies framed as sustainable development. Certainly, the global normative weight of sustainable development provided the context within which mining multinationals came to frame their CSR policies. Yet, what is interesting is that there were early movers and late movers in terms of the adoption of CSR policies, and a small number of mining companies felt it necessary to take on a leadership role in the late 1990s, to bring other firms along. To account for these developments, firm-specific factors need to be brought into the explanation. An approach that is able to explain how norms work their influence on mining companies, and how mining companies themselves disseminate norms, becomes a central part of the explanation. Organizational processes and managerial leadership need to be factored in to explain the leadership roles undertaken by a small number of mining multinationals. At the same time, important studies have noted the dynamic and interdependent relationship between internal influences, external influences (including institutional dynamics), and

[2] KPMG surveyed forty-four companies in total, of which thirty-one are headquartered in the advanced industrialized economies.

intra-organizational factors (Galaskiewicz in Powell and DiMaggio 1991; Gunningham et al. 2003; Hoffman 1997). Attempts to isolate variables operating at the global level are therefore misguided, given the interdependence between macro and micro-level influences (Fuchs 2007; Levy and Prakash 2003).

Corporate social responsibility and sustainable development in mining: emerging patterns

CSR: a brief definition

There is no single definition of corporate social responsibility, and other terms have been used to describe roughly similar activities, such as business ethics, corporate citizenship, corporate governance, and sustainable development or sustainability. CSR is understood as the beyond-law obligations which companies must adhere to because their economic activities affect the social and ecological systems in which they are embedded (Culpeper and Whiteman 1998; Prakash 2000). Abiding by existing regulations represents the baseline of good corporate behavior (Carroll 1999). The notion that CSR is voluntary is misleading, because it can imply that CSR is philanthropy, in the sense that companies can simply choose which charity they might support. There is tension between what a firm's responsibilities are, and what it is deemed they should be. As the late Friedman famously postulated, so long as the firm's activities are legal, then the firm's primary responsibility is to maximize profit and shareholder value (Friedman 1970). Firms have a fiduciary responsibility towards their shareholders, but since Friedman first advanced his arguments, states have introduced regulations that impose legal requirements on firms respecting the treatment of labor, human rights, and the environment.

The term CSR connotes duties that, even if not legally required, entail obligations that resonate with societal norms and values. Not all of these norms are regulated. In short, CSR expects that organizations engage in a combination of self-regulation, active promotion of the public interest, and an awareness of their fiduciary responsibility to stockholders, as well as to society and the natural environment (Carroll and Bushholtz 2006).

CSR is understood as distinct from sustainable development, in that it refers to a narrower range of responsibilities that corporations can act upon. Sustainable development implies that companies are but one actor in a larger project undertaken together with governments and civil society to promote development in the economic, social, and environmental realms (the three pillars of sustainable development). Sustainable development is a broader concept, which has provided the normative underpinning for mining companies' CSR policies. Separating out CSR from sustainable development allows this study to trace how mining companies' self-regulatory initiatives evolved over time. Sustainable development can be understood as a broad norm of appropriate behavior, while CSR norms can be understood as industry-specific standards.

The normative weight of sustainable development

Global initiatives that brought the environment and sustainable development onto the international agenda, and efforts at the national level among the advanced industrialized economies, led by the early 1990s to a consensus among the majority of states on the norm of sustainable development. The establishment in 1983 of the World Commission on Environment and Development (WCED) set the stage for a lengthy process of consultation that culminated in the report, *Our Common Future* (better known as the Brundtland Report after the Chair). The report defined sustainable development as "development that meets the needs of present generations without compromising the ability of future generations to meet their own needs" (WCED 1987: 43). While much ink has been spilled in attempts to clarify what this means in practice, sustainable development refers to the economic, social, and environmental dimensions of development.

Sustainable development has been variously defined, but it is generally understood to encapsulate two principles: the Earth's finite capacity to accommodate people and industrial development, and the need to refrain from depriving future generations of the natural resources necessary for life (Smith 1995). Sustainable development further implies that profit maximization must be squared with measures that promote ecological and human well-being. In the context of non-renewable mineral resources, sustainable development can be broadly understood as the efficient use of such resources, while encouraging environmental, social, and economic preservation (Jenkins and Yakovleva 2006; Pring 1999). In the developing country context, mining's role in poverty alleviation and socio-economic development is considered a necessary component of sustainable development (Bird 2004).

Sustainable development gained wide credibility at the 1992 United Nations Conference on Environment and Development (better known as the Rio Conference). Through the Rio Declaration and Agenda 21, principles and actions for achieving sustainable development were established, thereby cementing the normative validity of sustainable development as a means to guide action on the part of governments, international organizations such as the World Bank, and global civil society as represented by NGOs. In the same year, the UN Commission on Sustainable Development (CSD) was established, in order to ensure follow-up on the Rio conference, and to ensure forward movement on the sustainable development agenda. The development of subsequent laws regulating mining at both the national and international levels have been informed by the consensus over sustainable development (Pring 1999).

The 2002 World Summit on Sustainable Development in Johannesburg reaffirmed sustainable development as the central element of the international agenda. The Plan of Action flowing from the World Summit included a section dedicated to mining (Part IV), a victory for the mining sector, as it had not been included in the 1992 Plan of Action. Significantly, the section covers provisions on mining framed in terms of sustainable development, acknowledging both the role and contribution mining can make to sustainable development, but also outlining the many concerns associated with the life cycle of mining operations, from exploration to closure (Dalupan 2005).

Explaining the mining industry's response to sustainable development

The mining industry was slow to appreciate the normative significance of sustainable development. Although sustainable development was a well-established global environmental norm amongst states by the mid-1990s, most mining companies were dubious at best, and highly critical at worst, of the concept (Dashwood 2007a). In fact, in the early 1990s, fewer than half a dozen mining companies around the world were reporting on their CSR policies (Walde 1992; Warhurst 1992). With the exception of a small number of leaders, the majority of mining companies had not taken serious steps to address the environmental and social impacts of their operations. By the mid-1990s, a gap had thereby emerged between larger societal normative expectations, and the policies and practices of mining companies.

Within the period of a decade and a half, the mining industry has undergone a dramatic transformation in terms of both its thinking and practices around sustainable development. By the mid-2000s, most major mining multinationals headquartered in the advanced industrialized economies had come to adopt the principle of sustainable development as a means to frame their CSR policies, pointing to the global influence of that universally accepted norm (Dashwood 2007b; Jenkins and Yakovleva 2006; KPMG 2006). This reflects a significant shift in attitudes on the part of mining executives in a little over a decade. Throughout the 2000s, the diffusion of best practices in such aspects as environmental management systems and community engagement protocols became a marked feature of the mining industry. It had become an accepted norm of business practice to report on environmental and social performance. The theoretically relevant question arising from this finding is to what extent mining companies' CSR policies can be explained by global normative developments.

Convergence: common response to external systemic constraints

At a broad level, the near-universal framing of CSR policies as sustainable development would appear to support the claims of convergence theorists, who argue that economic integration associated with globalization induces companies to adopt common corporate practices (Berger 1996; Ohmae 1991). Convergence in the context described here refers to the adoption of similar policies framed around the broad norm of sustainable development, as opposed to convergence in the political, economic, and cultural institutions of different countries that is argued to be the result of globalization (Kollman and Prakash 2001: 410). It could be argued that the common external pressures experienced by large mining multinationals in the advanced industrialized economies, including NGO activism, tightening environmental regulation, and growing public awareness, induced them to respond in similar ways, pointing to systemic or global dynamics at work. Such a conclusion would be consistent with the findings of other research, such as Hoffman's study of the US oil and gas industry, where companies within the same industry tend to adopt similar strategies in response to common external pressures (Hoffman 1997).

As Table 1.1 reveals, a growing number of major[3] mining companies with headquarters in the advanced industrialized economies of Canada, the US, Japan, Australia, and the UK, came to refer to their CSR reports as "sustainable development" reports, or "sustainability" reports. (A condensed version of this discussion can be found in Dashwood 2011.) To trace how this process occurred, the major mining companies with headquarters in Canada, the US, the UK, Australia, and Japan were identified, drawing on data from *Corporate Register* (companies headquartered in these countries make up the vast majority of the membership of the ICMM). Only companies with *stand-alone* CSR reports were tallied, as this is inferred to indicate a stronger commitment to CSR framed as sustainable development. While information in the reports themselves cannot be taken at face value in the absence of external verification (Guthrie and Parker 1990; Neu et al. 1998, cited in Yakovleva 2005: 53), they are important indicators of the normative affirmation by mining companies of their environmental and social obligations.

Table 1.1 reveals that there was a significant increase in the number of companies framing their CSR policies as sustainable development in the early-to-mid 2000s. Although a few of the twenty-nine companies recorded in the table have merged or been taken over, it can safely be observed that there was a significant up-swing in the number of major mining companies reporting on their CSR policies framed in terms of sustainable development. This is confirmed by KPMG's (2006) *Global Mining Reporting Survey*, which found that forty out of the world's forty-four major global mining companies counted were reporting according to sustainable development indicators.

The data presented in Table 1.1 is consistent with the expectation of institutional approaches in organization theory, which observe a tendency

---

[3] This study follows the Metals Economics Group's classification of junior, mid-tier, and major mining companies. A junior company is one engaged primarily in exploration, and a mid-tier company is one with annual revenues of at least US$50 million, and a major company is one with annual revenues of more than US$500 million. (See Metals Economics Group, *Special Report on World Exploration Trends*, www.metalseconomics.com/pdf/PDAC%202009% 20World%20Exploration%20Trends.pdf, p. 2.)

Table 1.1 *Number of major mining companies with sustainable development/sustainability in the title of their reports, by first year of use of term*[a]

	1998–2000	2001–3	2004–6	2007–9
Canada	Noranda Falconbridge Placer Dome	Alcan Teck Cominco HudBay	Cameco Inmet Goldcorp Kinross Lundin	IAMGOLD
United States		Alcoa Freeport-McMoRan	Newmont Southern-Copper	
Australia	BHP	WMC Newcrest	BHP-Billiton Oxiana Roche Zinifex Downer EDI	OZ Minerals
United Kingdom		Anglo American	Rio Tinto Lonmin	Antofagasta
Japan	–	–	–	–
Total no. of co's	4	8	14	3

[a] The date starts in 1998 because no mining companies reported according to sustainable development prior to that time. Note that some companies already had pre-existing CSR reports, and later changed their name to "sustainable development" report. For example, Noranda first issued a stand-alone CSR report in 1990 (see Table 1.2 below) and in 1999 changed the name of its report to sustainable development.

Source: Corporate Register: www.corporateregister.com.

towards "isomorphism," where striking similarities in institutional forms, procedures, or symbols have been observed across organizational fields and nations. They have noted, for example, the similarities in organizational form and practice that Education Ministries display throughout the world, regardless of differences in local conditions or between firms across industrial sectors (DiMaggio and Powell 1991; Hall and Taylor 1996: 947; Meyer and Rowan 1997; Scott and Meyer 1994). Scholars working within the constructivist tradition in international relations theory have observed the global diffusion of norms and organizational practices, drawing on examples of the diffusion of Science and Technology Ministries, the laws of war (Finnemore 1996), and the adoption of international development assistance policies and institutions across countries (Lumsdaine 1993). The transnational and global context has facilitated the diffusion of CSR norms amongst mining companies. Consistent with the observations of theorists noted above, most have also adopted CSR policies framed as sustainable development, and most have created the position VP, Sustainability/Sustainable Development.

Confounding the convergence explanation, however, is that although mining companies in advanced industrialized countries were facing similar constraints, they produced different responses in terms of the timing and degree of commitment to CSR both between and within countries. In the early 1990s, a small number of mining and metals companies from the advanced industrialized countries began reporting on their environmental policies and practices (Scott 2000). As Table 1.2 shows, in all such countries, there have been early movers and late movers in terms of the uptake and disclosure of CSR policies and practices. As has been found in research on other industries, some companies are leaders in terms of their CSR policies and practices, while others are laggards (Campbell 2006: 926; Gunningham 2003).

Table 1.2 shows the number of major companies by the date that they *first* began CSR reporting, in five-year cohorts. The date that these companies first started issuing stand-alone reports on their CSR policies was noted, and those that were the first to start reporting, beginning in the early-to-mid 1990s, are referred to as the "early movers." The early movers tended to be the same companies that by the mid-to-late 1990s began pushing for global CSR standards, and adopting sustainable development as a means to frame their own policies. In 2009, there were fifty-six major (revenues over US$500m) mining companies with headquarters in Canada, the US, the UK, Australia, and Japan, of which forty published CSR reports. The data shows a significant increase in the number of companies reporting on CSR for the first time from the late 1990s to 2009.

Of the fifty-six major mining companies with headquarters in Canada, the US, Australia, the UK, and Japan in 2009, forty published CSR reports. It should be noted that this data does not show the fact that there is variation between companies that have adopted CSR

Table 1.2 *Mining companies' CSR reports, by date of first release and country headquarters*[ab]

	1990–4	1995–9	2000–4	2005–9
Canada	Noranda Falconbridge	Cambior Placer Dome Alcan	Teck Cominco Cameco HudBay Inmet Goldcorp Barrick	Kinross Lundin IAMGOLD
United States	Alcoa Homestake	Freeport- McMoRan	Newmont	Southern Copper
Australia	WMC BHP	North MIM Holdings Normandy	Macmahon Newcrest Oxiana Roche	Zinifex Downer EDI OZ Minerals
United Kingdom	–	Rio Tinto Anglo American	Billiton Antofagasta Lonmin	Eurasian
Japan	–	Mitsubishi	–	Sumitomo Nippon
No. of co's	6	10	14	10

[a] Data collection was greatly complicated by the large amount of M&A activity. Data on major mining companies was obtained from Mergent Online: www.mergent.com, which provides information on the Merger and Acquisition (M&A) activity of the members of the ICMM from the advanced industrialized economies. Where merged companies had annual revenues over US$500m, and had commenced CSR reporting, they were included in the database (e.g. Placer Dome, which was subsequently taken over by Barrick).
[b] In 2001, BHP and Billiton merged, and this new company is headquartered in both the UK and Australia. M&A activity means that some of the companies counted no longer exist. The combination of M&A and bankruptcies also means that the total number of major mining companies changes, making it difficult to express the above numbers as a percentage of the total number of major mining companies accurately.

Source: Corporate Register: www.corporateregister.com.

policies, in terms of how committed they are to those policies. Jenkins' and Yakovleva's research revealed considerable variation in the reporting styles and maturity of content of ten leading mining companies surveyed between 1999 and 2001 (2006). Furthermore, KPMG (2006) in its survey found marked variation between companies in terms of the degree of disclosure (in terms of amount of detail) on sustainability information, a reality which can only be captured by examining individual companies.

Country-of-origin effects

In light of the variation between companies noted above between early movers and late movers, and in terms of the adoption of stand-alone CSR reports, an alternative explanation for significant differences in the response of mining companies to common external pressures could stem from country-of-origin effects. Theorists point to country-of-origin effects that produce significant differences in the corporate strategies of firms in response to economic integration. Country-of-origin effects stem from different historical and institutional legacies among the advanced industrialized economies (Berger and Dore 1996; Doremus et al. 1999; Kollman and Prakash 2001; Pauly and Reich 1997; Prakash and Potoski 2007a). In their study of corporate strategies in Germany, the US, and Japan, Pauly and Reich found that enduring national attributes produced by the institutional and ideological legacies of different historical experiences result in important differences in the way in which firms adapt to dynamic and highly competitive global markets (1997: 4). Prakash and Potoski found that variation in the uptake of the ISO 14001 management standard between countries such as Japan and the United States influences whether or not Japanese and American firms adopt such standards in the developing host countries where they invest (2007a: 724–7). Divergence theories predict that due to enduring institutional arrangements, there will be greater homogeneity among companies headquartered in the same country, while producing heterogeneity among companies from different countries (Sethi and Elango 1999). Home country heterogeneity will be reproduced in host countries where multinational corporations invest, rather than producing convergence.

The research findings support the impact of country-of-origin influences on firm behavior. In-depth interviews with senior management revealed that the experience of mining in the countries in which they were headquartered as well as abroad was the single most important influence on their CSR policies. This finding suggests that institutional context remains very important, even as firms are influenced by emerging global CSR norms such as sustainable development. In seeking to adapt to changing societal expectations, and to make sense of the normative shift to sustainable development, firms had to find practical ways related to their own experiences of mining to respond to external pressures. The research findings suggest that *both* country of origin as well as country of operation influenced CSR strategies.

The data presented in Table 1.2 shows that there is significant variation in corporate responses to common external pressures not just between countries, but *within* them as well. Other studies have also found variability in the environmental strategies of companies operating in similar institutional contexts (Aragon-Correa 1998; Hart and Ahuja 1996; Russo and Fouts 1997) and within the same industry (Sharma and Vredenburg 1998). In a review of the literature on CSR adoption, Campbell argues that it is not clear whether observed differences are the result of nationally specific institutions (2006). Some studies do suggest that country-of-origin effects have a bearing on whether companies adopt CSR policies. Maignan and Ralston (2002), for example, have found that managerial attitudes towards CSR vary cross-nationally. Doh and Guay (2006) point to the impact of political structures on the access of NGOs to the policy-making process, which is significant because of their role in advocating on behalf of the environment.

In their conclusion to their study on the cross-national diversity of corporate governance practices, Aguilera and Jackson argue that the range of internal variation among firms within the same country is growing, due largely to the growing salience of cross-border and multi-level interactions between stakeholders, which can have an uneven impact within national institutional contexts (Aguilera and Jackson 2003: 462). As such, convergence and path dependence may be "false theoretical alternatives," in a context where processes of continuity and change are occurring simultaneously. This book concurs with this observation, and argues that implementation of more sustainable practices by major mining companies is institutionally conditioned; a function of both the home country where mining companies are headquartered, and the host countries where they invest (Campbell 2006; Fligstein and Freeland 1995). The book contributes to the convergence/institutional divergence debates by arguing that both convergence and institutional/path-dependent/country-of-origin effects are at play.

Weighing the evidence

The central argument advanced in this book is that, although emerging global CSR norms are necessary to the explanation of why mining companies adopted CSR polices and came to frame them in terms of sustainable development, the influence of global norms is not sufficient to explain the policies and intentions of these companies. To understand how firms interpret their external environment, including their perceptions of global dynamics, intra-organizational factors, including organizational learning and the critical role of internal leadership, must be brought into the explanation. Variation in managerial perceptions and interpretations of the environmental and social challenges affecting their operations (Bansal and Penner 2002; Egri and Herman 2000; Sharma 2000) and organizational culture around CSR (Forbes and Jermier 2002; Howard-Grenville 2006; Welford 1997), produce differing responses to external pressures. This study has observed variation both between and within countries, in terms of the timing of mining companies' adoption of CSR policies, and in terms of which companies were leaders in promoting CSR globally. To explain this variation, as well as to understand varying degrees of commitment to CSR framed as sustainable development, it is necessary to look at factors internal to the companies themselves, including leadership, learning processes, and the corporate culture as it relates to CSR (Gunningham et al. 2003).

This book concurs with the findings of other studies (Gunningham et al. 2003; Prakash 2000) that the role of managerial leadership, where senior executives take on the role of norms entrepreneurs, is central to understanding the policies and intentions of mining companies. This argument addresses a long-standing debate in both constructivist and institutionalist literatures, about the relative importance of structure and/or agency in explaining state/firm behavior, with this book leaning on the agency side of the debate. The approach could be identified as "actor-centered institutionalism," where the institutional embeddedness of firms is accounted for, but where change agents or policy entrepreneurs play a decisive role (Aguilera and Jackson 2003: 448, citing Scharpf 1997).

The research also addresses a central and ongoing debate within international relations scholarship, on the relative importance of systemic, as opposed to state-level, explanations for behavior. This book extends this debate to the realm of firms, by pointing to the fact that emerging global CSR norms are not sufficient to explain firms' CSR policies, because norms can be disseminated from the "bottom-up" as much as from the "top-down" (for an opposing view, see Kollman 2008). A key finding of the research is that some global mining companies from the advanced industrialized economies took on a leadership role in disseminating CSR norms applicable to the mining sector globally. They did so by collaboration not only within industry associations, where they sought to promote sustainable development as a normative framework for mining companies' CSR policies, but also by participating in major global governance processes in inter-governmental organizations that were developing global CSR standards applicable to mining. They were engaged in a bottom-up process of disseminating global CSR norms, that would then be expected to filter from the top on down. The support and active role of industry leaders was critical to the dissemination of emerging CSR norms in mining. Following on Flohr et al. (2010), industry leaders played two roles simultaneously: that of norm entrepreneurs, in disseminating global CSR norms, and that of norm leaders, in leading by example through their own policies and practices.

It is suggested here that the fact that mining companies have adopted sustainable development to frame their CSR policies is evidence of acceptance of the normative validity of sustainable development at the discursive level. These developments could be interpreted as being the result of rhetorical framing or "symbolic adoption" in order to manage their public image (Campbell 2007; King and Lenox 2000; Meyer and Rowan 1997). It is argued here that both strategic and normative dynamics were at play (see also Sell and Prakash 2004).

In seeking to demonstrate the interplay between normative and interest-based motivations for behavior, this study builds a bridge between rationalist and interest-based orientations and interpretivist approaches where ideas and norms play a central role in shaping interests and preferences. In some cases, early movers were driven not simply by strategic interests, but out of normative conviction that sustainable development should serve as a guiding principle or value underpinning business conduct (Dashwood 2007a). As such, individual norms entrepreneurs relied on *rationalist* appeals drawing on market considerations in order to win internal consensus, as well as on appeals to the *intrinsic* value of sustainable development in its own right (see Flohr et al. 2010).

Research design and method

The patterns observed above, with respect to the commencement of CSR reporting, and the acceptance of the normative validity of sustainable development, informed the research design of this study. Having observed that an understanding of firm-level dynamics is necessary to the explanation of mining companies' CSR policies, this study opted for rich case-study analysis of three major mining companies with global operations. Recognizing the major differences in institutional contexts between developed and developing countries, the companies were chosen with headquarters in advanced industrialized economies. With the possible exception of South Africa (Hamann 2003; Hamann et al. 2011; Thauer 2009) there is a dramatic difference in corporate attitudes towards CSR between countries such as India and China, on the one hand, and countries such as Canada, the US, Australia, Japan, and the UK on the other. Although this might suggest convergence along an Anglo-Saxon model, the presence of Japan confounds such a conclusion (Aguilera and Jackson 2003: 461).

It is argued here that a best practices convergence is taking shape within the mining industry among major companies from the advanced industrialized countries. At the same time, there is considerable variation between mining companies *within* and between advanced industrialized economies, pointing to the institutional embeddedness of CSR. In all of the advanced industrialized economies, there were early movers and late movers in terms of when they first started reporting on CSR. To control for possible country-of-origin effects, three major mining companies headquartered in the same country were selected as case studies.

The three major mining multinationals selected include Placer Dome (now Barrick Gold – Barrick Gold acquired Placer Dome in 2006), Noranda (now Xstrata), and Barrick Gold. The choice of major Canadian mining multinationals is appropriate, as Canada is a major global player in the mining and minerals sector.[4] Canadian companies operate over 130 mines abroad, and exploration companies have 2,800 properties in over 100 countries (Natural Resources Canada 2006). The

---

[4] Despite the recent spate of foreign takeovers of Canadian mining multinationals, Canada continues to be a major player, because of the growth of junior Canadian mining companies, and because Canada continues to be a center of financial, technical, and legal expertise related to mining.

experiences of these companies are transferable to similar large mining
multinationals operating in industrialized economies, such as Australia,
the UK, Japan, and the United States.

Noranda and Placer Dome were early movers in adopting CSR
policies, and were also leaders in promoting sustainable development
within the mining industry in the late 1990s. Barrick was a late mover
relative to Noranda and Placer Dome, both in terms of commencement
of reporting and acceptance of the normative validity of sustainable
development. The choice of these companies provides variation on the
dependent variable (whether an early or late mover; uptake of sustainable development; degree of commitment to CSR) (King et al. 1994).
The decision to look at two positive examples of norms leadership
strengthened the reliability of the independent variables found to be
causally significant (George and Bennett 2005: 23).

Noranda was the first of the two early mover companies, having well-
established environment, health, and safety (EHS) policies by the late
1980s, and was the first company in Canada industry-wide to begin
reporting on EHS in 1990. Placer Dome was an early mover compared
to the majority of major mining companies in terms of the timing of
CSR adoption in the early 1990s, the release of the first stand-alone
report in 1998, and the framing of that report in terms of sustainable
development. Barrick Gold is a late mover relative to Noranda and
Placer Dome, although it moved in sync with most major mining
companies in terms of the commencement of reporting (2002) and the
reference to sustainable development as informing CSR practices
(2005).[5] In contrast to Noranda and Placer Dome, Barrick opted out
of a leadership role in promoting industry-wide collaboration through
the Global Mining Initiative and the ICMM. Significantly, its annual
CSR reports are not framed as "sustainable development" reports, but
rather, as "responsibility" reports. Placer Dome framed its CSR policies
as sustainable development from the outset, while Noranda changed the
title of its annual EHS reports to sustainable development reports
starting in 1998. Table 1.3 shows how the early mover concept is
operationalized in this study.

[5] In this respect, referring to Barrick as a "late mover" is somewhat of a
misnomer for what is a more complex scenario, and should therefore not be
construed as meaning the same as "laggard." The term "late mover" is a
convenient broad-brush phrase that captures nuances that are spelled out in more
detail in subsequent chapters.

Table 1.3 *Key indicators of early mover status*

Structural	• Expansion beyond North America • Prominence in industry (size, production, earnings)
Internal/organizational	• Committed leadership • Release of stand-alone CSR reports • Creation of EHS/CSR positions • Introduction of EHS management systems • Adoption of sustainable development • Adoption of voluntary standards
External engagement (local/national/global)	• Leadership in industry collaboration • Degree of external engagement (with stakeholders, critics)

This book is concerned with the processes by which major mining companies became committed to operating in an environmentally and socially responsible way. It documents the change in CSR policies and intentions over time, and then traces domestic and international normative, political, and institutional developments to explain the changes observed. It seeks to trace the influences on them, their impact on management decision-making procedures, and how thinking about their responsibilities evolved over time. The focus is on process-tracing of decision-making, and shifts in cognitive frames (George and Bennett 2004), as opposed to outcomes in terms of actual environmental performance. In order to assess the role of global norms, the relative importance of global developments is weighed against domestic (Canadian) and internal company factors.

To weigh the impact of global CSR norms on mining companies, three indicators can be identified. The first indicator is the significant shift in thinking amongst mining executives on CSR. The cognitive change that would produce shifts in thinking suggests a learning process, as evidenced by norms- and self-interest-based dialogue that took place within these companies on the issue of CSR (Haufler 1999; Prakash 2000; Ruggie 2002). The second indicator of the influence of global CSR norms is the adoption of the concept of sustainable development by mining companies to frame their CSR policies. In the absence of global norms, mining companies would not have had a reason to frame their CSR policies in terms of sustainable development. As such, the global normative weight of sustainable development provided the normative context in which the companies' thinking and policies evolved. These indicators are addressed in the case-study chapters. The third indicator is the collaboration amongst mining companies to promote policies, practices, rules, and norms around CSR. This has been done both within Canada and globally, resulting in the creation of nationally linked, global private governance structures. They serve as an indicator of global normative influence because companies felt the need to coordinate a position on CSR that could be represented at global conferences, and at international organizations where policies affecting mining were being developed. These efforts have resulted in a transnational network of mining multinationals (Dashwood 2005). Mining multinationals have assumed a degree of private authority in the dissemination of CSR norms, derived from their knowledge and technical expertise (Cutler et al. 1999: 19). This third indicator is addressed in the chapter on the mining industry's global standard-setting initiatives.

International collaboration is both an *indicator* of the impact of global norms, but also a *marker* of the role multinational corporations are playing in shaping CSR norms relevant to mining. At one level, mining companies felt the need to create a global mining association in order to address (and counter) global developments affecting all mining companies. At another level, mining companies have worked through the ICME and then the ICMM to structure dialogue, influence company behavior towards higher standards, and influence global governance processes affecting mining. Collaborative behavior runs counter to the assumption of firm behavior based on individualistic, competitive self-interest. Yet, as has been documented, there is a long history of cooperation amongst firms in order to realize common goals (Cutler et al. 1999: 6–9).

Data sources

Consistent with the argument that it is necessary to look at factors internal to the companies themselves, this study examined the role of leadership, learning processes, and the corporate culture as it relates to CSR. Given the critical importance of decision-making and cognitive understandings to this research, interviews with key corporate officials were a key source of evidence. The empirical analysis benefited greatly from access to, and cooperation from, senior executives in Noranda and

Placer Dome, making it possible to conduct multiple interviews with a number of key officials over different time periods. Some interviews were also conducted with officials in Falconbridge (majority-owned by Noranda), since these companies began producing joint CSR reports in 2003. Since some of these officials are now retired, it was possible to get unusually candid accounts of thinking around CSR and sustainable development from officials with a long institutional memory of their companies. This access made it possible to trace in detail cognitive processes, including shifts in thinking about the nature of the companies' obligations, learning, and the decision-making processes in these companies. In the case of Placer Dome, access to internal documents concerning the progression towards sustainable development policies greatly enhanced the richness of information available. This access is an important part of the contribution of this study, as mining companies are typically disinclined to grant open-ended access to researchers.

Upon initial contact in 2003, access to key people at Barrick was more limited and it was originally envisaged that the chapter on Barrick would be more of a vignette, to highlight the contrast with early movers, and the role of internal company factors in explaining this. However, when a follow-up interview was conducted in May 2011, the author found that the interviewee was much more open and responsive. Access was granted to a number of other people responsible for CSR, allowing for a more substantial case-study analysis than was originally thought possible. In addition to public company documents, extensive feedback through interviews provided a window to thinking within the organization, and management perceptions of issues relevant to CSR.

Table 1.4 shows interviews conducted in person, unless otherwise specified. In the interests of consistency, company interviewees are not identified, even where permission was granted for identification. In addition to interviews with corporate officials, supplemental interviews were conducted with officials knowledgeable about the mining industry, as outlined in Table 1.5.

Separating out instrumental and normative motivations is a challenging empirical task but one that is useful to attempt for analytical purposes. Norm conformance is often self-interested and what appears as rational action reflects a normative understanding that it is permissible to act in that way (Sell and Prakash 2004: 150). To understand the interplay between normative and strategic considerations, one needs to contend with managerial perceptions, interpretations, and organizational culture as it relates

Table 1.4 *Timeline of interviews conducted, by company*[a]

Company	Interviewees	Date
Noranda	Executive 1	February 13, 2006; February 16, 2006; March 2, 2006; August 20, 2008; December 9, 2011 (phone) (5)
	Executive 2	April 22, 2003; October 28, 2003; August 26, 2008; October 23, 2011 (email); December 2, 2011 (phone) (5)
	Executive 3	September 11, 2008
	Executive 4	August 28, 2008
	Manager 1	April 3, 2003
	Manager 2	April 1, 2003
Falconbridge	Executive 1	February 22, 2006
	Manager 1	February 22, 2006
Placer Dome	Executive 1	July 31, 2002
	Executive 2	July 30, 2002; June 21, 2003; December 7, 2005; January 25/26, 2006; August 11, 2011 (phone); November 13, 2011 (email); December 6, 2011 (phone) (7)
	Executive 3	August 12, 2002; January 26, 2006 (2)
	Executive 4	July 31, 2002 (phone)
	Executive 5	April 1, 2003
	Manager 1	April 3, 2003
	Manager 2	April 2, 2003
Barrick	Executive 1	May 6, 2003; October 14, 2011 (phone) (2)
	Executive 2	May 28, 2003
	Executive 3	May 5, 2011
	Executive 4	August 23, 2011
	Manager 1	August 18, 2011 (phone); November 3, 2011 (email) (2)
	Manager 2	August 18, 2011 (phone); August 23, 2011; August 25, 2011 (phone); November 3, 2011 (email) (4)
	Manager 3	August 18, 2011 (phone)

[a] Confidential documents are listed in the References. See, for example, 'Executive 6 (Placer Dome)'.

Table 1.5 *Timeline of supplemental interviews*

Company	Interviewees	Date
Northwest Ethical Investments	Official 1	August 30, 2011 (phone)
	Official 2	August 30, 2011 (phone)
International Council on Metals and the Environment (ICME)	Gary Nash	May 26, 2006; November 29, 2011 (email)
	Executive 1	May 25, 2006; December 2, 2011 (phone)
Mining Association of Canada (MAC)	Executive 1	May 26, 2006

to CSR. Ethnographic observation through in-depth interviews was the key means employed to discern managers' understandings of what they were doing and why they were doing it. Public addresses of managers, as well as internal documents the author had access to, helped shed further light on the decision-making process, to determine what mindsets were driving corporate behavior around CSR. Content analysis of CSR documents, including company reports, also help reveal how beliefs changed over time, and how interests came to be redefined. This information was supplemented with industry-wide reports, industry conference proceedings, trade journals, NGO reports, and secondary academic sources.

Case selection

The choice of cases was driven by the key research objective of this book, to trace the role and importance of global CSR norms on the policies and practices of global mining companies. Both Placer Dome and Noranda (the early movers) had developed progressive CSR policies, were committed to improving performance, and sought to lead industry in the promotion of better standards. A study of mining companies represent "hard" or "least likely" cases (George and Bennett 2004: Chapters 1 and 6), because the conditions under which mining companies operate makes them unlikely to undertake significant investments in CSR policies. Given the structural constraints within the mining industry, one would expect companies to be defensive, or to have CSR policies that are intended for public relations purposes, with an emphasis on low-cost initiatives with high visibility. Few mining multinationals demonstrate the degree of commitment to CSR that Placer Dome and Noranda did (Rio Tinto, Newmont, and BHP-Billiton being among the notable exceptions). This makes them very interesting and theoretically important cases.

Within the mining sector, there remain significant differences between mining companies that influenced the case selection. The companies were chosen, in part, because they have not been subjected to intense public scrutiny on the scale of, for example, Talisman.[6] This controls for the possibility that they were simply responding to a public relations crisis, an important consideration, as companies are often accused of adopting CSR policies merely for public relations purposes. These companies were also similar in that they have/had global operations, but do/did not have operations in zones of conflict, which dramatically changes the conditions under which companies must operate.

To make the findings comparable, the companies selected were/are major mining multinationals, with annual revenues over US$500 million and global operations in two or more countries. The lessons learned from these companies are relevant and transferable to other mining companies with global operations.

Company profiles

Noranda

Noranda was a global corporation which as of 2004 employed 16,000 people in seven countries around the world. In the early years, Noranda was a diversified natural resource company, with operations in forestry and oil and gas, in addition to its mining and metals business. In the mid-1990s, management decided to concentrate Noranda's business in the mining and metals industry. In 1995, Brascan (now Brookfields) acquired 40 per cent of Noranda's public shares, becoming the major shareholder. Its mining and metals businesses were comprised of aluminum, nickel, zinc, primary copper and secondary copper recycling, and recycling of other metal-bearing materials. Copper accounted for

---

[6] Talisman Energy Inc., based in Alberta, was the subject of a government inquiry and the target of much negative publicity over allegations that it was complicit in human rights abuses at its operation in Sudan. Talisman subsequently divested from Sudan.

about 40 per cent of its US$11 billion in capital assets. Noranda's copper business included the Horne copper smelter in Rouyn-Noranda, Quebec, the Altonorte smelter and the Collahuasi and Lomas Bayas mines in Chile, and the Antamina copper-zinc mine in Peru. Its zinc operations consisted of the Brunswick mine and smelter in Bathurst, New Brunswick, and the Bell Allard mine in Matagami, Quebec.

Noranda had a majority stake in Falconbridge, owning 55 per cent of its shares. Noranda's nickel revenue was derived from Falconbridge's Integrated Nickel Operations in Sudbury, Ontario, Raglan, Quebec, and a refinery in Norway. Falconbridge's copper business consisted of its Kidd Creek operations, including a mine, smelter, and refinery in Timmins, Ontario, and the Collahuasi mine and the Lomas Bayas mine and refinery in Chile. Falconbridge employed 6,400 people in thirteen countries.

Until 2002, Noranda and Falconbridge operated as separate public companies, with each having their own board, management, policies, management systems, objectives, and reporting practices. Starting in 2002, the two companies began to amalgamate their business services, which led to the integration of their corporate functions and policies, including their environment, health and safety, and sustainable development policies. In 2005, the two companies merged under Falconbridge's name, which was considered to represent better value for shareholders.

Table 1.6 below provides a snapshot of the two companies in 2002.

Placer Dome

Placer Dome Inc. (PDI) was a major gold-mining company headquartered in Vancouver, British Columbia, Canada. Placer Dome was the result of a merger in 1987 between Ontario-based Dome Mining, and

Table 1.6 *Comparative data on Noranda and Falconbridge, 2002*

	Noranda	Falconbridge
Sales CAN$ millions (2001)	6,152	2,138
Assets $ millions	12,032	5,069
Employees	16,000	6,400
Activities	Cu, Zn, Mg, Al, Pb, Au, H_2SO_4, Recycling	Ni, Cu, Zn, Co, Pd, Pt, Ag

British Columbia-based Placer. In addition to the corporate office in Vancouver, PDI had separate business units for its regional operations; Placer Pacific (PPI) in Asia, Placer America (PA) in North America, and Placer Latin America (PLA) in Latin America. As of 2004, PDI employed 13,000 people in eight countries across four continents. PDI was a publicly listed company, with listings with the Toronto Stock Exchange, New York Stock Exchange, and Australia Stock Exchange.

PDI's business was in gold, copper, and silver, but in the late 1990s, the company made a strategic decision to concentrate its operations primarily in gold. This decision prompted the sale of PDI's share (39 per cent) of the controversial Marcopper mine in the Philippines in 1998, which was the scene of a major tailings failure in 1996. In 2004, Placer Dome produced 3.65 million ounces of gold, and 413 million pounds of copper. PDI's major operations included the Campbell, Porcupine, and Musselwhite gold mines in Ontario, the Bald Mountain, Cortez, Golden Sunlight, and Turquoise Ridge gold mines in the US, Zaldivar (copper) and La Coipa (gold and silver) mines in Chile, the Misima and Porgera gold mines in Papua New Guinea, the Granny Smith, Henty, Kalgoorlie West, Kanowna Belle and Osborne gold mines in Australia, the South Deep gold mine in South Africa (which it acquired in 1999), and the North Mara gold mine in Tanzania (acquired in 2003) (Placer Dome 2005a: 21).

Barrick Gold Corporation

Barrick Gold Corporation is a major gold-mining company founded in 1983 by Peter Munk. Its headquarters are in Toronto, and it is listed on the Toronto and New York stock exchanges. African Barrick Gold (ABG) is listed on the London Stock Exchange.

Through a merger and a series of acquisitions, Barrick grew from a company based in North America, to a major international company, with operations in South America, Australia, and Africa. Significant milestones for the company included the merger in 2001 with Homestake Mining Company, a 125-year-old American company, and the acquisition in 2006 of Placer Dome, solidifying Barrick as the world's largest gold-mining company, with operations on four continents. The early 2000s saw the development of new mines, as Barrick made new discoveries and/or developed new mines on existing properties from previous acquisitions. Table 1.7 reveals the trajectory of Barrick's growth from a North American company to a global player.

Table 1.7 *Barrick's operations by date of acquisition/merger and continent*

	Continent			
Year	North America	Central America	Africa	Australia
1983	Camflo Co.[a] (Quebec)			
1985	Mercur Mine (Utah)			
1987	Goldstrike Property (Nevada)			
1992	Betze-Post Mine (JV with Newmont-Nevada)			
1994		Lac Minerals Ltd. (Pascua-Lama, Chile)		
1996		Arequipa Resources Ltd. (Pierina, Peru)		
1999			Sutton Resources (Bulyanhulu, Tanzania)	
2000			Pangea Goldfields (Tulawaka, Tanzania)	
2001	Eskay Creek, BC; Hemlo (Ontario); Round Mountain (Nevada)	Pascua-Lama, Veladero (Chile/ Argentina);		Homestake merger (Kalgoorlie, Plutonic, Darlot, Lawlers, Cowal, Australia)
2002		Lagunas Norte (Peru)		

Table 1.7 (*cont.*)

		Continent		
Year	North America	Central America	Africa	Australia
2006	Cortez, Turquoise Ridge, Bald Mountain (Nevada), Golden Sunlight (Montana)	Zaldivar (Chile)	South Deep (South Africa), North Mara, Tanzania	**Placer Dome** (Porgera, PNG; Kanowna, Kalgoorlie, Granny Smith, Osborne, Henty, Australia)
2007		**Arizona Star** (Cerro Casale)		
2008	Cortez Hills (Nevada)	Pueblo Viejo (Dominican Republic)	Buzwagi, Tanzania	

[a] Company names are marked in bold, and are placed where their acquisition denotes a new continent for Barrick.

Source: Barrick Gold Corporation, Annual Reports, various years.

Table 1.8 *Financial highlights: 1999, 2001 (data includes Homestake) and 2010*

	1999	2001	2010
Gold sales (US$ millions)	1,421	1,989	10,924
Total employees	3,500	4,500	20,000
	(approx.)	(approx.)	(approx.)
Dividends paid per share	0.20	0.22	0.44
Gold production (000s oz)	3,660	6,124	7,765
Proven and probable gold reserves (000s oz)	59,283	82,272	139,786

Source: Barrick Gold Corporation, Annual Reports, 1999, 2001, 2010.

Table 1.9 *Comparative data for Noranda, Placer Dome, and Barrick: 2004*[a]

	Noranda	Placer Dome	Barrick
Business	Copper, nickel, zinc, aluminum	Gold, copper	Gold
Employees	16,000	13,000	15,000 (est.)
Operations	10 mines; 3 refineries; 7 smelters, 5 recycling facilities	17 mines	12 mines
Countries of operation	Canada, United States, Peru, Chile, Jamaica, Norway, Dominican Republic	Canada, United States, Australia, Papua New Guinea, Chile, South Africa, Tanzania	Canada, United States, Australia, Peru, Tanzania
Financial (US$ millions):			
Sales	6,978	1,888	1,932
Cash from operations	1,380	376	506
Net income	551	284	248
Earnings per common share (actual amount)	1.78	0.68	0.95

[a] The year 2004 was used because in 2005, Noranda merged with Falconbridge.

Source: Noranda, Annual Report, 2004; Placer Dome, Annual Report, 2004, Barrick, Annual Report, 2004.

Barrick's growth in the 2000s has been exponential, as reflected in the number of employees, number of projects, proven reserves, and annual earnings. Table 1.8 shows financial data from 1999, 2001, and 2010.

Table 1.9 provides comparative data for the three case-study companies.

Organization of book

Having set out the research topic, central research question, and research agenda, Chapter 2 is devoted to elaborating a theoretical framework for analyzing the role and importance of global CSR norms on the policies and intentions of mining multinationals. A three-level institutional approach is presented, incorporating rational choice institutionalism, "new" institutionalism, and historical institutionalism. The chapter then draws on constructivist insights from international relations theory, and charts the firm-level variables that are considered important in explaining the variation observed between the three cases.

Chapter 3 outlines major developments in the global mining industry. It then explains the external environment common to all mining companies regardless of nationality, including domestic (Canadian) and global influences or drivers. Key among the global drivers was the emergence of sustainable development as the universal normative basis for progress on environmental protection. All mining companies were facing common constraints, such as increased domestic and global regulation, growing public opposition in the face of the bad reputation experienced by the mining industry as a whole, and increased risks associated with NGO targeting of their operations around the world. The point of this exercise is to outline the external constraints experienced by all major mining companies, as the basis for the argument that these external factors are not sufficient to explain the behavior of mining companies with respect to CSR.

Chapters 4, 5, and 6 analyze how Noranda, Placer Dome, and Barrick, respectively, responded to the common developments in their external environment, focusing on internal and organizational variables to explain their CSR policies to highlight the variation between them. These chapters trace how the early movers (Noranda and Placer Dome) became committed to operating in an environmentally and socially responsible way. They document the change in CSR policies and intentions, and trace the internal debates around sustainable development. Where relevant, the chapters trace the domestic and global normative, political, and institutional developments to explain the changes observed in policies. The tracing of the evolution of CSR policies over time is very important to this analysis, as it allows internal changes to be linked to external developments at the national and global levels

(Dashwood, 2007a). The chapter on Barrick serves to provide a contrast to the early movers, to highlight the differences in the role of senior management and in corporate culture around CSR, which is considered critical to explaining CSR adoption and to explain Barrick's different approach to sustainable development.

The role and motivation of the early movers in promoting private global norms for the mining sector is examined in Chapter 7, to capture the norms-disseminating role of private actors. The chapter will seek to capture the dynamic and interactive learning process taking place among major global mining companies, and identify the global subset of sustainable development norms applicable to mining that have emerged. The purpose of this chapter is three-fold. First, it sets out the reasons Noranda and Placer Dome (along with other mining companies such as Rio Tinto) sought to stake out a leadership role in the promotion of global CSR standards for the mining industry, initially through the ICME (based in Ottawa), and then its successor organization, the ICMM (based in London). Second, this chapter traces the process by which consensus was reached on the normative validity of sustainable development as a means to frame mining companies' CSR policies. Third, it identifies the sub-set of global CSR norms that have now been institutionalized, as a result of the leadership of individual mining companies, and the efforts of the ICME, and later, the ICMM. The concluding chapter reiterates the theoretical implications of the research, and identifies areas for future research.

2 | Theoretical explanation of CSR adoption

Introduction

This chapter sets out the conceptual, theoretical, and methodological approach adopted to analyze the impact of global CSR norms on mining companies. The argument presented is that emerging global CSR norms are important to the explanation of why Noranda, Placer Dome, and later, Barrick, came to adopt CSR policies and how they evolved over time. To explain how these companies adapted, and why Noranda and Placer Dome took on a leadership role in promoting CSR norms globally, factors internal to the companies themselves, including managerial leadership, learning processes, and the corporate culture as it relates to CSR, need to be accounted for. There is a dynamic and interdependent relationship between internal influences, intra-organizational factors, and external influences operating at the local, national, regional, and global levels. This chapter draws on the theoretical literature from international relations, public policy, and management in order to accommodate the need to simultaneously account for dynamics at the global or macro level, and at the micro level of the firm.

While not rejecting the rational choice literature, it is argued that firms are responsive to normative shifts within the larger society, seek to promote organizational values that are not always directly tied to tangible benefits, and can themselves play a role in the dissemination of progressive norms. The theoretical literature that best fits this argument is institutionalism from organization theory and constructivism from international relations theory. Constructivist approaches in international relations theory mirror institutional approaches in organization theory, in that emphasis is placed on cognitive processes, such as learning, to explain state/firm behavior. Values, norms, and identity are understood to shape interests/preferences, which are not fixed, but change over time. Norms are inter-subjective understandings of appropriate behavior, and are used here to refer to all standards of behavior, including principles and rules (see Porter 2005: 218).

By the early 1990s, companies such as Placer Dome and Noranda were actively seeking to improve their environmental and social practices. The evidence points to the importance of internal company and domestic level (Canadian) dynamics as key determinants of the decision to adopt CSR policies. Barrick was also influenced by domestic dynamics in the early years of its CSR, but was later much more influenced by global CSR norms as they relate to mining. These findings support research in the organization and business literature, which has examined both strategic and normative dynamics in explaining firm behavior (for example, Aguilera and Jackson 2003; Campbell 2006; Sell and Prakash 2004; Suchman 1995). Yet, the organization and business literature tends to ignore global dynamics. A major contribution of this study is to draw on constructivist scholarship to analyze the role and importance of global norms in influencing corporate responsibility policies.

Noranda and Placer Dome were leaders within the mining sector, both in terms of the adoption of their own CSR policies, and the role they played in bringing practices in the global mining industry into closer alignment with societal expectations. They were not simply reacting to global developments, but were themselves participating in the shaping of global CSR norms, through their involvement in global mining industry associations and other organizations. This finding runs counter to assumptions held by scholars working within the global civil society literature, who focus on transnational NGOs as global norms-disseminating agents (Keck and Sikkink 1998). Keck and Sikkink look at how norms are disseminated at the macro level, inducing states to change their behavior. This study adds to that scholarship by examining how similar logics and dynamics apply to not just states, but non-state actors such as multinational corporations (see also Flohr et al. 2010). Like states, multinationals can be socialized into accepting new norms, values, shared terms of discourse, and perceptions of interest. As a late mover, Barrick's CSR policies have been influenced by global CSR norms established by other mining companies. The major push by Barrick in the mid-2000s to improve its CSR was the result of change in senior management, rather than the inevitable outcome of structural forces.

Keck and Sikkink discount the role that "interested" actors might play in the dissemination of global norms. As such, their work does not explain why companies chose to promote CSR norms. Research on non-state actors demonstrates that failure to account for private-sector norms presents an incomplete picture of how global norms are disseminated through global governance mechanisms (Porter 2005: 217–19). Also overlooked is the interaction between state and transnational actors (including firms) in the dissemination of global norms, and the entanglement of private and public sector norms (Porter 2005: 236; Ruggie 2002, 2004). Borzel and Risse suggest that self-interested actors will only promote norms for strategic reasons, in response to societal pressures (2010). It is worth considering whether, in the process of doing so, firms may come to accept the intrinsic value of certain norms (Flohr et al. 2010).

Elaboration of the three-level institutional approach

This study employs a three-level institutional analysis, by drawing on insights from rational choice institutionalism, the "new" institutionalism in organization theory, and historical institutionalism to explain why the firms under study adopted CSR policies, and the extent and nature of their commitment to them (for a variation of this approach, see Kollman and Prakash 2001). It argues that it is necessary to combine these approaches to understand why, and under what conditions, firms seek to become more socially responsible (Campbell 2006). To flesh that argument out, this section outlines how mining companies' behavior might best be understood. The next section then draws on insights from the theoretical literature on organizational behavior and international relations to explain the firm-level and global-level dynamics that form part of the explanation for what has driven CSR adoption.

Rational choice institutionalism

Rational choice institutionalism seeks to understand how institutions mediate or structure the choices made by rational actors (Hall and Taylor 1996). Rational choice institutionalism assumes that firms are instrumental actors which are motivated by the self-interested desire to maximize profits and shareholder value, as dictated by the institution of the competitive market place. With its antecedents in microeconomics (Cohen 2007), the rational choice literature expects that, to the extent firms adopt CSR policies, they do so for strategic reasons in order to achieve organizational value-maximizing goals. According to this logic, the adoption of CSR policies can be largely understood as a strategic, calculated response to the need to improve the bad reputation of mining companies and ensure the continued viability of the mining industry. Since rationalist approaches take interests as given, interests are assumed to be exogenously defined, leading analysis to focus on the external constraints (including institutional context beyond the market) that firms are encountering to explain CSR policies.

Research does confirm rational choice expectations that mining companies were responding strategically to external constraints (Yakovleva 2005). A key external factor influencing mining companies is the institutional context of the countries in which they are headquartered. Mining companies headquartered in the advanced industrialized economies faced broadly similar institutional pressures in their home countries, so it is not surprising that the mining companies leading the push to improve the industry's environmental and social performance are/were headquartered in the advanced industrialized economies. In the 1990s, governments in countries such as Canada, the United States, Australia, the UK, and Japan tightened up existing environmental regulations affecting various aspects of mining, pertaining to safeguarding the quality of land, air, and water affected by mining and mineral processing (Dias and Begg 1994).

Although specific details may vary, at a broad level, mining companies also face similar institutional constraints in host countries, often developing countries. Since much capital expenditure is required even before the mine opens, and because companies have to locate where the ore is, mining companies lack the mobility of other sectors (such as textiles/clothing) when things turn sour. Mining companies are therefore vulnerable to local community opposition, which (often with the help of NGOs), can disrupt their operations. Mining companies operating in developing countries face strong pressures from local communities to promote normative values, such as the provision of public goods that ordinarily would be the prerogative of states (Bird 2004; Dashwood and Puplampu 2010; Idemudia 2007; Szablowski 2007). In areas of "limited statehood," contributing to governance becomes a matter of self-interest, as it pays off if a firm can set the industry standard with regard to environmental or human rights standards (Borzel and Risse 2010).

Mining companies employ risk management to address operational challenges. From the early 1990s, a major new risk for the mining industry was the assault on its reputation. Reputational capital takes years to build, but can be quickly destroyed (as the BP offshore disaster shows). Reputational concerns about socially accepted behavior induce firms to take norms more seriously, such that concerns about norms affect the utility calculations of an entire industry (Borzel and Risse 2010). The need for community acceptance of mining operations where companies cannot readily relocate, the need to meet growing environmental expectations of governments, lending institutions, and insurers, and the need to ensure markets for certain metals, point to strategic considerations as paramount in explaining the adoption of CSR policies. The publication of stand-alone CSR reports, and the framing of CSR as sustainable development would, according to this logic, be explained as an attempt to manage companies' public image.

There are limitations, however, to treating interests as given, and appropriate responses to external constraints as self-evident. Rational choice approaches do not leave much (if any) room for firm interests beyond the realization of profit, understood through a cost-benefit calculus. Since a company's *raison d'être* is to make a profit, it is often assumed that corporate responsibility is incompatible with profit maximization. Narrow, economistic views of firm behavior predict that unless firms calculate that they will profit from or enjoy cost-savings from CSR measures, they will not undertake such policies unless forced to do so through legal coercion (Gunningham et al. 2003: 20–1). In response to this understanding of firm behavior, much ink has been spilled putting forth a "business case" for CSR (for a good review, see Vogel 2005).

To be sure, companies that are able to realize cost savings through, for example, reducing the amount of energy consumed, enjoy a "win–win" situation that benefits both the company and the environment (*The Economist* 2008; Porter 1991). In the related field of OHS (Occupational Health and Safety), there is a clear business case in the mining industry for taking worker health and safety seriously, as injuries can cause significant disruption to production processes, increase worker compensation costs, and increase staff absences (Gunningham 2008). Vogel concludes that only under very limited conditions would firms choose to invest in CSR (2005). Yet, research demonstrates that firms will undertake expenditures even where the returns are not easily quantified (Gunningham et al. 2003: 21–23; Palan 2000; Prakash 2000). In the case of OHS in major mining companies from the advanced industrialized economies, for example, there is a very strong culture of commitment at the executive level to achieving high standards of OHS, a priority that goes beyond business case considerations (Gunningham 2008).

Rejecting the narrow view of the profit-maximizing firm does not, however, mean that firms can ignore the cost and market implications of costly CSR expenditures. Using the language of public/private goods, firms cannot provide costly public goods if it is unprofitable to do so. Companies, for example, that incur heavy costs in order to make their operations more environmentally responsible could compromise their competitive position. Companies will, however, incur socially beneficial costs if there are market incentives that allow firms to *transform* public goods into private (excludable) goods (Prakash 2000: 20–3). Companies, for example, may develop technologies that foster better environmental results, that they can market to other companies (Porter 1991). Or, companies might fund local schools or health clinics to promote community acceptance of their operations.

The structural imperatives of the competitive global marketplace serve to further constrain the extent to which expenditure on CSR can be rationalized. Within this structural imperative, however, there is significant variation between companies in terms of how, and the extent to which, they incorporate CSR into their policies and practices (Dashwood 2007a; Jenkins and Yakovleva 2006; Prakash 2000). Firms operate in a larger social and political environment beyond the market, and are pressured to respond to societal demands for a commitment to social and environmental responsibility. In the developing country context, socially embedded markets can provide a functional equivalent to the "shadow of hierarchy," where the state threatens to impose binding rules on private actors (Borzel and Risse 2010).

Potential early mover advantages are an important consideration in explaining unilateral CSR adoption, and global collaborative standard setting. In the economic meaning of the term, early mover advantages refers to the various benefits accruing to companies that are the first to move into a market, thereby pre-empting the gains to late movers (Lieberman and Montgomery 1988). In the case of mining, early mover advantages can be relevant in this sense, through spatial pre-emption in terms of gaining access to prime deposits in specific geographic locations (Frynas et al. 2000). Early mover advantages were a relevant consideration for mining companies as they expanded into developing countries in the 1990s.

There are other early mover advantages that are not as directly fungible in terms of cost-benefit calculations. For example, by showing leadership through voluntary adoption of EHS measures, firms may earn cooperative relations with government regulators and obtain greater flexibility in the enforcement of existing environmental regulations (Potoski and Prakash 2005). By extension, firms may enjoy advantages in negotiations over regulatory standards, directing regulation to fit their own CSR strengths, and potentially raising rivals' entry costs (Maxwell et al. 2000; Porter and van der Linde 1995; Potoski and Prakash 2005; Salop and Scheffman 1983). At the global level, firms who take on leadership roles in industry self-regulation can shape the standards that other firms will then feel pressured to adopt. Early mover considerations may overcome collective action problems when major companies take on the "privileged group" characteristics that lead them to assume the private costs of collective action (Olson 1965).[1]

If "value-maximizing goals" (a malleable concept) are understood to be consistent with cost-benefit calculations, then the rational choice approach provides an adequate framework for explaining companies' CSR policies. However, it misses a valuable and essential part of the explanation, which is how firms respond to changing societal norms, the cognitive process by which firms respond to changing norms, and the influences that lead firms to adopt CSR policies in response to evolving norms. To fully understand what was driving these companies, rational choice calculations need to be blended in with approaches that can better account for the role of values and norms in the decision-making process. As such, this work is situated at the intersection of a material ontology and instrumental, agent-driven approaches on one hand, and norms-based, institutional or social structure-driven approaches on the other.

---

[1] I am grateful to Aseem Prakash for bringing to my attention the applicability of the privileged group concept to the mining industry's global collaborative initiatives.

"New" institutionalism

The "new" institutionalism in organization theory, which emphasizes cognitive processes and the normative environment, highlights the ways in which firms interpret their external environment (Hoffman 1997; Powell and DiMaggio 1991). Drawing on March and Olsen, an "institution" is defined as a "relatively stable collection of practices and rules defining appropriate behavior for specific groups of actors in specific situations" (March and Olsen 1999: 306), a definition that is similar in meaning to the understanding of norms employed within the constructivist literature in international relations theory (Finnemore 1996; Keck and Sikkink 1998). As with institutionalism in organization theory, constructivist approaches emphasize cognitive processes, such as learning and cultural mindsets, to explain state/firm behavior. Values, norms, and identities are understood to shape interests/preferences, which are not fixed, but change over time. Furthermore, these approaches look at norms-socialization processes, which can be applied to firms to assess to what extent they have "internalized" global CSR norms, by, for example, determining to what extent they have incorporated CSR norms into corporate policies and management practices.

Borrowing the language of the institutional approach to organizational behavior, this study is broadly situated in an understanding of firm behavior that allows for a "logic of appropriateness" as the basis for action (March and Olsen 1999: 309). Such an approach acknowledges that firms will act according to a "logic of consequences," based on preferences or interests, while recognizing that firm behavior is informed by complex motives that include cognitive and ethical dimensions (ibid.: 311). Institutionalism, moreover, holds that firms are embedded in a larger social environment beyond the marketplace, which induces them to conform to societal norms.

How firms behave is a function of how accepted conceptions of corporate behavior are defined by the firm's social environment, understood as the "organizational field" (Hoffman 1997: 7). The organizational field consists of relevant actors, such as governments, environmental NGOs, industry associations, and chambers of commerce, that define acceptable corporate behavior. The firm's external environment includes societal norms, which are generated nationally and globally. The language of norms used in the international relations constructivist literature is similar to the meaning of institution employed by institutional approaches in organization theory (Finnemore 1996; Keck and Sikkink 1998). This study joins these literatures, by looking at institutional dynamics and global norms to understand why mining companies are promoting CSR. While firms are not completely devoid of choice in this context, the range of choice is constrained/shaped by the external environment.

The variation in firm responses to societal pressures for greater environmental and social responsibility suggests that firms exercise agency or choice in how they respond to those pressures. Given the dynamic and shifting nature of societal norms, firms must ask not only how they will benefit from adopting CSR policies, but also what is the appropriate response, given conflicting rules and norms (March and Olsen 1999). CSR involves choosing between different obligations, rights, and responsibilities, such that understanding how firms respond to external pressures requires an appreciation not just of utility maximization, but of the social norms and rules that structure their decisions (Finnemore and Sikkink 1999: 274). Such normative considerations are especially relevant for mining companies from the advanced industrialized economies operating in developing countries, where different values and cultural understandings present challenges in terms of what the "right" approaches are to CSR in the developing country context. Corporate culture plays an important role in mediating understandings of appropriate action (where culture is understood in cognitive terms, in relation to normative understandings of how one can behave) that influence firm behavior (Fligstein 1990; Hall 1997; Howard-Grenville 2006).

In the past fifteen years, there has been a dramatic shift in thinking (or learning) amongst mining executives, reflecting the broader shift in understanding as to whether a company has obligations beyond its immediate shareholders. Prior to the 1960s, it was assumed that the assimilative capacity of the environment would suffice to absorb effluents and emissions. Any environmental damage could thereby be treated as an externality, and companies did not have to bear the cost. It was further felt that a company's contribution came through producing its product and generating employment.

In the 1960s and 1970s, that thinking began to give way to the realities of greater public environmental awareness and the introduction of regulations in industrialized countries. This shift gained momentum in the 1980s and 1990s, as countries signed on to global environmental treaties, and transnational NGOs kept the environment on the global agenda and drew attention to corporate malpractice. Still, many mining companies were slow to come around, and as late as the mid-1990s, some mining executives remained very behind in their thinking on corporate responsibility (Dashwood 2007a). New institutionalism provides a means to explain how internal resistance to change was overcome, resulting in a dramatic transformation in managerial understandings about the nature of their social and environmental responsibilities.

Given the profit maximizing organizational logic of firms, change agents or norms entrepreneurs make sense of normative shifts within the larger society by identifying instrumental reasons for adopting CSR policies and changing practices. To ensure their CSR policies resonate and are recognized by society, firms frame their CSR policies so that they are aligned with societal norms (sustainable development in the case of mining companies). Strategic responses to normative shifts reflect a normative affirmation of the validity and appropriateness of the societal norm (sustainable development). The "new" institutionalism in organization theory, which emphasizes cognitive processes and the normative environment, is useful in enhancing understanding of how managers interpret their external environment, identify problems, and address challenges. Considerable room is allowed for agency, because the role of senior management is critical in supporting internal CSR initiatives. Research that looks solely at external pressures is not going to be able to account for the variation in firms' responses (Halme 2002).

Historical institutionalism

This study accepts that rationalist approaches provide an important part of the explanation for why firms would adopt CSR policies, and also that institutional context can mediate the instrumental, agent-driven choices of individual firms. Historical institutionalism improves upon methodological individualism, because it looks to how institutional structure conditions responses to external constraints (Hall and Taylor 1996). The research for this study confirms the importance of institutional context, specifically the countries where mining companies are headquartered, as well as where their operations are located, in influencing mining companies' CSR policies. It also provides an explanation for the timing of when mining companies started to report on their CSR obligations. Historical institutional approaches are useful here, because they emphasize the temporal ordering and timing of key developments (Thelen 1999: 388), and trace the unfolding of processes over time (Thelen 1999: 400).

The concept of "critical junctures" found in historical institutional approaches helps to explain the coming together of various external pressures that pushed the mining industry into accepting its social and environmental responsibilities. Critical junctures, "interaction effects between distinct causal sequences that become joined at particular points in time" (Pierson and Skocpol 2002), is a relevant concept to understanding how external constraints that had been increasing over time reached a threshold, triggering significant change within the mining industry (Thelen 1999).

One weakness of the critical-juncture argument is that there is the danger of tautology in identifying *ex ante* when a juncture might be critical: because significant changes took place within the mining industry, the juncture must have been critical.[2] A possible rival explanation can be found in the work of Baumgartner and Jones on punctuated equilibrium in social theory (Baumgartner and Jones 1993). Drawing from theories of biological evolution, the process of evolution is characterized by long periods of stability (equilibrium) "punctuated by compact periods of qualitative, metamorphic (revolutionary) change" (Gersick 1991). Policy change in organizations happens only incrementally, until the occasional sharp burst of policy change, resulting in fundamentally new policies (Baumgartner and Jones 1993). Organizational or policy change is brought about by significant change in the conditions that produce enduring or stable structures, where policy entrepreneurs play a key role. (Baumgartner and Jones 1993; Cioffi-Revilla 1998).

It is argued here that punctuated equilibrium also has an *ex ante* dimension to it: there were/were not dramatic changes in policy because the underlying conditions (or deep structure) did or did not change (see, for example, Givel (2006) on the American tobacco industry's policy monopoly). The key advantage of the critical-junctures approach for

---

[2] I am grateful to one of the anonymous reviewers for his/her insights on the matter of critical junctures versus punctuated equilibriums.

the purpose of this study is that it explains how a series of external pressures bore down on the mining industry in the late 1990s. These pressures did not produce a rapid change in policy on the part of mining companies, but rather, set the process in motion for serious efforts at the unilateral and collaborative levels to improve their CSR policies and practices. To the extent that there were changes in the underlying conditions governing the mining industry, their effects have been cumulative, and did not produce dramatic change in a short period of time. To paraphrase Gersick, the rules of the game have changed, but the game itself has not been up-ended (Gersick 1991: 19). The process of transformation in industry thinking has been neither smooth nor linear (Avant et al. 2010), so the concept of equilibrium does not fit developments still unfolding in the mining sector.

Many mining companies in the mid-1990s were caught with a significant gap between societal expectations and their institutionalized practices (Crossan et al. 1999). For the industry as a whole, the gap had widened so much that companies experienced a legitimacy crisis, and it was recognized that measures needed to be taken to repair legitimacy (Suchman 1995). Mining companies in the 1990s were affected by a range of global developments that negatively affected their access to finance, markets, and land. The critical juncture experienced by mining companies in the mid-to-late 1990s provided the necessary push that led leading companies to advocate for improved environmental and social practices in the mining industry.

One weakness of historical institutional interpretations is that they can be overly deterministic in emphasizing path dependency or structural accounts that seem to push actors in certain directions with little room left for agency (Hall and Taylor 1996). The role of agency is an important part of the explanation for the actions of mining companies. Not only did a number of external pressures come to bear on the mining industry in the late 1990s, but CEOs in major mining companies themselves perceived that the industry had reached a crisis, prompting them to promote a fundamental transformation through industry collaboration at the global level and to improve their unilateral CSR policies and practices.

The importance of agency to this analysis speaks to larger debates within both institutional approaches within organization theory and constructivist approaches in international relations theory, about the relative importance of structure and agency. At one extreme, a firm can be seen as acting completely autonomously, free from external constraints (agency). At the other extreme, the firm is seen to be constitutive of its social environment (structure). Institutional approaches within sociology lean heavily towards the structure side of the debate, by questioning whether individuals can choose freely, and pointing to the cultural and historical frameworks within which individual choices are embedded (Powell and DiMaggio 1991: 9–11). These debates are mirrored in the constructivist approach within international relations theory, with structurally oriented explanations broadly represented by the scholarship of Wendt (1999). To propose that both social structures and agency need to be considered is to argue that the two are mutually constitutive. Social structures are constructed by agents, which in turn influence and condition the behavior of agents (Finnemore 1996: 24). Structural and agency dynamics are both relevant to the explanation of the role and importance of global CSR norms on mining companies.

Weighing the influence of global CSR norms

The central argument advanced in this book is that, although emerging global CSR norms are necessary to the explanation of why mining companies adopted CSR polices and came to frame them in terms of sustainable development, the influence of global norms is not sufficient to explain the policies and intentions of these companies. Most major mining multinationals have adopted the discourse of sustainable development in framing their CSR policies, an important indicator of the weight of this global norm. As will be elaborated upon in Chapter 3, major mining companies with global operations experienced a range of common external pressures, ranging from stricter domestic environmental regulation to sustained targeting from NGOs with transnational linkages. These common external constraints did not elicit a common response, however, in that there were early and late movers in terms of the adoption of stand-alone CSR reports. Furthermore, not all mining companies have exhibited the same degree of commitment to sustainable development, as evidenced in their policies and practices. As will be demonstrated, the crucial factor accounting for variation between mining companies in terms of when they adopted their CSR policies, and the degree of commitment to them, depends very much on the role of senior management and intra-organizational attributes.

Firm-specific or micro-level explanations must work alongside systemic-level explanations to gauge a firm's degree of commitment to

CSR. The role of senior management is especially crucial, and when this book speaks of the impact of global and domestic influences on mining companies, it is the impact on a company's senior management that is being referred to. While the Board of Directors is (or should) be responsible for the oversight of CSR policies, this book focuses on senior managers as the key individuals who influence the company's overall direction and shape CSR policies (Cooksey 2003).

A multi-level framework for explaining CSR norms socialization

To explain the differences between Noranda, Placer Dome, and Barrick, the range of possible influences on CSR can be broadly divided into internal (company) factors, intra-organizational factors, and external factors. Each set of factors can be separated out analytically, but in reality, are best understood to be interdependent. While external factors are often understood to refer to the domestic operating environment, global influences have come to play an increasingly important role, and should be factored in to the analysis.

Internal factors

Internal variables include the role of leadership and managerial attitudes towards CSR. The preferences and strategies of key managers are central to an explanation of why companies would adopt CSR policies (Gunningham et al. 2003; Hemingway and Maclagan 2004; Hoffman 1997; McGuire and Hutchings 2006). The role of managerial leadership in bringing about change is important to understanding how companies come to adopt CSR policies (Chemers and Ayman 1993; Northhouse 1997). Research has demonstrated the crucial role of managerial leadership in determining the extent of a firm's commitment to CSR (Galaskiewicz 1991; Gunningham et al. 2003; Hoffman 1997; Prakash 2000). Furthermore, an individual's professional training and orientation can have a decisive influence on approaches to problem-solving and perceptions of the operating environment (Chwieroth 2007; Downs 1957; Haas 1990, 1992). This is certainly the case in mining, where engineers who work their way up the company can end up in leadership roles.

Variation in managerial perceptions and interpretations (Bansal and Penner 2002; Egri and Herman 2000; Sharma 2000) can influence a company's approach to CSR. As such, the values and beliefs of senior management and the role of managerial leadership is critical in explaining how companies move forward on CSR (Dodge 1997). For example, managers who view environmental challenges as threats or risks to be avoided are likely to be reactive and take a conformist approach to environmental strategy that would entail complying with regulations and other external pressures (Russo and Fouts 1997; Sharma 2000). At the other end of the spectrum, managers who view environmental challenges as opportunities, because they see environmental protection as an integral part of their company's identity, are more likely to take a proactive, or values-based approach to environmental strategy, involving consistent actions to reduce the environmental impact of the company's operations (Sharma 2000).

The contrast between Barrick on one hand, and Placer Dome and Noranda on the other, serves to nicely illustrate the difference between a compliance-driven approach to CSR, as opposed to a values-driven approach. Barrick released its first CSR report in 2002, and did not take on a leadership role in industry-wide global standard setting. In fact, Barrick pulled out of the ICMM in 2002, over concerns that ICMM members were moving too far, too quickly, on initiatives to improve the performance of the mining sector (Executive 1, May 6, 2003). Barrick's initial approach to CSR appeared to focus on minimizing risks and liabilities, and management tended to be defensive, rather than responsive to societal concerns. Barrick in the early 2000s did not yet have the size and profile it has today as the world's largest gold-mining company, which partly explains its late mover status, relative to Noranda and Placer Dome. Leadership in the early 2000s tended to be reactive and defensive, rather than proactive in the face of societal pressures. A cultural shift in terms of external engagement and responsiveness to stakeholder concerns has only started to take hold in the past few years, under a new CEO.

Gunningham et al. identified criteria for evaluating managers' commitment to CSR, including their attitudes towards environmental problems, their environmentally relevant actions and implementation efforts, and their explanations for those actions (Gunningham et al. 2003: 97). Management's attitudes influence whether they see environmental innovation as a cost to be avoided, or an opportunity where environmental investments will bring economic returns, or improve a firm's reputation, where the economic returns may be less immediate. This in turn influences the extent to which management "scans" for information that will improve their company's environmental performance. Management's commitment to CSR can further be gauged by its responsiveness to societal pressures to become more environmentally responsible, such as from neighbors, regulators, customers, and environmental activists, as well as the extent of collaborative interactions with stakeholders. Another dimension of managerial commitment is the nature of implementation efforts, including self-auditing, employee training, and integration of environmental and production-oriented training and decision-making (ibid.: 98).

To get a sense of *why* management chooses to move companies in a more environmentally responsible direction, Kingdon's model can be employed (Kingdon 1995). His insight suggests that for organizational change to occur, a number of variables must come together. Kingdon identifies three separate streams: problem identification or recognition, policy alternatives generation, and politics. When companies encounter problems, it presents "policy entrepreneurs" with the opportunity (policy windows) to introduce new ideas, get them on the corporate agenda, and propose policy options to resolve the problem. Problems need not take the form of a crisis, but they have to be serious enough to grab the attention of senior executives. While Kingdon's model was intended for government bureaucracies, it is applicable to companies as well. Within Placer Dome and Noranda, policy entrepreneurs at the senior level responded to the serious damage to the mining industry's reputation as an opportunity to promote change, both within their organizations, and globally. Policy entrepreneurs can operate both inside and outside the corporation (for example, in the form of environmental NGOs), but the presence of policy entrepreneurs within the corporation is critical to whether action is taken or not.

Research on organizational culture reveals that transformative leadership may not be sufficient to change a firm's CSR practices if there is a dominant culture that resists taking action on CSR issues (Howard-Grenville 2006). Galaskiewicz's work on how firm contributions to charity in Minneapolis-St. Paul became institutionalized highlights the importance of the preferences and strategic actions of individual actors (Galaskiewicz 1991: 293–310). Galaskiewicz points to the critical role of "change agents" in addressing situations where firms are confronted with societal pressures that run contrary to the dominant ideology or culture of the firm. Stressing the role of agency, Galaskiewicz demonstrates that meanings, values, and norms within a company can change through the conscious efforts of change agents (as opposed to external structural pressures).

The critical juncture the mining industry experienced in the mid-to-late 1990s provided the "policy window" or opportunity that enabled policy entrepreneurs within individual mining companies to push for change. Using the language of norms, norms entrepreneurs within the industry worked to alter mindsets, and a steep learning curve ensued as attempts were made to render sustainable development meaningful to mining. Although external pressures were clearly important at this stage, essential to bringing about change was the need for norms entrepreneurs *within* mining companies to set in motion a transformation of beliefs and shared meanings; a cultural shift (Halme 2002).

Organizational factors, culture, and the learning process

Margolis and Walsh suggest a broad framework that points to organizational dynamics to explain the variation in firms' responses to pressures to promote CSR (Margolis and Walsh 2003: 286–90). For example, firms make judgments about whether to respond to pressures (or stimuli), and which ones to respond to. Problems may be framed as a cost or investment, a burden or responsibility, a threat or opportunity, or a combination of these traits. Firms will evaluate options either according to the logic of consequences (weighing costs and benefits) or a logic of appropriateness (weighing the fit of potential options with conceptions of the company's role identity). Management challenges arise from the fact that CSR initiatives may be both legitimacy-seeking and legitimacy-threatening, depending on the interests of various stakeholders and the degree to which they come into conflict.

CSR initiatives can also be "identity-bridging" and "identity-begging" because of the lack of consensus on the proper role of firms in society. Furthermore, a mix of motives is likely to complicate managerial responses, as a desire to aid society is likely to be combined with a desire to secure a company's legitimacy, reputation, and ability to function. Finally, the consequences of CSR initiatives must be weighed, both in terms of their impact on a firm's financial performance, and the extent to which society benefits from such initiatives.

Corporate culture

Variation in companies' commitment to CSR can be traced to internal structure and corporate culture. As Hoffman argues, beyond environmental expenditures and environmental performance indicators, organizational structure and culture are an important measure of a firm's long-term commitment to (environmental) CSR (Hoffman 1997: 8). According to Hoffman, corporate culture includes the existence of environmental goals, the extent of their support by senior management, the incentive structure for employees around achieving those goals, and what positions exist for managing environmental affairs (1997: 8; see also, Gunningham et al. 2003: 97–9).

Another dimension of corporate culture is the cultural framing of CSR initiatives (Howard-Grenville and Hoffman 2003). Corporate cultural attributes have an important influence on how committed companies might be to CSR. In this context, culture is understood from a cognitive perspective, where it refers to the shared meanings held by individuals that shape their understandings of situations and guide their actions within an organization (Howard-Grenville and Hoffman 2003: 71–2). The key insight here is that CSR initiatives that are framed according to a firm's dominant culture are more likely to be taken up and executed. Cultural frames could include operational efficiency, risk management, capital acquisition, market demand, strategic direction, or human resource management (ibid.: 73). In the case of mining companies, risk management is often an important guide to management actions. CSR initiatives framed in terms of risk avoidance, for example, provide a means for specific initiatives to make sense to mining executives and plant managers.

Norms entrepreneurs in mining companies wanting to bring about change have to frame CSR (and later, sustainable development) in a manner consistent with the dominant corporate culture (e.g. risk avoidance) and by challenging accepted meanings and strategies for action (Howard-Grenville 2006: 69). How well they realize that potential depends on the skill with which change agents can draw upon or work around cultural dimensions to promote CSR within the organization (Howard-Grenville 2006).

Differences in organizational culture (Forbes and Jermier 2002; Howard-Grenville 2006; Welford 1997) produce differing CSR responses to external pressures. In her study on how firms respond to environmental challenges, Howard-Grenville found that organizational culture plays a significant role in explaining idiosyncratic firm responses to external pressures on the environment (Howard-Grenville 2006: 49, 64–7). Furthermore, Howard-Grenville finds that subcultures may exist within organizations, such that even if firms present a united external front with a coherent set of environmental policies, they may mask internal turmoil over the nature of the issues, and the responsibility of the organization to act on them (ibid.: 67). These findings are relevant in the case of mining, where many companies have adopted sustainable development to frame their CSR policies, but there is ongoing debate about what sustainable development should mean to the company.

Important scholarly research on the related issue of occupational health and safety in mining provides further insights on the role of subcultures, and even "counter-cultures" within an organization (Gunningham 2008; Gunningham and Sinclair 2009). Gunningham and Sinclair's research on a major mining company in Australia with multiple mine sites found significant variation in the quality of implementation of management-based systems (Coglianese and Nash 2006) for OHS between different mine sites in the same company (2009). Gunningham and Sinclair found that even where senior management was committed to the implementation of effective OHS systems, subcultures based on professional affiliation, geographic location, and management hierarchy (Gunningham and Sinclair 2009) strongly influenced the extent to which systems and standards devised by management were carried out in practice.

Their findings are highly relevant to major mining companies with far-flung facilities in different countries where heterogeneous facilities face heterogeneous conditions (Coglianese and Lazar 2003), with applicability beyond OHS to the full range of CSR initiatives. A key variable identified by Gunningham and Sinclair as influencing the efficacy of management-based systems for OHS is the level of trust between workers and middle management on the mine sites, and between middle management and corporate executives devising the audit, reporting, and monitoring systems (Gunningham and Sinclair 2009). Trust is affected by the degree of commitment of middle management, the extent to which workers and middle management are consulted on the development of management systems (giving workers a sense of ownership), and the extent to which any bad blood (perhaps due to past labor disputes) between workers and all levels of management are overcome or addressed. Individual mine sites run as personal fiefdoms are likely to challenge even the most committed corporate management. These dynamics are especially salient for Barrick, which expanded rapidly in the 2000s after the merger with Homestake and the acquisition of Placer Dome, influencing the desire of management by the mid-2000s to institute more uniform OHS and CSR practices across the organization.

This study confirms the research that demonstrates that professional occupations shape identities and role perceptions and influence the identification of, and approaches to, problems (Howard-Grenville 2006; Huang et al. 2003; Jermier et al. 1991; Van Maanen and Barley 1984). As Gunningham and Sinclair (2009) noted, professional orientation at the mine site, where mine managers have engineering backgrounds, influences the approach to OHS management systems. The predominance of engineers in mining companies means that people may tend towards narrow, specialized, technically oriented roles, with a practical, results-oriented approach to knowledge. Problems are understood as technical challenges to be resolved in a hard-working, "get on with it" environment involving the application of technical expertise (drawn from Howard-Grenville 2006). The requirements of CSR, which entail dealing with dynamic, evolving, and often ambiguous societal expectations, are not always a good match for the traditional mining mindset.

Data is not available on the proportion of employees in mining companies with mining engineering backgrounds that would allow for a systematic analysis of the impact of professional background (see, for example, Chwieroth 2007). There are few engineering schools in Canada devoted specifically to mining engineering, and mining companies hire different types of engineers, including chemical, mechanical, and civil engineers, in addition to those trained specifically in mining engineering. As documented in Chapter 7, and following on Chwieroth, an individual's professional training can serve as a reasonable proxy for the ideas and values that individual holds (Chwieroth 2007: 6). For the industry as a whole, the preference of engineers for science-based approaches presented problems when addressing societal values and perceptions that diverged from that approach. In the 1990s, this dynamic hindered the ability of the industry as a whole to respond adequately to reputational damage stemming from negative societal perceptions.

When confronted with the types of challenges typical of CSR, where the nature of the problem (especially social issues) is not clear-cut, and where technical solutions are not always applicable and where social expectations are dynamic and changing, the technical, "get on with it" approach to problem-solving presents challenges for mining companies dominated by engineers. Norms entrepreneurs in mining companies wanting to bring about change had to work within this cultural context, by framing CSR in a manner consistent with the dominant corporate culture (e.g. risk avoidance and preference for technical problem-solving) and challenging accepted meanings and strategies for action (Howard-Grenville and Hoffman 2003; Howard-Grenville 2006: 69). Leading companies such as Noranda and Placer Dome can be differentiated by the fact that engineers led the push to change attitudes within their companies about CSR, thereby overcoming the mining mindset.

Role of learning

The critical role of senior executives and the dynamics behind a cognitive learning process have been widely documented in the organizational and business literature (for example, Argyris 1990, 1999; Cooksey 2003; Crossan et al. 1999; Hoffman 1997; March and Olsen 1999; Senge 1990). This literature stresses the importance of unpacking the "black box" of the firm, of not treating interests as fixed (even in the context of competitive markets), of not assuming a strict demarcation between firms and the surrounding environment; and that norms, beliefs, and identities (cognitive forces) can influence decision-making as much as technical or material imperatives. The literature addresses the challenges of learning in a context of complexity and uncertainty (Cooksey 2003; Stacey 2000).

Learning has been variously defined, but is understood here to refer to an organization skilled at creating, acquiring, and transferring knowledge, and at modifying its behavior to reflect new knowledge and insights (Garvin 1993). As learning is a slow and incremental process, a gap can occur between changing social environments and institutionalized practices (Crossan et al. 1999: 530). If the gap widens too much, firms can experience a legitimacy crisis (Suchman 1995). Individual mining companies, and the mining industry as a whole, had reached this point by the mid-1990s, as devastating environmental practices became unacceptable to society. Yet while all mining companies were experiencing similar pressures, they did not all respond in the same way. (A condensed version of this discussion can be found in Dashwood 2012.)

Crossan et al. provide a useful framework for thinking about how learning might proceed within a firm (Crossan et al. 1999). Learning is understood to consist of four interrelated processes: intuiting ("the preconscious recognition of the pattern and/or possibilities inherent in a personal stream of experience"), interpreting ("explaining, through words and/or actions, an insight or idea to one's self and to others"), integrating ("the development of shared understanding through dialogue and joint action"), and institutionalizing ("the process of ensuring that routinized actions occur"), whereby learning is embedded into the organization through the establishment of systems, structures, procedures, and strategy (ibid.: 525). Importantly, three levels are identified through which this process occurs: individual, group, and organizational.

The authors envisage that intuiting and interpreting occur at the individual level, interpreting and integrating occur at the group level, and integrating and institutionalizing occur at the organizational level (Crossan et al.: 524–5). Only individuals can intuit, and only individuals and groups can interpret, not organizations, pointing to the central role of individuals in bringing about change in firms. Individual "entrepreneurs" discern future possibilities that have not been identified previously, and through conversations and interactions with others, develop a common language to interpret their vision. Through conversation and dialogue, shared understandings evolve and deepen. To entrench new understandings, new practices must be engendered (through training) and enhanced (through innovation) (ibid.: 529). As practices become routinized through structures, systems and procedures, routines and rules emerge that exist independently of any one individual. As Crossan et al. stress, the learning process is a dynamic one, such that new learning ("feed forward") is affected by what has already been learned and institutionalized ("feed back") (ibid.: 532–4).

This approach to learning, which recognizes the critical role that individual policy entrepreneurs (or change agents) play, is relevant to the experience of the mining companies under study. Policy entrepreneurs in key positions worked at the group and organizational levels to promote CSR policies and institutionalize practices. In the case of Placer Dome and Noranda, sustainable development came to serve as a common language for promoting CSR policies and practices within the organization.

In an important and enlightening article, Antal and Sobczak (2004) draw on the literature detailing the multiple types of learning processes, to identify those learning processes most relevant to CSR. Part of the learning process involves improving on current ways of doing things, what Antal and Sobczak (citing Argyris and Schon 1978, 1996) call "single loop learning" (2004: 81). For mining companies with already engrained ways of thinking (or not) about CSR, some "unlearning" was necessary in order to meet society's shifting expectations (Antal and Sobczak 2004: 82, citing Hedberg 1981). Mining companies undergoing substantial change with respect to CSR have to re-think internal procedures and introduce new measurement techniques to reflect their environmental and social obligations, what Antal and Sobczak (citing Argyris and Schon 1978) call "double loop learning."

In practice, all mining companies had to engage in "unlearning," in order to address mindsets and practices that had become outdated. Noranda and Placer Dome were among the earliest companies to get to this point. Both companies also had to learn how to engage in "deutero" learning (Antal and Sobczak 2004: 81–2, citing Argyris and Schon 1978), the ability to "learn how to learn." Grappling with CSR entails responding to shifting societal expectations, to the emergence of new issues, and to the shifting constellations of stakeholders. Learning is an ongoing, dynamic process, requiring the ability to adapt to evolving societal norms. To facilitate this process, deutero learning requires interactive learning processes between organizations at the local, regional, national, and international level. National industry organizations such as the Mining Association of Canada (MAC), as well as international organizations such as the ICMM, facilitate such learning. Existing research confirms the importance of industry collaboration for changing mindsets and influencing the world views of corporate managers (Galaskiewicz 1991; Hardy et al. 2003).

Galaskiewicz's research points to the importance of professional roles and professional networks in promoting social learning and in institutionalizing an ethic of commitment to corporate responsibility. This process includes the creation of professional positions specifically responsible for corporate responsibility, and the existence of organizations, such as professional associations, committed to corporate responsibility. Galaskiewicz found that the effect of a network of professionals committed to corporate responsibility is two-fold: 1. professional networks shape one another's priorities and those of their respective firms; and 2. a system was created whereby consensus could be reached on where charitable dollars would be expended (Galaskiewcz 1991: 306).

Collaboration through mining–industry associations at the national and global levels served to institutionalize normative shifts within industry. As opportunities for learning about CSR increased, more corporate managers were brought along. To the extent that companies were prepared to engage with their external critics, there was increased sensitization to the concerns of other actors, such that new patterns of interaction affected how companies perceived their situations (Campbell 2006: 933). For example, interaction with community groups sensitizes companies to the perspectives of the communities in which they operate. This process was initially nationally based, but became increasingly globalized, as NGOs and business associations began to operate transnationally.

Research has demonstrated that participation in professional networks and industry associations supportive of CSR allows the potential for short-term profit maximizing views to be superseded by views that look to long-term value (Campbell 2007: 959; Galaskiewicz 1991). For example, reputation concerns prompted some mining companies to contemplate the long-term business benefits of caring for the communities in which they operate, and not harming the environment. The Mining, Minerals and Sustainable Development (MMSD) initiative, which grew out of the Global Mining Initiative (GMI), facilitated multi-stakeholder dialogue, allowed mining companies to interact with their external critics, to appreciate their concerns, and take them into account when making corporate policy (Campbell 2007: 960). Such patterns of interaction affect how actors perceive and define their situations, such that the definition of their interests can change over time (Fligstein 1990; Ostrom 1990; Prakash and Potoski 2007b).

The ICME, and later, the ICMM, created an institutionalized environment, where normative calls for more socially responsible behavior could be invoked (King and Lenox 2000). The creation of the Responsible Care® program in the chemical industry, and the fact that mining companies are heavy users of chemicals, influenced thinking within the mining industry about the need for similar collaboration in the mining sector. The ICME, however, was a very "weak sword" (Prakash and Potoski 2007b: 781), as its mandate was not to promote industry self-regulation. It was in large part the crisis the mining industry faced in the mid-1990s that set in motion the developments that led to the creation of the ICMM in 2001. The ICMM has progressively moved from a weak sword club to a medium sword, with the introduction of third-party certification and public disclosure (McPhail 2008).

The above discussion highlights how social learning within mining companies might occur. Left out of the explanation, however, is where the ideas come from that are ultimately acted upon by change agents, or norms entrepreneurs. To better understand learning on CSR, it is necessary to turn to influences operating in the external environment.

External environment

The external environment includes a wide range of potential variables, encompassing political, legal, and economic factors. External variables frequently identified in the business literature include the level of regulatory and public scrutiny, the extent of environmental risks inherent in the company's operations, the degree of local community concern and pressure, a company's stake in reputational considerations, the extent to which market opportunities exist for adopting "green" processes, the extent to which industry associations are encouraging CSR (or not), the impact of parallel initiatives in other sectors, and the role of locally, nationally, or transnationally based NGOs (for summary, see Campbell 2006 and Flohr et al. 2010). Within the external environment, this study makes a further distinction between domestic (Canadian) influences on mining companies, and global (or international) influences.

Gunningham et al. organize external variables according to the concept of a "license to operate," derived from the expectations of economic, legal, and social stakeholders (Gunningham et al. 2003: 35–8). Consistent with institutional insights, the concept of a license to operate captures the fact that firms are dependent on various economic, regulatory, and social stakeholders, who define the nature of the license. The regulatory license, economic license, and social license interact with each other in a dynamic relationship, such that no single component can be isolated out as "driving" CSR. Furthermore, the different components of the license are malleable, and firms negotiate with key stakeholders to set the terms of the license. Significantly, corporate managers interpret similar regulatory, economic, and social expectations differently.

For mining companies, a most salient risk is opposition from the local communities in which they operate. Unlike manufacturing multinationals, which have greater mobility, mining companies choose their locations based on the availability of metals to extract. Failure to establish and maintain good community relations could result in a company losing its "social license to operate," even where the company possesses a regulatory license to operate. This can drive mining companies to adopt beyond-compliance measures, in order to meet social expectations. As Gunningham et al. (2003) correctly note, social actors, such as environmental NGOs, can influence firm behavior directly through the social license, but can also influence firms indirectly by seeking leverage over the terms of the economic license (through consumer boycotts, for example) as well as the regulatory license (by pressuring regulators to tighten regulations).

Stakeholder theory

The view that firms operate within a social and ecological framework, such that they rightly have responsibilities that extend beyond their shareholders, is reflected in stakeholder theory (Freeman 1984). Stakeholder theory extends the realm of actors to whom firms are responsible, to include local communities affected by a firm's operations, the natural environment, employees, NGOs, governments (all levels), contractors, the media, and industry associations (Donaldson and Preston 1995; Jacobs and Getz 1995).

Firms have a broad constituency, and stakeholder theorists advance both instrumental and normative arguments to explain why firms seek good relations with external stakeholders (Donaldson and Preston 1995). Instrumental arguments focus on how stakeholders may affect a firm's objectives, while normative approaches focus on how stakeholders may be affected by a firm's activities. Consistent with the rational choice approach, the instrumental variant of stakeholder theory argues that firms will factor in the interests of stakeholders in efforts to maximize profit, as failure to do so could negatively affect the bottom line. The building of strong stakeholder relations is believed to improve profitability, through heightened brand reputation, positive media coverage, and less extreme opposition (Wheeler et al. 2003). In this respect, CSR is understood as a stakeholder risk-management strategy.

According to Donaldson and Preston, all stakeholder theory, even that with an instrumental basis, has an implicit or explicit normative dimension (1995). Stakeholder theory requires a fundamental shift in managerial objectives away from an exclusive focus on shareholder value, towards a consideration of the rights and interests of all stakeholders (although not all stakeholders are given equal priority) (ibid.: 80). When firms are concerned with reputation or value-adding activities, the benefits of good stakeholder relations are difficult to measure in straightforward cost-benefit terms.

Legitimacy theory lends insights into the strategies firms employ to foster good relations with external stakeholders. Legitimacy theory recognizes the importance of societal norms, and the need for firms to respect both widely acknowledged norms, such as sustainable development and respect for human rights, as well as norms specific to local communities where they operate (Taylor et al. 2001; Waddock and Boyle 1995). For example, firms adopt voluntary standards in order to earn legitimacy and goodwill from stakeholders (Potoski and Prakash 2005; Taylor et al. 2001). Firms will also employ communications strategies, such as stand-alone sustainability reports, to address threats to their legitimacy arising from conflicts in the communities where they operate (Jenkins 2004).

Wheeler et al. (2003) suggest that societal norms can be used strategically by firms to promote value-maximizing goals. They argue that the norm of sustainable development serves as a bridge between the firm-centric approach of stakeholder theory and the societal level in which the firm is embedded (ibid.: 16). Sustainable development serves as a "safe linguistic haven" for previously antagonistic actors (business, government, NGOs) to promote a common vision for the future. Critical to the success of this strategy is the recognition that value creation must be understood to reside beyond the confines of the firm. According to Jenkins, the widespread adoption of sustainable development to frame their community relations policies is a strategic response to social challenges designed to earn, maintain, or regain legitimacy (2004: 32).

Sustainable development was certainly employed by mining companies for strategic reasons, but the logic of sustainable development requires a normative understanding about the value of promoting economic, social, and environmental sustainability. Firms may well have to employ frames that resonate with their institutionalized practices to justify strategies that address stakeholder concerns, such as risk management in the case of mining (Cragg and Greenbaum 2002). Instrumental logics can be used to appeal to internal constituencies while also recognizing the intrinsic value of external stakeholder rights. As such, sustainable development fits well with an approach to stakeholder theory that understands the normative embeddedness of instrumental claims.

Conceptualizing global norms

How do global norms fit into this analysis? The constructivist literature in international relations provides insights into how evolving global CSR norms might influence corporate managers and firm behavior (Dashwood 2012). Norms can be defined as shared (or inter-subjective) expectations about appropriate behavior held by a community of actors (Finnemore 1996: 22). Evidence for the existence of norms can be found in the patterns of behavior that are consistent with their prescriptions, as well as in discourse (ibid.: 23). Norms can emanate from states, NGOs (often conflated with civil society), international organizations, firms, and private sector actors such as industry and business associations (Cutler et al. 1999; Porter 2005). Norms vary according to the degree to which they are universally accepted and the extent to which they are contested as new, emerging norms. Firms themselves promote norms, through their own actions, which can encourage institutional "isomorphism," as other firms model themselves on successful firms engaging in CSR, and through industry associations (both national and global ones) (Flohr et al. 2010). Norms are reflected in broad shifts in societal attitudes about issues such as the environment, which influence the social, economic, and regulatory license to operate (Wapner 1995).

Evidence for the existence of global CSR norms is present at both the behavioral and discursive levels. They vary in their degree of specificity, from broad principles to specific rules (Porter 2005: 219). It can be said that a hierarchy of global CSR norms exists, depending on whether they are codified as "hard" law in the form of treaties, reflect "soft" law (Kirton and Trebilcock 2004), such as United Nations declarations or global conference proceedings, or are strictly voluntary or quasi-"voluntary" in nature.

At the top end of the hierarchy is "hard" law, in the form of environmental and human rights treaties. While these treaties are legally binding on states, not firms, they nevertheless reflect a near universal consensus on standards of behavior applicable to CSR and the social environment within which firms operate. At the "soft" law, or nonbinding level, there is a huge range of CSR-relevant norms, through such state-sponsored processes as the Organisation for Economic Co-operation and Development (OECD) Guidelines for Multinational Enterprise (MNE), the International Labour Organization (ILO) regulations, and the UN Global Compact, whose guiding principles reflect CSR norms in the areas of human rights, labor, and the environment. Important conferences such as the World Summit on Sustainable Development (2002) and the Conference on Climate Change in Bali (2007) release declarations that reflect an emerging consensus on the part of a wide variety of actors, including states, civil society actors, and firms. Wide-ranging consensus is reflected in such initiatives as the International Finance Corporation's (IFC) Performance Standards (2006, revised 2011), which are effectively mandatory for any mining company seeking financing for operations in developing countries. Another example is the work of the Special Representative of the Secretary General (SRSG) on the issue of human rights and transnational corporations and other business enterprises, which sets out the obligation of international business to *respect* human rights (Ruggie 2008).

CSR norms which are strictly "voluntary" are evident in a large and growing number of standards that range from CSR-reporting indicators and environmental-management procedures, such as the Global Reporting Initiative (GRI) and the International Organization for Standardization (ISO), respectively, to industry initiatives that set out specific standards relevant to that particular industry. Within the mining sector, there have been a number of initiatives since the late 1990s stemming from the Global Mining Initiative (GMI) that led to the MMSD multistakeholder consultations process to the creation in 2001 of the ICMM. Even within the "voluntary" realm, there are initiatives that could be considered quasi-regulatory in the sense that they entail outside, third-party verification that standards are being adhered to. The Forestry Stewardship Council (FSC) is a prime example of this and there are many other initiatives with varying degrees of rigor in terms of monitoring compliance (Cragg 2005).

Norms socialization and sustainable development

Keck and Sikkink shed light on the process of norms socialization in their seminal work on transnational advocacy networks (Keck and Sikkink 1998). Transnational advocacy networks consist of advocates (often NGOs) that are "organized to promote causes, principled ideas and norms, and they often involve individuals advocating policy changes that cannot be easily linked to a rationalist understanding of their 'interests'" (ibid.: 8–9). Although they limited their discussion to transnational advocacy networks and their impact on state behavior, the dynamics they describe can be related to firms as well.

Transnational advocacy networks most commonly employ persuasion and socialization to influence state behavior, employing such strategies as reasoning with opponents to bring about change. Just as often, networks will take a confrontational stance, by bringing pressure to bear, arm-twisting, encouraging sanctions, and shaming (Keck and Sikkink 1998: 16). Keck and Sikkink identify four tactics employed by networks, including: 1. information politics: the dissemination of information about an issue or cause; 2. symbolic politics: the use of symbols, actions, or stories to give an issue resonance for a larger public; 3. leverage politics: calling upon powerful actors to exert pressure or influence on the target; and 4. accountability politics: holding powerful actors to their previously stated policies or principles (ibid.: 16).

Local, national, and transnational NGOs have used these tactics effectively in targeting mining companies. With the tendency for mines to be located in remote, rural areas, mining operations used to be out of sight (and out of mind) of all but the local communities directly affected by them. Since the late 1980s, NGOs have been able to take advantage of information technologies to widely disseminate information about the environmental impact of mining activities. Mining companies' reputations can be damaged if NGOs are able to draw attention to gaps between publicly stated policies on CSR and actual practice.

The actual influence of NGOs, whether directly or indirectly, is a question of degree. As disseminators of global norms, NGOs can influence the discursive positions of mining companies, whereby they acknowledge that environmental degradation is bad and must be avoided. NGO efforts can also result in companies changing their policies, and ultimately, their behavior (Keck and Sikkink 1998: 25). The degree of influence of NGOs depends on how vulnerable companies are to normative pressure (ibid.: 29). Material incentives clearly figure into why companies would change their policies and behavior. Individual mining companies are vulnerable to direct targeting by NGOs in communities in which they operate, because they lack mobility and must locate where the ore is. But companies may be vulnerable if they are sensitive to moral leverage, if they are concerned about reputation, or if they wish to be seen as good corporate citizens. Such sensitivity may not be the result of purely material concerns, but rather, of cognitive preferences on the part of managers. At this level, the role of management becomes an important determinant of how a company might respond to normative pressure.

Firms that adapt in response to normative pressure are likely to do so either as instrumental, strategic adaptation, or because they see CSR norms as consistent with their interests and/or identities. Rather than being fixed, material interests may come to be interpreted in light of collective understandings of appropriate behavior in a given realm (such as the environment). Stakeholder theory implicitly acknowledges this process when it identifies a wider range of stakeholders to whom firms are accountable. It is also the case that norms initially adopted for instrumental or strategic reasons may gradually be maintained out of conviction that they are the appropriate basis for action, ultimately influencing understandings of interests.

Building on Keck and Sikkink's work on transnational advocacy networks, Risse et al. developed a framework of norms socialization, whereby states (in our case, firms) change their behavior in accordance with societal expectations (Risse et al. 1999: 11–17). When faced with normative pressures, firms may engage in instrumental, or strategic, interest-based adaptation to counteract them. The common response of the majority of mining companies up to the mid-1990s was to deny the fact of serious environmental degradation, often by questioning the validity of the science behind the claims. Some firms chose to start "talking the talk" about the need to protect the environment, adjusting their behavior without necessarily believing in the validity of the norms. Such a response usually takes the form of a policy statement on CSR, which is often discounted as a mere public relations exercise.

Some firms may also begin to engage in discussions with societal actors, such as states, NGOs, and international organizations, seeking to persuade them to change their behavior. Persuasion can take different forms, including dialogue and argumentation, but also shaming and the exertion of pressure. Firms that saw it in their interest to make tactical concessions may find themselves becoming "entrapped" by their own words. Over time, as firms engage in dialogue with NGOs, states, and international organizations, they may become persuaded to see their interests in new ways, which are consistent with CSR norms. At this point, for example, firms might recognize that investing in environmentally sound processes can both save on consumption costs and serve a broader public good. As firms engage in internal discussions around issues of CSR they may develop a consensus that corporate responsibility is appropriate. Policies that were initially adopted for instrumental, strategic reasons, may subsequently be sustained through conviction of their normative validity. Firms' identities may be transformed where they wish to be seen as good corporate citizens, as opposed to corporate pariahs.

Argumentation and persuasion involves a learning process amongst individuals, and change in behavior is dependent on their having reached a consensus about the validity of CSR norms. Senior managers may be convinced of the appropriateness of CSR norms, but for changes in firm behavior to be durable, a gradual process of institutionalization must occur. Risse et al. (1999) draw on institutional approaches to show that the final stage of norms socialization is when norms acquire a "taken for granted" status, independent of individual beliefs (ibid.: 17). For institutionalization to occur, it is necessary that institutional practices, or "standard operating procedures" be in place.

Risse et al. (1999) identify two phases in the institutionalization process that are useful in explaining the degree of commitment of firms to CSR norms. The first, "prescriptive status," is applicable when firms regularly refer to CSR norms to describe and comment on their behavior. "Prescriptive status" is achieved when the validity claims of CSR norms are no longer controversial, even if actual behavior is inconsistent with CSR norms (ibid.: 29). Firms that have reached prescriptive status would need to demonstrate a sustained effort to improve their CSR practices and performance. Firms are often accused of not matching words with deeds. Many mining companies have reached a stage of CSR norms socialization where the validity of norms is no longer controversial, but where actual behavior is still inconsistent with CSR norms (prescriptive status). Evidence that Noranda and Placer Dome had reached this stage by the late 1990s can be discerned from their sustained effort to improve their CSR policies and practices, a willingness to engage with external critics, and the leadership role they played in promoting sustainable development in the context of mining at the global level. For a variety of reasons, Barrick did not achieve prescriptive status around global CSR norms until the late 2000s.

The final phase of norms socialization or institutionalization is "rule-consistent behavior," where practices are consistent with CSR norms. Few, if any, mining companies have reached this stage, because of the inherently damaging nature of their operations to the environment, the challenging social context in which mining operations are located, and continuing debate as to the appropriate social role for mining companies, especially in developing countries and when dealing with indigenous communities.

Table 2.1 applies a selection of key phases in the norms-socialization process to the corresponding organizational responses of a typical mining company. Although it is not being suggested here that there is an

Table 2.1 *Phases of sustainable development (SD) norms socialization*

Denial	Strategic adaptation	Conviction	Prescriptive status
– Environment treated as externality – No consideration of social impact	– Talk the talk/ lip service – Tactical concessions	– Normative validity of SD accepted – Committed leadership (senior executives, Board)	– Institutionalization; "walk the walk"
Organizational response – Questioning of science	**Organizational response** – Release of SD policy; – Reference to SD in annual report	**Organizational response** – Organizational changes, e.g. creation of VP, sustainability; – EMS established; – Release of stand-alone EHS/SD reports	**Organizational response** – Ongoing effort to improve performance – Continuous engagement with stakeholders

automatic linear progression, the table points to the sorts of organizational arrangements that would have to be in place to gauge the degree of a company's commitment to sustainable development.

The norms life cycle

The process by which norms have been disseminated in the mining sector is broadly consistent with the literature on the "life cycle" of norms, as applied to states (Finnemore and Sikkink 1999; Keck and Sikkink 1998; Risse et al. 1999). According to the life cycle theory of norms development, domestic support/pressure is crucial in the early stages of norms development (Finnemore and Sikkink 1999). The literature on the dissemination of human rights norms shows that the initial pressure came from transnational advocacy networks of NGOs with a global reach, but based in the "West."

In the case of firms, domestic pressure would refer to the countries in which mining companies are headquartered. The fact that leaders emerged from the advanced industrialized economies points to the salience of the domestic context in which normative propositions originate. By this logic, considerable explanatory weight must be assigned to the domestic (or state-based) sources of norms that eventually become accepted at the global (or international level) (Katzenstein 1996; Meckling 2011). Also crucial in the early stages of the life cycle of norms is the leadership role taken by early movers headquartered in the advanced industrialized economies.

Once a critical mass of firms come to accept the normative validity of sustainable development, a critical threshold or tipping point is reached, after which a norms cascade occurs (Finnemore and Sikkink 1999: 255). This second stage of the norms life cycle occurred in the mid-2000s, when a critical mass of mining companies came to accept sustainable development as a normative framework for their CSR policies. Evidence of the acceptance of sustainable development norms comes both from discourse and patterns of behavior that are consistent with their prescriptions (Finnemore 1996: 23).

Figure 2.1 reproduces the aggregate data from Table 1.1, to show that for mining companies, sustainable development began to emerge as an accepted norm in the mining industry in the late 1990s to early 2000s. In the mid-2000s, the data clearly suggests that a norms cascade had occurred, what Finnemore and Sikkink refer to as Stage 2 of the

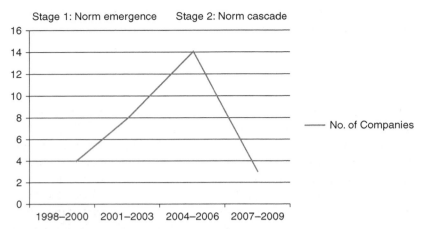

Figure 2.1 Number of major mining companies with sustainable development/
sustainability in the title of their reports, by first year of use of term.

norms life cycle (Finnemore and Sikkink 1999). Stage 3 of the norms life
cycle entails internalization of the sustainable development norm, but
this cannot be discerned from the data alone and is therefore not
presented in the figure.

The role of norms entrepreneurs, or change agents working within
individual mining companies, was important in bringing sustainable
development norms to a critical threshold from whence a norms cascade
could occur. The efforts of leaders working through industry associations to persuade other mining companies also played a critical role.
Consistent with research on other voluntary associations, such as
Responsible Care® in the chemical industry, a range of sociological
pressures (informal coercive, or peer pressure; normative; mimetic;
dissemination of best practices) served to encourage the framing of
CSR policies in terms of sustainable development (King and Lenox
2000; Prakash and Potoski 2007b). Not all mining companies chose
to frame their policies in terms of sustainable development because they
believed in the normative validity of the concept. For some, the motive
was one of rhetorical framing or "symbolic adoption" in order to
manage their public image (Campbell 2007: 950; King and Lenox
2000; Meyer and Rowan 1997). Where reputation is at stake, companies are more likely to mimic successful peers (isomorphism) (Howard
et al. 1999: 285). Some mining companies were also mimicking what

other firms were doing in order to gain legitimacy among them (Campbell 2007: 959; Margolis and Walsh 2003: 286; Orlitzky et al. 2003: 426). These dynamics are consistent with the overall argument that a combination of instrumental and normative motives were at play.

Conclusion

This chapter has identified what are considered to be the key variables at both firm and global levels which influence the CSR policies of mining companies. At the firm level, managerial leadership, cultural attributes, and learning processes are key to explaining how mining companies respond to external pressures. At the global level, the dissemination of norms through a variety of means is central to understanding the influence of sustainable development on mining companies' CSR policies. Interspersed between the global and firm levels is the domestic level, where institutional context plays a vital role, encapsulating such actors as states, NGOs, and industry associations (and their global

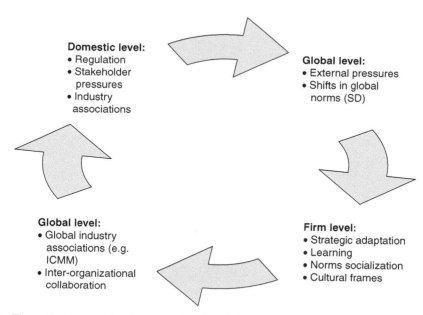

Figure 2.2 Interaction between global and firm levels in explaining influences on mining companies' CSR policies.

counterparts). Figure 2.2 seeks to capture the dynamic and interdependent relationship between variables operating at the global, national, and firm levels.

The next chapter will begin to operationalize the three-level institutional approach, by accounting for the structural changes in the mining industry, as well as major developments affecting the industry, and their implications for CSR adoption. The subsequent three chapters will turn to the individual case studies of Noranda (Chapter 4), Placer Dome (Chapter 5), and Barrick (Chapter 6), where firm-level responses to domestic and global contexts will be explained. Noranda and Placer Dome, as early movers, and Barrick, as a relative late mover, will be contrasted in terms of their approaches to environmental and social challenges, as reflected in the role of managerial leadership and their corporate culture as it relates to CSR. Chapter 7 will then return to global-level dynamics, by exploring the role of industry leaders and the impact of their efforts through the global mining industry associations.

3 | Major developments in the global mining industry

Introduction

This chapter sets out the major changes that occurred in the global mining industry from 1990 onwards and their implications for CSR adoption. There were structural changes in the industry that influenced CSR adoption, the most significant of which was the opening up in the 1990s of new investment opportunities in the developing world. It is argued that mining companies were not attracted to developing countries because of lax environmental laws. Rather, it was precisely because of regulatory deficiencies that major mining companies sought to establish global standards for the industry in a context where serious mining accidents tarnished the reputation of the industry as a whole. The three-level institutional approach helps to explain the impact on CSR adoption of major global developments, as well as growing restrictions on mining in the advanced industrialized economies. Rational choice institutionalism explains the incentive structures in the advanced industrialized economies that led mining companies to adopt CSR. The critical-juncture concept in historical institutionalism accounts for how various pressures came together in the mid-to-late 1990s, prompting unilateral CSR adoption, collaborative initiatives, and the acceptance of sustainable development. The critical juncture facing the mining industry is a necessary part of the explanation for significant change in the policies and practices of mining companies.

Structural changes in the global mining industry

The 1990s were marked by a significant expansion in opportunities for mineral resource development. Mining companies with headquarters in the advanced industrialized economies, while facing growing restrictions at home, benefited from a number of major global developments. With the end of the Cold War, new market economies opened up in Eastern Europe, Latin America, Asia, and Africa (Cohen 1996; Warhurst 1994). Structural adjustment programs (SAPs) imposed on/recommended to indebted developing countries by international financial institutions (IFIs) encouraged the privatization of state mining assets. Mining laws in many countries were revised and/ or enacted, with a view to providing incentives to encourage foreign direct investment (FDI). The scope of these changes can be seen in the fact that between 1985 and 1995, over thirty-five countries made changes to, or enacted, mining laws, while another thirty-five made changes to national policy and laws, with a view to attracting FDI (Clark 1997). The result has been significant geographic shifts in exploration and development, away from the United States, Canada, and Australia, and towards South America, starting in the early 1990s (most significantly in Chile) and to a lesser extent in the Asia-Pacific region and Africa (Clark 1997). The results of new exploration and development were borne out in the late 1990s and 2000s, with significant new projects coming on stream in various parts of the developing world.

Some of these trends, such as privatization, began in the early 1980s, in response to low metal prices and metal demand, which dramatically reduced cash flows for state mining companies and access to exploration and development funds. The magnitude of the privatization effort was that in 1995 alone, over US$2 billion in funding was raised (*Mining Journal* 1996). Subsequent developments in the 1990s changed the structure of the industry, as major mining companies significantly expanded their global operations. This process included the expansion of already large mining companies (such as RTZ), and the development of large new companies through the merger and acquisition of other medium and large mining companies (e.g. Teck Corporation) (Clark 1997). Mergers and acquisitions continued at a frenzied pace in the 2000s, with some significant ones, including the merger of BHP and Billiton, the acquisition of Placer Dome by Barrick Gold, the acquisition of WMC by BHP-Billiton, and the acquisition of Inco by CVRD, now Vale. Table 3.1 shows the industry leaders in a selection of metals, as of 2009.

Industrial development in emerging economies such as India, China, and Brazil ensured increased consumption of the majority of minerals. Key industries on which the metals industry depend, including appliances, automobiles, and beverages, have performed well in light of

Table 3.1 *Industry leaders by type of metal and largest producers, 2009*

Metal	Company	Largest producers
Gold	Barrick (Can), Newmont (US), Anglo-Gold Ashanti (SA)	South Africa, United States, Australia, China, Canada
Iron ore	Rio Tinto (Aust/UK), BHP/Billiton (Aust/UK), Cleveland Cliffs (US), CVRD/Vale (Brazil)	China, Brazil, Australia, India, Russia
Copper	Codelco (Chile), Phelps Dodge (US), Freeport-McMoRan (US)	Chile, United States, Indonesia, Peru
Aluminum	Rio Tinto (Aus/UK), RTZ	Guinea, Australia, Brazil, Jamaica, India
Zinc	CVRD/Vale (Brazil), Teck Cominco (Can), Xstrata (Switz)	China, Australia, Peru, Canada, United States
Nickel	Xstrata (Switz), CVRD/Vale (Brazil)	Canada, Australia, Russia, Cuba, Indonesia

Source: Stueck, *Globe and Mail,* 2009.

increased demand in the emerging economies, especially China (Gale Group 2007). China has been responsible for a significant increase in demand for iron ore, copper, gold, zinc, and lead (which had declined dramatically from the 1970s due to environmental and health regulations). New technologies have further increased the demand for certain metals, such as gold, silver, aluminum, lead, copper, iron, zinc, and tin, used in computers; and cobalt, nickel, zinc, gold, silver, lead, and copper, used in cell phones. Figures 3.1 and 3.2 show the global trend in production of a selection of metals (copper, gold, nickel, silver, and zinc).

Since 2006, there have been further seismic shifts in the mining industry. Metals such as copper, aluminum, zinc, nickel, and gold enjoyed exponential price increases, followed by a collapse in the metals market in the second half of 2008, with the financial crisis. There were record levels of merger and acquisition activity in 2006 and 2007 (Xstrata/Falconbridge, CVRD/Inco, Freeport/Phelps Dodge, Barrick/Placer, BHP/WMC, Rio Tinto/Alcan) (McMillan LLP 2009). China, which has been investing in developing countries for a decade now, to meet its demand for metals, has recently moved into developed countries, such as Australia and Canada.

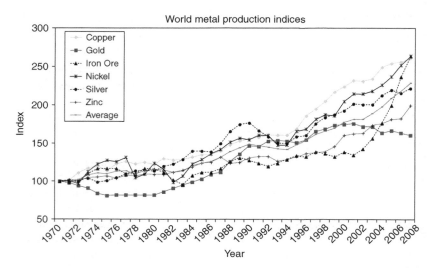

Figure 3.1 World production of selected metals, 1970–2008.
Source: US Census Bureau, 2009.

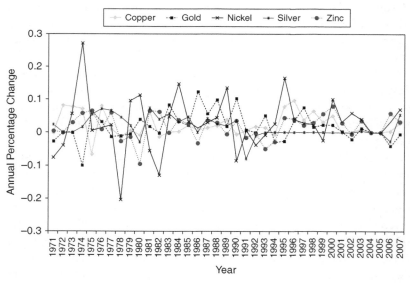

Figure 3.2 Percent change in production levels, selected metals, 1971–2007.
Source: US Census Bureau, 2009.

Canada's place in the global mining industry

Canada is a major player in the global mining industry. Canada is a leading miner of uranium, nickel, titanium, zinc, aluminum, gold, copper, and lead. Canada is also a major player in certain non-metallic minerals, including diamonds and potash (world's number one producer) (Natural Resources Canada 2004). Canada is the world's largest exporter of minerals and metals (US$46.6 billion in 2003), with the US remaining Canada's principal trading partner (Gale Group 2007). Canada is the world's third largest source of capital for the global mining industry, after the UK and Australia (with the US fourth largest), with most of the world's major mining companies listed on the Toronto Stock Exchange (PricewaterhouseCoopers 2004). Canadian mining companies (mostly juniors) play a major role in the global exploration side of the mining industry (Natural Resources Canada 2004).

Hard-rock mining and smelting process

Although there is much romance associated with some of the fruits of mining, such as gold and diamonds, there is nothing romantic about the manner in which the ore is extracted.[1] Hard-rock mining involves the displacement of large amounts of earth in order to extract the desired metal ore. The discarded earth, or waste rock, is then stored in huge piles, which can leach toxic metals or acid produced when previously unexposed rock is exposed to the air and water. Acid produced by mine waste leaches and releases other highly toxic compounds, such as arsenic, mercury, cadmium, and lead. Acid-rock drainage can seep into groundwater, streams, and rivers, endangering potable water supplies, aquatic and human life.

Toxic chemicals used to extract ore, such as cyanide in the case of gold, must be stored in tailings ponds, which if not properly maintained can spill, destroying rivers and the human and animal life dependent on

---

[1] Information for this section is drawn from Earthworks/Oxfam America 2004 – a good layperson's source on the mining and smelting process. Readers interested in a more technically savvy analysis of the mining process and its environmental effects should consult UNEP 2000. See also Eggert 1994; Cohen 1996; Warhurst 1992. For details on environmental effects, see Balkau and Parsons 1999. For details on socio-cultural effects, see Clark and Clark 1999. See Yakovleva 2005 for a comprehensive overview of environmental and social effects.

them. Tailings dam failures are the most common major accident associated with mining. Where tailings disposal on site is unfeasible (for example, where mining takes place in areas prone to earthquakes), tailings are pumped into nearby rivers (riverine tailings disposal) or oceans, destroying aquatic eco-systems and coral reefs. Both acid-rock drainage and tailings disposal present expensive and technologically demanding challenges, which is why these problems continue to persist even where companies seek to address these issues responsibly.

Many metals, such as copper, zinc, bauxite, and nickel, must be subjected to smelting and refining before they are ready for market, a major source of air pollution in the form of sulfur dioxide emissions. Some smelting processes produce "persistent organic pollutants" (POPs), which do not break down readily and tend to bio-accumulate. Smelting processes consume large amounts of energy, encouraging the construction of hydroelectric dams (themselves a source of environmental and social disruption). Mining typically also consumes very large quantities of water, which can cause substantial hydrological disruption.

In the past two decades, the mining industry has transitioned away from underground mining to surface mining, to cut costs. Surface mining entails blasting so as to remove the soil and surface rock, producing massive craters. Surface mining has caused social disruption of the communities in the vicinity of the mines, through noise and vibrations from the blasting, and displacement when communities are moved to make way for mining. In many parts of the developing world, many people lack legal title to the land, making them vulnerable to eviction to make way for mining companies, as occurred on a massive scale during the 1990s in the Tarkwa District of Western Ghana, which lies along the prolific Ashanti Gold Trend (Dashwood and Puplampu 2010). Indigenous communities in both the industrialized and developing world are often negatively affected by mining when it takes place on traditional territories, degrading cultural and religious sites.

Implications for CSR

Sectoral idiosyncrasies within the mining industry may be a factor that has pushed mining companies to address common constraints in a similar way. The nature of the market for minerals, with its boom–bust quality, has often pushed mining companies to behave irresponsibly. The literature predicts that firms whose financial performance is weak, or who operate in a difficult economic environment where near-term profitability is in question, are less likely to act in socially responsible ways (Campbell 2007; Margolis and Walsh 2003; Orlitzky et al. 2003). Research has also clearly shown that firms that operate in a highly competitive environment will be tempted to take short cuts, including compromising worker safety and damaging the environment (Campbell 2007; Dore 2000; Roe 2003; Schneiberg 1999). Furthermore, the very severe and long-lasting nature of pollution problems associated with mining increases the financial burden of environmental responsibility. The disincentives for mining companies to assume the costs of environmental protection would seem overwhelming. Why then, would mining company executives assume such costs?

The three-level institutional analysis provides a means to develop an understanding of how and why mining companies responded to major developments affecting their industry.

Historical institutionalism: the critical juncture

An important part of the explanation for CSR adoption is that mining companies were facing a crisis in the mid-to-late 1990s. (A condensed version of this discussion can be found in Dashwood 2011.) Consistent with historical institutionalism, it is argued that the mining industry had reached a "critical juncture," as a number of distinct, yet interrelated, developments came together at this time to produce a crisis for the mining industry. The industry as a whole suffered from a bad image due to widely publicized mining accidents in the 1990s. The serious negative social impacts that can arise from mining led to protracted NGO activism against the industry. Coupled with these developments were changes to international environmental treaty law and the advent of "green conditionalities" attached to financing. The coming together of these developments negatively affected the mining industry's access to land, finance, and markets.

Mining's bad reputation

Major environmental disasters associated with mining badly damaged the industry's reputation, and the legitimacy of the industry as a whole was called into question. From the early 1990s, a number of widely publicized environmental disasters cemented the bad reputation of mining companies (Warhurst 2001). In 1996, Placer Dome's (now Barrick) Marcopper mine in the Philippines had a major accident when the plug to the tailings dam gave way, causing serious damage to rivers downstream and disrupting the livelihoods and health of people living nearby. In another example, in 1998, the tailings dam at the Aznacollar mine (owned by Swedish/Canadian Boliden-Apirsa) in Spain collapsed, killing almost all life in the river, and threatening the nearby Donana National Park, a UN World Heritage site. In one legendary case, at the Summitville mine in Colorado, Galactic Resources (a Canadian company) declared bankruptcy and walked away from a tailings pond failure that was deemed to be imminent by the US Environmental Protection Agency (EPA). Such well-publicized disasters served to damage the already tarnished reputation of all mining companies, not just those directly implicated in such events.

Role of NGOs

The expansion of mining companies globally in the face of new opportunities heightened international awareness and concern about the negative environmental and social effects of mining (Cohen 1996; Prince and Nelson 1996). These growing concerns reflected broad shifts dating from the 1970s in societal expectations around care for the environment (Wapner 1995). Where once it might have been acceptable to treat pollution and waste as an externality, global civil society came to demand constraints on industrial activity causing environmental harm. Environmental NGOs such as Greenpeace and the World Wildlife Fund (WWF), operating nationally and globally, helped to mobilize public opinion against mining. By the early 1990s, NGOs were increasingly involved not just in setting the environmental agenda, but in participating in decision-making, as became clear at the 1992 Rio Conference on Environment and Development. NGOs were able to adeptly use information technologies to raise awareness about mining company operations in far-off places, and to mobilize local community opposition to mining.

At the domestic level, influential NGOs operating in the advanced industrialized economies played a critical role in informing the public of issues, in launching litigation, and in putting pressure on governments to take steps to protect the environment. Institutional investors in these countries with advanced capital markets have also played an increasingly important role in promoting socially responsible investment, another form of pressure on companies. As such, NGOs played a critical role both nationally and internationally in exerting pressures on companies, and are considered a key factor driving companies' CSR policies (Vogel 2005). They are also able to influence policy through their participation in processes such as the World Bank Extractive Industry Review, and indirectly, can influence regulations through their advocacy of tougher international standards for mining (Walde 2005).

Role of international organizations, international treaties, and "soft law"

A number of other developments at the global level affected mining companies directly or indirectly. Early pressure came from the United Nations Environment Program (UNEP, created in 1974), which, through various programs initiated in the 1990s, sought to improve the environmental performance of the mining sector through engagement with national governments and the mining industry (Yakovleva 2005: 42). National governments which had signed on to international environmental treaties, began to restrict mining companies' access to mining sites in an attempt to meet their treaty commitments (see Pring 1999 for a comprehensive review). The UNESCO World Heritage Convention (1972), for example, can restrict access to areas that could negatively affect natural or cultural values, which is of particular significance to companies wishing to extract ore from lands deemed of outstanding natural significance, or claimed by indigenous peoples. The Biodiversity Convention (1992) restricts access to land with fragile ecosystems (Balkau and Parsons 1999; Yakovleva 2005). Such treaties came to be used to block mining companies' access to new sites, as happened in the early 1990s when the provincial government of British Columbia turned down the Windy Craggy mine proposal by listing the Tatshenshini-Alsek Region in northern British Columbia as a World Heritage Site (Pring 1999).

The Basel Convention (1989) restricted the use of certain metals and minerals in consumer products, affecting mining companies' (especially those engaged in smelting) access to markets, particularly in Europe. For example, in 1993 under the Basel Convention, the EU adopted regulations strictly limiting hazardous waste shipments within, into, and out of, EU member countries. By allowing for the ban of importation of products deemed to harm the environment, such treaties effectively make environmental controls legitimate grounds for trade discrimination (Pring 1999). The Heavy Metals Protocol of the 1979 Convention on Long-Range Transboundary Air Pollution (LRTAP) placed restrictions on the use of lead, cadmium, and mercury in products, and restricted or banned certain metal production processes that cause transboundary air pollution.

Conditions attached to financing

In the mid-1990s, under pressure from northern-based NGOs, the World Bank began to strengthen its environmental lending criteria. Environmental impact assessments (EIAs) became an international standard for major developments such as mines, required by multilateral development banks, development assistance agencies, and various UN bodies (Pring 1999). Public insurance institutions also began to institute "green conditionality" (Walde 1992). The Multilateral Investment Guarantee Agency (MIGA), for example, was shamed into considering environmental criteria after disasters at two gold mines it had insured: Omai, Guyana (Golden Star Resources) and Irian Jaya, Indonesia (Freeport McMoRan). Commercial banks and private insurers, concerned about liability risks in light of high-profile litigation against several mining companies in the mid-1990s, began to attach environmental conditions to their loans through the Equator Principles (Danielson 2005). The Extractive Industry Review (EIR), launched under World Bank auspices in the early 2000s, was a multistakeholder series of negotiations that ultimately resulted in the International Finance Corporation's (IFC) Policy and Performance Standards on Social and Environmental Sustainability (IFC 2006). In light of the dependence of mining companies on financing for their large, capital-intensive projects, conditionalities attached to lending were a major source of concern.

These various developments, a bad reputation, threats to its very legitimacy as an industry, NGO activism, and the development of international environmental treaties affecting mining and "green" conditionality came together in the mid-to-late 1990s to produce a critical juncture for the industry. As the next section will demonstrate, increased regulatory scrutiny and public opposition to new mining projects in the advanced industrialized economies provided the domestic backdrop to the critical juncture the industry was facing.

Rational choice institutionalism

Rational choice institutionalism draws attention to the domestic institutional context that influenced the incentive structures of major mining companies. Initially, developments in the countries in which they were headquartered exerted pressure on mining companies to internalize the environmental and social costs of their operations. Later, in the 1990s, when major mining companies expanded their global operations in response to new investment opportunities, they found that many of the developing countries lacked the institutional capacity and/or will to protect the environment and the rights of people affected by mining. It is argued that institutional context in both the advanced industrialized economies and developing countries where mining companies expanded their operations influenced CSR adoption.

Domestic institutional context

The fact that early CSR adoption and initial efforts at industry collaboration came from major mining companies with headquarters in the advanced industrialized economies reflects the changes in regulation and values of voting publics in those countries. In the 1990s, governments tightened up existing environmental regulations affecting various aspects of mining, pertaining to safeguarding the quality of land, air, and water affected by mining and mineral processing (Dias and Begg 1994). New regulations were introduced, such as environmental impact assessments for new projects, which set limits on discharges of waste and contaminants to water, required monitoring, and incorporated legal penalties in the event of violation of permit conditions. The timing and nature of environmental regulations in countries such as Australia, Europe, Japan, and North America share common elements in terms of regulatory instruments (Yakovleva 2005). In these countries, national parks and wildlife management areas were established that were off limits to mining. For example, in 1996 Noranda (now Xstrata) had to walk away from its New World mine project, after public outcries over the development of a mine only three miles from Yellowstone National Park.

The domestic context in which major mining companies from countries such as Canada, the US, Japan, the UK, and Australia were based produced pressures on these companies to improve their own CSR practices (Jenkins and Yakovleva 2006), and to work globally to develop CSR norms. In these countries, firms have responded to "domestic push" factors (by political actors and concerned domestic constituencies) as well as "external pull" factors (transnational forces) (Boardman 1992). In Canada, as elsewhere, domestic push has come from domestic and transnationally organized NGOs, responding to the Canadian public's desire for long-term and lasting solutions to complex environmental problems (Doern and Conway 1994). Developments at the global level, outlined above, reverberated in the advanced industrialized economies where major mining companies are headquartered.

Institutional context in developing countries

Regulatory deficiencies in developing countries, widespread poverty, and weak or non-existent protection for the rights of people in local communities affected by mining produced serious environmental and social challenges for mining companies investing there. During the Cold War, mining companies might have negotiated with authoritarian regimes to deal with attendant opposition to their operations. With the end of the Cold War, and the advent of political liberalization in many developing countries, NGO scrutiny and local community opposition made this strategy unviable for mining companies with long-term investments. The fact that companies must locate where the ore is, and lack mobility, made them vulnerable to community opposition. The need for a "social license to operate" influenced CSR adoption on the part of mining companies.

There have been some serious large-scale social and cultural impacts as a result of mining in developing countries. Salient examples of serious negative social impacts include the Ok Tedi mine in Papua New Guinea (1994) and the Grasberg mine in Indonesia (1995). The forced closure of the Bougainville mine by the peoples of Bougainville Island in Papua New Guinea (PNG) resulted in armed struggle (Clark and Clark 1999). Although these examples could be said to be extreme cases, they illustrate the fact that the mining industry faces significant environmental and social challenges as a result of its operations. Table 3.2 identifies the main problems that the mining industry has sought to address in the past decade.

Mining companies typically understand their social and environmental responsibilities in terms of the risks they present to their operations and the viability of their business. Up until the early 1990s, mining

Table 3.2 *Major challenges facing the global mining industry*

Viability of minerals industry	• Need to secure access to capital, land, and markets • Need for social license to operate • Ability to attract good people • Return on investment
Control, use and management of land	• Conflicts over compensation, resettlement, land claims of indigenous peoples, protected areas
Minerals and economic development	• Need to demonstrate that mining can contribute to economic development
Local communities and mines	• Social tension caused by inequitable distribution of costs and benefits within communities • Lack of planning for after mine closes
Environmental impacts	• Need to internalize costs of environmental degradation • Need to improve impact assessment and environmental management systems • Need for rehabilitation after mine closure
Integrated approach to using minerals	• Recycling, reuse, and remanufacture of products • Development of product stewardship and supply chain assurance
Access to information	• Need to reduce information asymmetries • Need for public participation in decision-making
Artisanal and small-scale mining	• Address conflict with large-scale (usually foreign) companies
Sector governance	• Need for integrated governance systems to ensure mining contributes to sustainable development • Need for voluntary standards to compensate for weak capacity in developing countries

Source: Adapted from MMSD, *Breaking New Ground*, 2002: xvii–xviii.

companies faced a range of what could be called traditional political and economic risks. From the time of initial exploration, through to mine construction, and on to the life of the mine and finally, closure, many years, often decades are involved. Since much capital expenditure is required even before the mine opens, and because companies have to locate where the ore is, mining companies are especially vulnerable to political and economic risks. Over the course of a mine's life, companies must be concerned about potential political instability, and possible changes in a country's economic policies affecting mining (of which recent developments in Venezuela would be a prime example). Most salient of these is the risk of expropriation. Add to these the complications arising from operating in developing countries noted in Table 3.2 above, and mining companies face a complex range of "risks" that elicited a strategic response from the industry. Rational choice institutionalism would explain CSR adoption as strategic adaptation on the part of the mining industry.

Canadian institutional context

This section provides more detail on influences arising from the institutional setting in Canada, the headquarters of the three case-study companies. Institutional arrangements to address public concerns started in 1970, when the Federal Department of Environment was established. Within this institutional nucleus, the stage was set for the first round of environmental and pollution control regulations, a path replicated in Australia, the US, Japan, and Western Europe (Brenton 1994; Warner 2006). Canada's first environmental legislation was the Clean Air Act (1971), reflecting the preoccupation at the time with air pollution. In 1977, the Metal Mining Liquid Effluent Regulations came into force, to be later subsumed under the Fisheries Act (1985) as the Mining Metal Effluent Regulations, which were later amended in 2002. The Metal Mining Effluent Regulations apply to all operating metal mines in Canada, imposing limits on releases of cyanide, metals, and suspended solids (e.g. tailings), and prohibiting the discharge of effluent deemed lethal to fish and fish habitat.[2] The Canada Wildlife Act (1985) provides for the acquisition of lands by the Federal Government for wildlife research and conservation, and for the establishment of protected marine areas.

In the 1980s, there was an expansion in the number of Canadian environmental NGOs, which became increasingly transnationalized. Where environmental groups had earlier tended to focus on discrete

---

[2] Detailed information on Canada's environmental regulations can be found at Environment Canada: www.ec.gc.ca/EnviroRegs

environmental issues pertinent to Canada, such as the problem of acid rain in Canada's bilateral relationship with the US, NGOs came to focus on a more holistic national and international agenda (Warner 2006). This process ran parallel to, and was reinforced by, the consensus reached around sustainable development in the late 1980s. NGOs were invited with increasing regularity to participate in global debates through the World Commission on Sustainable Development, as well as domestically with national governments. For example, Canada's Task Force on Environment and Economy 1986 Report led to a series of Roundtables designed to entrench consultative processes, and sought to institutionalize dialogue between NGOs, business, and government (Doering and Runnells 1993). These Roundtables were informed by global developments on sustainable development, as reflected by the release in 1990 of Canada's Green Plan.

Starting in the 1990s, a new wave of environmental regulations ensued, and existing ones were tightened up. In 1992, the Canadian Environmental Assessment Act came into force, requiring environmental impact assessments (EIAs) where the project involves federal funding, permit, or license. In 1999, the comprehensive Canadian Environmental Protection Act (CEPA) came into force, with detailed provisions for controlling pollution and industrial wastes (Part 7), for institutionalizing public consultation and participation in matters involving the environment, and for establishing nationally consistent standards to protect the environment. The CEPA also seeks to bring Canadian environmental law in accordance with international agreements signed by Canada to protect the environment. Since natural resources are a provincial prerogative under the constitution (BNA Act 1867), a further array of provincial laws address environmental protection measures. As such, each province and territory has its own mining act, governing exploration, development, construction, production, closure, reclamation, and abandonment of mines through permitting. Furthermore, each province and territory has enacted its own environmental laws, such as Ontario's Environmental Assessment Act (1990 – EIAs), and Environmental Protection Act (1990), which governs allowable discharges and emissions through Certificates of Approval.[3]

---

[3] The full range of Ontario environmental laws can be accessed at: www.e-laws.gov. on.ca

In the face of growing public pressure to respond to concerns about the activities of Canadian mining companies in developing countries, the Canadian government preferred to facilitate voluntary initiatives to promote CSR. As reports continued to surface of bad practices on the part of Canadian mining companies abroad, the voluntary initiatives favored by the Canadian government became the subject of much criticism from such NGOs as Mining Watch Canada and the Halifax Initiative.

A particularly significant development was the tabling, in June 2005, by the Parliamentary Standing Committee on Foreign Affairs and International Trade (SCFAIT), of a report on the activities of Canadian mining companies in developing countries (SCFAIT 2005). The report singled out the activities of Canadian mining company TVI Pacific Inc. in Mindanao, Philippines, with respect to alleged abuses of the indigenous rights and human rights of people in the area. Concern was expressed about the lack of Canadian laws to regulate the activities of Canadian mining companies in developing countries, and the report called for legislation to hold companies accountable for their activities overseas (SCFAIT 2005).

In response to the SCFAIT report, the government agreed to a number of the recommendations, but shied away from enacting legislation that would entail the extraterritorial application of Canadian law in foreign jurisdictions (Government of Canada 2005). A key outcome of the government's response was the launching of a major series of Roundtable consultations with industry associations, NGOs, aboriginal peoples, academic experts, and company and government representatives to discuss the issues raised in the report, and make recommendations. The National Roundtables on Corporate Social Responsibility and the Canadian Extractive Sector in Developing Countries entailed public consultations in four major cities across Canada throughout 2006.

Although the Roundtable process was deemed to be a success, bringing together as it did civil society, industry, and government, the outcome has been disappointing from an NGO perspective, because the government continues to resist enacting legislation that would regulate the activities of Canadian companies abroad. One immediate outcome of the Roundtable process was the government's announcement in February 2007 of its support of the Extractive Industries Transparency Initiative (EITI). Two years later, in March 2009, the government announced its strategy for promoting CSR in the Canadian extractive sector. Called "Building the Canadian Advantage," the government sets out initiatives it proposes to take to promote CSR in the extractive sector, and commits resources to that end (Government of Canada 2009).

Considerable emphasis is placed in the government's CSR strategy on encouraging Canadian companies to adhere to widely recognized international CSR guidelines. In addition to the OECD Guidelines for MNEs (which the government has long supported) and the EITI, the government committed to support the Voluntary Principles on Security and Human Rights. An initiative originally launched by the US and Britain in 2000, this is a significant development, as the Voluntary Principles provide guidelines on the use of private and public security forces, such that operations can be protected without excessive force or human rights violations. The government's strategy also endorses the IFC's Performance Standards on Social and Environmental Sustainability, and the Mining and Minerals Sector Supplement to the Global Reporting Initiative (GRI 2007).

The intense pressure to regulate the activities of Canadian mining companies abroad has influenced CSR adoption on the part of Canadian mining companies, inducing them to engage with government and NGOs in the development of voluntary standards. These more recent developments have been especially significant for Barrick, in light of the fact that the Canadian government now endorses several global standards that Barrick has aligned its practices with.

Canadian private sector response to external pressures

The trajectory of the Canadian mining industry's response to reputational and other risks reflects the domestic and global developments outlined above. Since the global collaborative industry response is documented in Chapter 7, national collaborative efforts of the Canadian mining industry are briefly documented here.

A noteworthy early effort on the part of the mining industry to respond to growing public concerns about the effects of mining was the Whitehorse Mining Initiative (WMI). Launched in 1992 by the Canadian mining industry, it entailed a two-year multistakeholder national consultation process with industry, indigenous, and environmental representatives, government, labor, and academia (McAllister and Alexander 1997; Miller 1997). As a multistakeholder consultation process, the WMI was precedent-setting and unique, the first of its kind anywhere in the world (Weitzner 2010: 88). Although the process did not solve difficult socio-cultural issues associated with mining, it nevertheless signified recognition on the part of Canadian mining companies that stakeholder concerns, especially those of aboriginal peoples in Canada's north, where much mining takes place, would have to be taken into account. The WMI served as a model for subsequent collaborative efforts at the global level and explicitly sought to address how mining in Canada might contribute to sustainable development (Weitzner 2010: 88).

Some of the lessons learned from the WMI were promoted at the global level by leading Canadian mining companies. As Tony Hodge, now President of the ICMM, noted with reference to the WMI, the "continued defensive posture that has characterized the industry for most of the second half of the 20th century will drive the industry into perfect storm conditions" (cited in McAllister 2007). The mining industry learned about process in terms of possible models for engaging with external critics (Cooney 2008; Weitzner 2010), as well as about substance, through engaging in extensive dialogue and searching for common ground. As the then President of the Mining Association of Canada (MAC), George Miller, explained, the mining industry hoped to gain allies and form partnerships by fostering better understanding about mining, but at the same time, also recognized the need to understand other groups' attitudes and values (Miller 1997).

Fitzpatrick et al. argue that the WMI fostered "conceptual" learning about the norm of sustainable development, and how it might apply to mining (Fitzpatrick et al. 2011). A major weakness of the WMI, however, was that, given the broad-based nature of the commitment to "sustainable development," and the failure to follow up on, or monitor, the commitments made, the perception on the part of stakeholders was that few tangible results were realized (Cooney 2008; Weitzner 2010). According to Gordon Peeling, past President of MAC, "industry was so fatigued by a very intense two-year process that it did not have the will to take on leadership in the absence of government ... this was seen as a lost opportunity" (cited in Fitzpatrick et al. 2011). With no mechanisms in place for industry to act on what it had learned from the WMI, there was no way for mining companies to demonstrate the significant impact the initiative had on their understanding of stakeholders' perspectives, and how their approach to issues had changed (Executive 1, MAC, 26 May, 2006). The need to act upon stated objectives was an important lesson carried over to the Global Mining Initiative (GMI) a decade later. As leading companies in the GMI, Noranda and Placer Dome, brought lessons learned from the WMI in Canada to the global level.

Canada's national mining association, the MAC, took the lead in organizing the WMI. In the aftermath of the Whitehorse Initiative, MAC revised and updated its environmental policy (first released in 1989), making its endorsement a condition of mining companies' membership.

In the early 2000s, in keeping with efforts at the global level to align the mining industry with sustainable development, MAC began to develop a voluntary reporting mechanism for Canadian mining companies. The Towards Sustainable Mining (TSM) initiative was launched and the first report released in 2005 for the 2004 reporting year. The TSM consists of a set of four performance indicators against which member companies report, including tailings management, energy use and greenhouse gas emissions management, external outreach, and crisis management planning. Companies' performance are ranked according to five levels, with level 1 being the lowest, where no systems are in place. Level 3 indicates a good performance with systems/processes developed and implemented, and level 5 denotes excellence and leadership (MAC 2005). In an effort to improve the credibility of these performance indicators to external stakeholders, MAC implemented an external verification system in 2007, with member companies being submitted to external verification on a three-year rotating basis (MAC 2008).

Conclusion

The concept of a critical juncture in historical institutionalism provides a compelling explanation for the range of developments that bore down on the mining industry. A variety of developments at the global and national levels conspired to restrict mining companies' access to mining sites, to markets, and to finance. Due to the fact that they must operate where the ore is, mining companies are especially vulnerable to community opposition to their operations. The combination of widely publicized environmental disasters, restricted access to new mine sites, tighter regulations in developed countries, the closing off of markets, sustained NGO targeting, and the conditionalities attached to loans by private and development banks, created a critical juncture for mining companies in the late 1990s.

Rational choice institutionalism further enriches the explanation, by accounting for the strategic response of the mining industry to broadly similar external pressures emanating from the domestic and global environments. The strengthening regulatory context in mining companies' home countries, as well as the risks associated with their operations in developing countries, induced a strategic response on the part of the industry. Rational choice institutionalism expects that mining companies would respond in the same way to these broadly similar risks and constraints.

However, mining companies did not all respond in similar ways, rendering rational choice institutionalism on its own an insufficient explanation for the response of the mining industry to external pressures. Research on CSR that looks at internal dynamics has confirmed that when faced with similar environmental issues, companies do not respond in the same way (see Howard-Grenville 2006 for review). In some, but not all companies, the coming together of these disparate developments provided the opportunity for change agents/norms entrepreneurs to overcome internal resistance and push for better practices both within their own companies, and through global initiatives among all companies (Kingdon 1995; Pierson 2004). Growing awareness of the need for a "social license to operate" (Gunningham et al. 2003), coupled with ongoing environmental challenges, made sustainable development an increasingly attractive means for some, but not all, mining companies to address their reputational problems. "New" institutionalism needs to be brought into the analysis, in order to account for both isomorphic pressures within the industry, but also variation in terms of the timing and nature of individual mining companies' responses.

By drawing attention to cognitive and normative processes, "new" institutionalism turns the focus of analysis to the level of the firm. Only through detailed case-study analysis can shifts in attitudes and interests on the part of the mining industry be adequately explored. Rich case-study analysis sheds light on the normative choices confronting the industry in terms of determining appropriate courses of action to meet social and environmental responsibilities. Isomorphism can be observed in the near universal framing of CSR initiatives in terms of sustainable development. Yet there was nothing inevitable about this outcome,

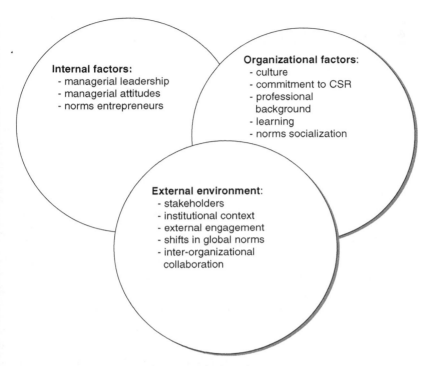

Figure 3.3 Multi-level explanation of CSR adoption.

pointing to the need to analyze managerial interpretations of their environment to explain the emergence of normative consensus within the mining industry around sustainable development. The interplay of instrumental and normative logics is a necessary part of the explanation for the varied responses of firms to common external pressures.

In the next three case-study chapters, the multi-level framework will be applied to the case studies. The interaction of internal, organizational, and external factors makes it possible to account for a crucial part of the explanation for CSR adoption that would otherwise be missed. Chapter 7 will then apply relevant elements of the framework to global collaborative initiatives. Figure 3.3 above summarizes the broad factors to be considered in the multi-level analysis as applied to Noranda, Placer Dome, and Barrick Gold.

4 | *Noranda Inc.*

Introduction

This chapter will look at the various influences that informed CSR adoption at Noranda. The role of senior management is central to the explanation, both in providing internal leadership and promoting a proactive approach towards environmental challenges facing the company. The proactive approach was informed by an appreciation of early mover advantages, both in terms of anticipating environmental regulation and in promoting voluntary standards for the mining industry nationally and globally.

As a major mining and smelting corporation with global operations, Noranda had a significant range of environmental challenges to manage, and was one of the largest polluters in Canada. Issues included mine wastes (such as tailings) and reclamation, air and water effluents (such as sulfur dioxide, mercury, and arsenic), and energy usage. To add to the challenge, these issues had to be handled at multiple sites, with different technologies, equipment of various ages, diverse effluent streams, and differing provincial and national (Canada) and state (US) regulations. There are between forty and fifty effluent discharge standards applicable to metal mining operations in Canada (Vietor 2002). These standards apply to the metals themselves (copper, lead, zinc), as well as oils and greases, phenols, total dissolved solids, and volatile organic compounds. There are standards applied to the chemicals used in, or generated by, smelting and refining, and for Noranda, the most difficult of these to address was sulfur dioxide (SO_2). Noranda's operations also generated fluorides, various hydrocarbons, nitrogen oxides, and perfluorocarbons.

The nature of Noranda's business, covering both mining and smelting processes, produced structural incentives to address wide-ranging environmental challenges. The highly polluting nature of Noranda's business made the company a target of regulatory scrutiny, promoting senior management to both anticipate potential regulation, but also work with government and NGOs in the development of standards. In addressing these challenges, Noranda sought to promote a win–win situation, where improvements in environmental performance would improve efficiency, reduce costs, and enhance the company's competitive position. The highly decentralized organization of Noranda was a further structural feature, which presented challenges at the operational level in terms of implementing CSR policies from head office. The decentralized organizational structure presented the most difficulties when Noranda sought to address (or failed to adequately address) the social effects of its operations.

Noranda recognized that its CSR (and later, sustainable development) policies had to be informed by long-term considerations, not just by short-term quarterly profits. Management was not content with mere environmental compliance, but also sought to promote long-term value. This philosophy was informed by the fact that in the mining sector, capital investments are for thirty-plus years, and long-term planning needed to be factored in to protect Noranda's investments. Senior management sought to create a value company that would be around for a long time, and was not fixated solely on profit-making (Executive 3, September 11, 2008; see Table 1.4 for full list of company interviews).

Institutional setting: external pressures (global and domestic)

Up until the 1960s, Noranda operated in an external environment that could be described as permissive, in so far as acceptance of its operations was concerned. Prior to the 1960s, industry as a whole assumed that the assimilative capacity of the environment would suffice to absorb effluents and emissions. Any environmental damage could thereby be treated as an externality, and companies did not have to bear the cost. It was further felt that a company's contribution came through producing its product and generating employment. Indeed, belching smokestacks were a symbol of prosperity and industrialization, and Noranda's original corporate logo was of five smokestacks. This logo was changed in the 1970s, when smokestacks came to be associated with pollution.

In the 1960s and 1970s, that thinking began to give way to the realities of greater public environmental awareness and the introduction of regulations in industrialized countries, including Canada. The enactment in the 1970s of legislation affecting worker health and safety and environmental externalities prompted Noranda to address the environment, health and safety aspects of its operations. With extensive operations in Ontario and Quebec, Noranda was subject to the respective Mining Acts of those two provinces. Noranda had to adjust to meet new environmental regulatory requirements.

Actual or impending government regulation is widely considered to be a prime motivator for companies in moving forward with CSR. While it is certainly the case that Noranda had to respond to stricter environmental requirements, managers were unanimous that this development alone was not a key driving force in the adoption of CSR policies. Noranda saw the value of working with industry, government, and NGOs in the development of standards, with a view to avoiding expensive adaptation after the fact, but not as a means to avoid regulation. As Noranda noted in its 1992 environmental report, its voluntary environmental auditing program "goes far beyond simply complying with government regulations" (Noranda 1993: 15). Since the cost of implementing new governmental requirements is very high, Noranda found it strategic to anticipate government regulation, a classic early mover consideration.

Growing public awareness and the expanded regulatory framework provided the context for Noranda's evolving CSR policies. An early influence on Noranda was the growing awareness and concern over acid rain, caused by sulfur dioxide emissions (Executive 4, August 28, 2008). In 1980, the Coalition on Acid Rain was created. Its membership included environmentally concerned Canadians, high-profile individuals, environmental groups, and federal and provincial Environment Ministers. The Coalition's influence grew over the course of the 1980s, as it gained support from former Prime Minister Brian Mulroney and the then US President, George Bush Sr. The coalition's efforts paid off when in 1990, Bush Sr. passed a revised Clean Air Act that committed the US to reduce its acid rain emissions (Heaps 2006: 17). In Ontario, the government's "Countdown Acid Rain" called on Ontario's four main sources of acid rain to cut their SO_2 emissions. The companies targeted included Falconbridge (Noranda's subsidiary), Ontario Hydro, Inco, and Algoma Steel. Noranda was responsive to these developments, but could not be described as reacting to them.

Starting in the late 1970s, several important developments had a direct impact on Noranda and thinking within the corporation. One noteworthy example of this was the 1979 Mississauga train disaster and the resultant mass evacuation (Executive 2, October 23, 2011). In November 1979, a large freight train derailed in Mississauga, a city twenty kilometers from Toronto. The train exploded because one of the tank cars carried propane, and a mass evacuation was ordered because some tank cars carried chlorine (other cars carried styrene and toluene). The evacuation of 218,000 people from the surrounding area made it the largest peacetime operation in North America until the New Orleans evacuation after Hurricane Katrina (Slack 2009). The resultant public outrage and questions about the safe transport of dangerous chemicals sensitized Noranda to potential long-term vulnerabilities in its operations (Executive 2, October 23, 2011).

The second significant incident was the chemical accident in 1984 in Bhopal, India, when a chemical spill at one of Union Carbide's plants led to thousands of deaths. In the view of one executive, Bhopal was the trigger that set in motion a major review and reform of Noranda's management systems (Executive 1, December 9, 2011). As a company that handles, produces, and transports dangerous chemicals, management was concerned whether such a tragedy could happen to Noranda (Executive 1, February 13, 2006). In fact, the very next day, a senior executive sought to establish what chemicals Noranda stored in large volumes. Disconcertingly, he found that Noranda did not have this information readily at hand in corporate office (Executive 4, August 28, 2008).

Plant managers were asked what emergency response plans were in place, and suppliers were spoken to. Attention turned to the Brunswick smelter in Belledune, Quebec, which had a plant that stored large amounts of ammonia to make fertilizer. It was discovered that there was a plan in place for emergency response, but that it had not been kept active (Executive 4, August 28, 2008). This proved to be an eye-opener, as it showed that even when a plan is in place, ongoing steps had to be taken to ensure it could be effectively activated. For example, personnel changes meant that people would not necessarily know what to do.

This realization prompted Noranda to launch an extensive training program for plant managers at all the plants, entailing regular drills and test trials of systems in place. Noranda brought in an expert from the United States to help properly train environmental coordinators. Noranda took steps to ensure that emergency response plans were in place at all operations, and developed an elaborate audit program covering four areas: environment, health, industrial hygiene, and emergency preparedness (Frantisak 1990: 8). The internal audits involved teams of three or four people, drawn from a pool of seventy people, who received continuous, specialized training. The teams would visit each plant at different times to review compliance with the four types of audits. A draft report on the findings would be prepared, and the plant would then have to develop an action plan in response (Executive 4, August 28, 2008). The action plans were reviewed at least once every quarter, and the results were presented at regular Board meetings. These audits, and the policy and programs supporting them, were developed as part of Noranda's overall management system, and pre-dated the development of the ISO management systems. ISO's subsequent 14000 environmental management system (EMS) was influenced by the system Noranda established, because Noranda participated in the development of the standards. Noranda's efforts, in turn, were reinforced because management saw other business leaders thinking the same way (Executive 1, December 9, 2011).

The costs to Union Carbide as a result of the Bhopal disaster were not limited to that company alone. The disaster proved very damaging to the reputation of the chemical industry as a whole. After Bhopal, Noranda approached the Canadian Chemical Producers' Association (CCPA), seeking help in the development of protocols for the handling, storage, and transport of hazardous chemicals (Noranda was a member of the CCPA as a result of its sulfuric acid business). Noranda also went to its suppliers, such as Dow Chemicals, seeking help in the development of protocols. A five-day session was held in Toronto, bringing together chemical suppliers, with one-day sessions devoted to the discussion of each chemical in turn. Noranda therefore worked in tandem with CCPA, both influencing the development of what became the Responsible Care® program, and interacting with suppliers in seeking help in developing its own standards (Executive 1, December 9, 2011).

Under the Responsible Care® program, companies undergo independent external audits, and can achieve certification that they are handling chemicals safely and responsibly. Noranda became the first, and for many years the only, mining and metals company to have its operations certified under the program, including its Mines Gaspé in Murdochville, the Horne smelter in Rouyn-Noranda, and the CEZinc operation in Valleyfield, Quebec (Five Winds 2000: 78). Noranda sought Responsible Care® certification for the transport of hazardous materials and achieved compliance by 1997. Membership in this professional association influenced Noranda's approach to public outreach and management systems for environment, health and safety (EHS) (Executive 2, October 23, 2011), while also influencing the development of internationally adopted standards for the chemical industry.

A third development which influenced thinking in Noranda was the 1989 Exxon Valdez oil spill. In a 1990 address, the then VP, EHS, Frank Frantisak, noted the huge costs to Exxon after the oil spill. At the time, the estimated cost to Exxon of the clean-up alone was US$2.5 billion, and 11 per cent of the US adult population stopped buying Exxon gasoline, and another 11 per cent said they were considering doing so (Frantisak 1990: 2). As of 2008, Exxon had paid US$3.4 billion in remediation, fines, compensation, and other costs (Anderson et al. 2008: B10). The message Frantisak brought home to senior management was that Noranda should seek to avoid such economic and legal risks, a clear business case for CSR adoption.

Global developments continued to have growing salience for Noranda in the 1980s and 1990s. During this time, environmental awareness and concerns gained momentum, as countries signed on to global environmental treaties, and transnational advocacy networks kept the environment on the global agenda and drew attention to corporate malpractice. The rise of management systems under the ISO influenced Noranda's efforts to improve its CSR performance. Noranda's CEZinc operation in Valleyfield, Quebec was the first zinc plant in the world to achieve product-quality certification under ISO 9000 (Executive 2, October 23, 2011). By the late 1980s, Noranda was also becoming aware of the growing significance of the emerging norm of sustainable development.

As opportunities for global expansion opened up in the 1990s, Noranda encountered a range of difficulties in gaining acceptance for its operations, and learned some difficult lessons in the process. As will be described below, the approach of senior management was to take a proactive stance to growing external pressures, seeking to exploit opportunities for corporate growth out of environmental concerns. Rather than being defensive, management recognized through such incidents as the Mississauga train derailment and Bhopal, that major polluting industries such as the chemical and mining sectors had lost society's trust (Executive 2, October 23, 2011). By contrast, most mining companies were reactive and defensive in response to shifting societal values.

From early on, Noranda took a proactive stance to mounting social pressures to improve its environmental performance and accept its responsibility toward society. Industry's image was seen to be poor, and it was recognized that social values were changing faster than corporate practices. Many companies had not yet appointed a VP Environment, and those that had done so had not yet come to the realization that this was the beginning of a process of change, not the end (Frantisak 1990: 3). In part because of Noranda's huge environmental footprint, but also because of management's approach to environmental challenges, the company came to the realization earlier than most companies that it was necessary to change its thinking.

Organizational and managerial response

The role of senior management is critical in explaining Noranda's response to its changing external environment. Since a corporation's main purpose is to make a profit, a culture of commitment to the environment has to be set by top management (Executive 1, March 2, 2006). Otherwise, people lower down the ranks are likely to be intimidated by the historical mentality of the company – its culture, in other words. At Noranda in the 1970s, senior executives, including Alf Powis (Chairman) and Adam Zimmerman (President and CEO of Noranda Forest Inc., 1967–92), began to take an active interest in the environment. Later, the succeeding CEO, David Kerr (1987–2003), Alex Balogh (Chairman of Falconbridge and Deputy Chairman of Noranda, 1989–2006), and Peter Bronfman (late founder of EdperBrascan Corporation) continued to provide strong support for CSR initiatives.

For some executives, interest in the environment was personal, as much as professional; their children cared about the environment and were active around environmental concerns. One executive's children, for example, were very involved with environmental issues, and supported Greenpeace (Executive 3, September 11, 2008). The executive's thinking on the environment was spurred by the experience of his eldest daughter, who got a summer job at one of Noranda's forest plants. She reported to him that there was gross pollution, and was convinced it was causing harm to people and the environment (Executive 3, September 11, 2008). The evidence was difficult to ignore. The executive recounted how, when playing golf near the Rouyn-Noranda smelter, he noticed the effects of sulfur dioxide blowing over, and turning the grass yellow (Executive 3, September 11, 2008). This executive, together with other senior management, formed a cohesive group who were on the same wavelength about the need for forward-thinking on the environment.

By the late 1970s, senior management recognized the need for centralized management of EHS policies. An important organizational development was the hiring in 1979 of Frank Frantisak from outside the company to the position Director, EHS. In 1982, that position was upgraded to Vice-President, EHS. From 1994 until his retirement in 1998, Frantisak served as Senior Vice-President, EHS. He was replaced by David Rodier, who had been President of Noranda's zinc operations (CEZinc). Rodier oversaw the initial merger of Noranda's and Falconbridge's EHS functions, until his retirement from Noranda in 2003.

Frantisak emphasized the importance of leadership from senior management in a 1990 address to Ontario Hydro (Frantisak 1990). Referring to the disastrous 1989 Exxon Valdez oil spill, Frantisak asked who was responsible for the spill; Exxon's Board, the CEO, President, VP for Environment, or the ship's captain (Frantisak 1990: 2). In answering his question, Frantisak declared that "Exxon's Corporate Environmental Culture and corresponding Environmental Management System, or its absence, is responsible for the disaster"(Frantisak 1990: 2). He identified the Board and senior officers as the architects of corporate culture.

Noranda's first environmental policy statement was adopted in 1965, and served as a broad statement of principles. Three components of CSR policy were identified, including environment, health, and safety. Until the end of the 1970s, EHS policies were implemented in a very decentralized fashion. Safety was considered an operational issue, and was dealt with directly by plant managers. Occupational health issues were dealt with by various people working independently, with local responsibilities. Site managers were responsible for implementing corporate policies and achieving specific goals. Strategic planning around CSR began in the late 1970s at CEZinc, which initiated external communications with local communities in 1987 (Executive 2, October 23, 2011; Executive 1, December 9, 2011).

The EHS management structure in the early years was very decentralized and specialized, much like the company as a whole. Noranda Inc. had four divisions covering mining, oil and gas, forestry, and manufacturing, with Frantisak responsible for the oversight of EHS in all four divisions. Noranda Minerals had separate and largely independent business units for each of its major areas of mining and metals activity, including copper, zinc, nickel, and aluminum smelting. (All documents are listed as 'Noranda Inc.' in the References.) Many of the mining and smelting operations had their own environmental managers. There were very few corporate policies for the mining groups of companies, but Frantisak was responsible for developing a corporate environmental policy. Upon his appointment in 1979, Frantisak brought in people who could coordinate the environmental, OHS, and industrial hygiene components of corporate strategy.

Throughout the 1980s, Frantisak worked on coordinating Noranda's EHS policies on a company-wide basis. In the mid-1980s, an environmental committee of the Board of Directors was established, with responsibility for setting the principles of corporate environmental practice. The senior VP, Environment, was responsible for presenting an environmental report to the Board on a quarterly basis. The report covered issues such as compliance or non-compliance with environmental laws, steps which needed to be taken in instances of non-compliance, progress of ongoing environmental audits, and any cases of environmental charges or convictions (Frantisak 1990: 5).

Frantisak sought to cultivate a uniform corporate environmental culture while, at the same time, respecting the highly decentralized management culture of Noranda. Given the fact that a corporation's primary purpose is to make a profit, it is very rare for change to come from the bottom up. The development of policies and programs was largely the result of a top-down process. However, given the decentralized nature of Noranda, the company relied on plant managers to implement policies set by senior management. Most plant managers were committed to environmental improvement and safety, but in 1999, one plant manager was let go because of lax safety attitudes (Executive 1, August 20, 2008; Executive 2, August 26, 2008; Executive 4, August 28, 2008). To promote consensus, Frantisak sought to build strong, positive relationships with the plant managers. He also conducted focus groups with employees before launching any new environmental initiatives. Extensive training programs, such as NEAT, the Noranda Environmental Awareness Training Program, helped to promote a culture of concern for the environment within Noranda (Executive 1, February 13, 2006).

Safety from early on was a top priority for Noranda, and remained so through the merger with Falconbridge. Beginning in the 1970s, regular on-site visits were conducted by the corporate safety committee. Twice a year, two or three senior executives would go to the sites to talk to plant workers and get verbal feedback on issues from workers and union representatives (Executive 2, August 26, 2008). Annual workshops were conducted on safety at all sites, and off-site meetings were conducted with site managers at the Noranda Technology Centre near Montreal.

In the 1980s, a similar but separate process was initiated for environmental issues. All plants received annual visits from senior EHS executives, and larger ones received visits two or three times a year (Executive 4, August 28, 2008). During each visit, the entire environmental program would be reviewed, and this would be discussed with the plant manager, and room for improvement identified. These visits provided the plant manager with the opportunity to ask questions and raise issues of concern. By the mid-1980s, most large plants had people in place whose sole responsibility was the environment, as well as health and safety. All plants had technicians in place who were responsible for monitoring and measuring emissions (Executive 4, August 28, 2008).

Policies on EHS issues tended to be driven by head office, and drafts were not sent to plant managers. However, annual meetings were conducted at head office with all environmental coordinators. The purpose of these meetings was to discuss current policies, but also future policies, which provided the opportunity for feedback from the people who would ultimately be responsible for implementing new policies. There was also a degree of policy coordination with people throughout the organization with responsibility for specific issues. These various measures were important in instituting a culture of commitment to CSR within Noranda.

Policy development

In a case study on Noranda conducted by the Harvard Business School, Frantisak divided the evolution of Noranda's EHS policies into five time periods. Prior to 1965, Noranda operated in an "era of innocence" when the environment was taken for granted and treated as an externality (Vietor 2002: 4). The period 1965 to 1980 was the "era of naivety," when Noranda was content to issue policy statements on the environment, such as the one adopted in 1965. The naive belief was that pieces of paper would be sufficient to move Noranda in the right direction.

The third period, from 1980 to 1990, marked the beginning of systematic efforts to address environmental concerns, which Frantisak called the "era of trying." Frantisak characterized the period 1990 to 1995 as the "era of action," when a range of initiatives were undertaken, both in terms of Noranda's internal policies, and the development of its external relations (Vietor 2002: 4). It was during this period that global environmental developments became more influential, as reflected in the growing international support for the principle of sustainable development. Frantisak characterized the period from 1995 on as the "era of culture," where attention to the environment was considered to be ingrained in Noranda's culture.

During the third period, the "era of trying," from 1980 to 1990, Noranda introduced a substantially revised environmental policy statement. Noranda's first environmental policy statement, adopted in 1965, was simply an expression of management's commitment to the environment (a summary of major policy developments can be found in Table 4.2). The revised 1985 statement enunciated five principles to which Noranda would adhere, including a commitment:

1. to meet or exceed applicable laws and regulations at all its sites;
2. to evaluate and manage risks to human health, the environment and physical property;
3. to conduct periodic environmental, health, hygiene, safety, and emergency preparedness audits;
4. to conduct environmental impact assessment studies for all new projects and for major expansions to existing facilities; and
5. to present a quarterly report to the Board of Directors on the state of the environment, health and hygiene, and safety and emergency preparedness at each operation.

(Noranda 1991: 4–5)

Principles three and five were clearly influenced by the need to avoid disasters, such as the one at Bhopal.

To implement this policy, Noranda introduced a comprehensive internal environmental auditing program, covering the four areas of environment, health, industrial hygiene, and emergency preparedness. Noranda also began to perform environmental impact assessments of its operations, and to prepare detailed emergency response plans and reclamation plans.

The period 1980 to 1990 was marked by an important strategic decision to incorporate recycling as a major part of Noranda's business plan. Noranda had reached a crossroads when, in the late 1970s, the local mines that supplied most of the feed to the Horne smelter in Rouyn-Noranda were nearing completion. Noranda had to decide whether to abandon the smelter (and the surrounding community, which owed its existence to Noranda) or become a custom smelter (Five Winds 2000: 69). At the same time, there was growing scientific and public concern about the effects of acid rain on forests and aquatic resources. There was also the prospect of regulatory pressure to reduce smelter emissions of sulfur dioxide. The thinking was to create a win–win situation, where environmental improvements would create financial benefits for the company. In approving projects, the Senior VP, EHS advised the Board to consider two factors: 1) what will the financial return be; and 2) how will the environment be enhanced (Executive 1, February 16, 2006). He believed that both goals could be accomplished.

To succeed in this transformation, Noranda had to take a long-term approach to technology development and smelter modernization. The 1980s witnessed substantial investments in environmental research and technologies at the Noranda Technology Centre, based in Montreal. The Centre's annual budget grew to US$50 million by 1990.

A series of major capital projects to strengthen the business and environmental performance of the copper smelter at Rouyn-Noranda ensued. An emerging and untapped source of feed for the smelter was identified in the form of electronic scrap and other secondary materials containing copper, gold, silver, platinum, and palladium (Five Winds 2000: 79). In 1984, special facilities were constructed for scrap processing at its Brunswick plant in New Brunswick. Noranda took a similar path with its copper smelter in Murdochville, Quebec. The smelter was modernized and expanded in 1996–7, but was shut down in 2002, due to the mine closure and high costs (Five Winds 2000: 70). By 2000, Noranda had become the world's largest custom processor of copper and precious metal-based feeds, processing scrap from used or obsolete products, such as phones, personal computers, children's electronic toys, printer cartridges, and costume jewelry (Five Winds 2000: 79).

Frantisak characterized the period 1990 to 1995 as the "era of action," when Noranda worked hard to clean up its operations and take the lead in environmental compliance (Vietor 2002: 4). In 1990, Noranda became the first Canadian company to publish an environmental report (for the 1989 reporting year), in which it reported on its environmental performance for its North American operations. In the preparation of the report, interviews were conducted with interested stakeholders, including NGOs, government, the academic community, and employees (Feltmate, Interview with Frantisak, 2008: 31). In order to respond to growing public environmental awareness and concern, Noranda expanded its communications with external audiences, including shareholders, governments, media, community, and special interest groups such as NGOs (Noranda 1991: 7).

According to one executive, the need to educate and inform Noranda's own employees was a major impetus behind the decision to start environmental reporting (Executive 4, August 28, 2008). With such a decentralized organizational structure, the EHS team in head office was aware that employees were not that well-informed about what the company's policies were, or about the environmental impact of the operations in which they worked. Generating awareness amongst employees would help them to see the role they could play in improving environmental performance. A second impetus for the reporting came from the recognized need to get information out to the local communities that were directly affected by Noranda's operations (Executive 4, August 28, 2008). Action plans published in the reports would put pressure directly back to the plant from the local communities. It was expected that the reports would encourage plant managers to hold meetings with local community members, and thereby promote ongoing dialogue (Executive 4, August 28, 2008).

A major commitment was made to environmental research, to develop cleaner and more efficient technologies, with CAN$4.4 million invested in 1990 (Noranda 1991: 7). In 1991, the Clean and Efficient Technologies (CETECH) research program was established at the Technology Centre in Montreal. Noranda invested CAN$4 million in the initiative, which addressed the question of how to make copper smelting more environmentally friendly. Research focused on how to reduce energy use, and it was found that it was possible to save 10 per cent of energy use without capital investment (Executive 1, February 16, 2006).

During the early 1990s, more data came to be included in the reports relating to water discharges and air emissions. Beginning in 1991, data was provided on the number of environmental audits conducted affecting environment, health, and safety, and, starting in 1992, on the number of environmental studies conducted. In the 1993 report, note was made of efforts to promote environmental best practices, and spending on environmental research in 1992 increased to CAN$24 million (Noranda 1994: 15). In 1995, Noranda began to publish emissions data on a per-site basis.

Throughout the 1990s, Noranda sought to reduce the amount of SO_2 emissions from its smelters. This was a difficult challenge, in light of increased smelter production in plants in Quebec and New Brunswick, as well as at its Altonorte copper smelter in Chile. To reduce the emissions of SO_2, and increase "sulfur fixation," Noranda made investments at its smelters in Rouyn-Noranda, Murdochville, and Altonorte. One way Noranda sought to reduce emissions was to use SO_2 to manufacture sulfuric acid, a saleable product. In an effort to improve its converter processes, Noranda developed the Noranda Continuous Converter, and the first one was installed at the Horne smelter at a cost of US$55 million. A similar installation at the Gaspe smelter allowed Noranda to expand production without increasing emissions. US$160 million was spent at Altonorte to boost sulfur fixation to over 90 per cent (Five Winds 2000: 72–3). Fully 50 per cent of Noranda's capital budget in the 1990s was spent on environmental improvements and clean-up, with a view to meeting the goal of full compliance with stricter environmental standards (Executive 2, August 26, 2008). Table 4.1 below shows Noranda's environmental expenditures during the 1990s.

Table 4.1 *Noranda's environmental expenditures (US$ millions)*

	1992	1993	1994	1995	1996	1997	1998	1999	2000
Reclamation	25	35	25	40	40	50	30	40	40
Operating expenditures	20	35	30	80	60	100	80	70	70
Capital expenditures	25	20	25	25	50	100	105	135	140
Total	70	90	80	145	150	250	215	245	250

Source: Noranda, various EHS reports.

Frantisak characterized the period from 1995 as the "era of culture," where attention to the environment was considered to be ingrained in Noranda's culture. As the then Chairman and CEO, David Kerr, was quoted as saying in the 1995 EHS report:

The important thing is that there is a strong core-value commitment from the senior management and the Board of Noranda. In addition, there is a manager at each site whose compensation, in part, is tied to how well he or she deals with environment, health and safety concerns. (Noranda 1996a: 3)

To integrate environmental awareness and performance into the corporate culture, it was recognized that commitment to the environment would have to emanate not just from senior management at the top, but down through the line to plant managers and all employees.

In the same report, Noranda launched its new environmental policy guidelines, which reflected Noranda's accumulated learning about its environmental capabilities. Key features of the updated environmental policy were the intention to act as "exemplary leaders" in environmental management, a commitment to the principle of sustainable development, and the design of control systems at all facilities to minimize risks to health, safety, and the environment (Noranda 1996a).

During this period, Noranda strove for continual improvement in its environmental management systems. In 1994, Noranda hired an independent consultant to review its EMS, and compare it against the environmental management standards then being developed by the International Organization for Standardization. Noranda's EMS was found to be highly compatible with the ISO 14001 standard that was published in 1996. This is not surprising, as Frantisak served as leader of the Canadian delegation to the ISO Technical Committee on the Environment that helped establish the ISO 14001 standard. The decision about whether or not to pursue ISO certification was left to the discretion of site managers (and as of 2003, none chose to do so). Noranda did not see the added value of the bureaucratic review, even though it could have self-declared to be compliant with ISO 14001 (Executive 2, December 2, 2011).

The review led to the identification of five areas requiring improvement, including:

1. a better definition of the concept of sustainable development
2. better plant-level adaptation of environmental, health and safety management systems
3. greater environmental input prior to capital expenditures and improved tracking
4. more tools for reviewing the environmental management system
5. a review of the reporting structures for environmental managers.

(Noranda 1996a: 5)

Noranda set up internal task forces to deal with each of these areas. Detailed discussions took place, and focus groups were established to explore the issues. Noranda made use of "scenario planning" as a decision-making tool, with a view to comprehending major trends likely to unfold over the long term.

Out of this process emerged in late 1996 a new environmental framework for the company, known as *Environment 2000 Plus* (1996b). As announced in the 1996 EHS report, *Environment 2000 Plus* was intended to ensure the complete integration of environment, health, and safety into every business decision, to ensure that environmental considerations were an integral and fundamental part of the business. As Trevor Eyton, Senior Chairman, EdperBrascan, explained in a 1997 address: "No major business decision is being made without first considering its environmental implications, and no major environmental expenditure is approved without first considering its economic impact" (Eyton 1997: 24).

The policy aimed to unify Noranda's environmental management systems within its various companies (mining, metallurgy, oil and gas, and forestry) across the corporation. To avoid the problem of "silo" management, environmental management was to be fully integrated "into all phases of business activities, from process research, new products, development of new facilities, operation of our plants, marketing/customer relations, and planning of the future" (David Kerr, as quoted in Vietor 2002: 6). Rejecting the concept of the "triple bottom line" (Elkington 1998), Noranda strove for one bottom line, with contributions from economic, environmental, and social areas. Senior management hoped that through this policy, Noranda could realize more on its environmental investment. A key objective of *Environment 2000 Plus* was "not to maintain our leadership only in the areas of environment, health and safety, but to use it for improved competitiveness" (Noranda 1996b: 7)

With the arrival of David Rodier to the Senior VP, EHS position in 1998, a major new initiative towards continuing improvement in EMS was the Environment, Safety and Health Assurance Process. Its goal was to provide a means to ensure that the root causes of problems were identified and addressed, so that deficiencies would not be repeated from one audit to the next (Noranda 1999a: 5). The transition to this new assurance process took several years, as each operation was expected to develop and implement an environmental framework. It was further revised in 2002, in preparation for the merger of Noranda's and Falconbridge's business services functions, including EHS.

Two major hurdles were encountered in the implementation of the ESH Assurance process. The first was that, consistent with Noranda's decentralized structure, site managers were expected to implement the process. This burden was an added responsibility without the benefit of additional resources, and site managers resented the prospect of increased bureaucracy and paperwork, resulting in considerable push-back. The second, and related, hurdle was that senior management was not prepared to devote significant new resources to this program (Five Winds 2000: 77). To address these problems, senior management reiterated its commitment to continual environmental improvement, and an effort was made to educate site managers on the economic benefits of sound environmental management. Staff compensation was linked, in part, to the implementation of the EHS framework, and site managers were made accountable for specific objectives and targets (Five Winds 2000: 77).

Another example of Noranda's win–win approach to environmental issues was with respect to the major challenge confronting Noranda of reducing its greenhouse gas emissions (GHGs). As with other aspects of its business, the challenge was approached as both a business and environmental issue. Since metallurgical processes are energy intensive, finding ways to reduce energy consumption reduces costs, as well as helping the environment. Despite substantial increases in refined-metal production since 1990, Noranda's total greenhouse gas emissions in Canada remained near 1,000 kilotonnes CO_2 per year, due to energy efficiency improvements, increased recycling, adoption of new process technologies, and mine closures (Five Winds 2000: 73). All the same, despite these improvements in energy intensity, the goal of actual reductions remained elusive. Canada's signing in 1998 of the Kyoto Protocol was therefore a major source of concern for senior management. Given the nature of Noranda's business, the realization of actual reductions was seen to compromise the company's competitive position.

Noranda advised the government that it should use Canada's Kyoto commitments to enhance the efficiency and competitiveness of Canadian industry on a global basis. Noranda felt that the government should enter into contract with industry, to help move it forward on meeting emissions targets (Executive 1, March 2, 2006). With a definite timeline and clear targets, such a process would allow industry to work with government on what would be expected in five years, and allow companies the time needed to make the necessary adjustments. In this respect, Noranda was far ahead of much of industry and the government of the day.

The aim to work with government in establishing emission reduction targets is consistent with the early mover logic of being in a position to shape eventual environmental regulation. Table 4.2 provides a timeline of the major changes put in place by Noranda to implement its CSR. In all of these initiatives, Noranda was an early mover, relative to other mining companies. In terms of environmental reporting, Noranda was an early mover not just in mining, but in industry as a whole.

Table 4.2 *Major organizational and policy developments: Noranda*

1965 Environmental policy statement
1979 Position created: Director, EHS
1979 Position created: Environment Officer
1982 Director, EHS upgraded to VP, EHS
1985 Environmental Policy Statement revised
1985 Environmental Auditing Program introduced (internal)
1987 CEZinc releases communications on EHS for 1986
1989 Environmental Committee of Board of Directors established
1990 First corporate-wide EHS Report published for 1989
1991 Environment Officer upgraded to VP, Environment
1992 Product Stewardship Statement released
1994 VP, EHS upgraded to Senior VP, EHS
1994 Position created: VP, Environmental Audits and Projects
1994 Position created: VP, Safety, Health and Hygiene
1995 Environmental Policy Guidelines updated
1995 Sustainable Development Principles released
1996 *Environment 2000 Plus* published
1998 Sustainable Development Indicators released
1999 First Sustainable Development Report released
1999 Code of Ethics
2002 Implementation of Environment, Safety and Health Assurance Process
2002 Release of first combined Noranda/Falconbridge Sustainable
       Development Report

Experiences that shaped the learning process

A most important influence on the early thinking of senior management on EHS was the experience of operating in remote northern communities (Executive 1, February 13, 2006). In 1973, a writ was served against Noranda and other companies by the Cree Indians in northwest Quebec. The Cree alleged that Noranda and other companies were responsible for acid rain and the discharge of mercury into the water system. Acid rain is caused by sulfur dioxide emissions, a by-product of copper, lead, and zinc smelting. Significant health claims were made. Frantisak was brought in as a consultant on the case (before formally joining Noranda in 1979).

Noranda took the allegations very seriously, and spent over US$1 million on studies, including a major epidemiological study of all plaintiffs (Executive 1, March 2, 2006). The case never went to court or discoveries, and there was no settlement, as the Cree were found not to have a case. All the same, Noranda realized that it could not ignore the environmental and social impact of its operations.

Another important case involving the James Bay Cree and the Quebec government was instrumental in influencing the decision of senior management to adopt a coherent approach to EHS. The Cree were opposed to the Quebec government's decision to expand hydroelectricity development in the James Bay region, and in 1973, succeeded in obtaining a court injunction stopping all work on the massive James Bay hydroelectric project (*Kanatewat v. James Bay Development Corp.* 1973). The injunction specifically referred to concerns about potential damage to the environment and natural resources. Although Noranda was not directly involved in this case, its heavy presence in northern Quebec meant that it was indirectly affected.

The Abitibi region, which is south of the affected area, is dominated by mining, with the main urban center being the company town of Rouyn-Noranda (originally two separate towns that amalgamated in 1986 and site of Noranda's Horne smelter). Noranda's mining and smelting operations are heavy users of hydroelectricity. Hydro-Quebec, which was cited in the James Bay case, is responsible for over 90 per cent of the hydroelectricity production in the Abitibi-Temiscamingue region (Alexander et al. 2004: 10). An injunction against further development of hydroelectricity would have clear implications for Noranda.

The case involving the James Bay Cree revealed that there could be circumstances where mining companies could be denied access to their claims. This was evident in the agreement that was reached between the Quebec government and the Cree in 1975, which provided for the lifting of the injunction against further hydroelectric development in the region. Known as the James Bay and Northern Quebec Agreement, it was a far-reaching agreement that confirmed Quebec's jurisdiction over its territorial boundaries, while at the same time accommodating the rights and needs of the Cree and Inuit communities. The agreement provided for a new land and administrative regime, including the designation of Category 1 lands (lands in and around the communities where the native peoples normally reside) for the exclusive use of the native peoples (Government of Quebec 1975: xvii). The agreement was formally enacted into law in 1977 (James Bay and Northern Quebec Native Claims Settlement Act, 1976–7).

The case was an early eye-opener for Noranda. Senior management realized that the company could not ignore the environmental impact of Noranda's operations. The provision requiring the prior consent of the Cree for mining activities on their lands, and the one requiring environmental impact assessments (EIAs), was seen by Noranda as an indication of what was coming for the mining industry.

By the 1990s, concerns around reputation had become an important issue for Noranda and the mining industry as a whole. Where once mining companies operating in remote northern communities in Canada and around the world were out of the public mind, advancing information technologies and NGO activism ensured public awareness about poor environmental practices. One example of this reality came on the forestry side of Noranda's operations. In the early 1990s, a proposed pulp and paper plant in Tasmania was blocked by environmentalists (Executive 2, April 22, 2003). Although an EIA had been approved for the project, Noranda learned that its Australian partner, which was left to manage the plant, had failed to adequately explain the project to people in the local community. The controversy over this project highlighted for Noranda the importance of addressing early on community concerns (it also demonstrated the perils of partnership arrangements, as Placer Dome was to learn after the Marcopper tailings spill in 1996 in the Philippines).

In the 1990s, mining companies began to encounter problems in gaining access to land for new projects, as Noranda experienced first-hand when it sought to develop the New World mine in the United

States. The New World property is located near Cooke City, Montana, a short distance from Yellowstone National Park. The New World mine experience was formative in driving home the need to integrate more fully the social implications of its operations.

In 1993, a subsidiary of Noranda, Crown Butte Mines Inc., became the object of a citizens' suit alleging water-quality violations. Crown Butte Mines was 60 per cent owned by Hemlo Gold Mines Inc., which is 44 per cent owned by Noranda. The suit cited discharges related to historic mine damage at the New World project site, as a result of actions from previous mining companies (Noranda 1995: 15). Crown Butte had been voluntarily reclaiming the historical mine workings and had committed to treat some of the historical adit discharges as part of the proposed plan of operations. Noranda invested millions in reclamation of old mine sites in the area.

In 1994, two US environmental groups, American Rivers and Trout Unlimited, initiated legal action to stop ongoing processing by the US Department of Interior of patent applications submitted by Crown Butte Mines Inc. for eleven hectares of the New World project. A variety of concerns were conveyed, but the main ones were that a mine located 2.5 miles from Yellowstone would disrupt the peace and tranquility of the area, and that the mine would adversely affect the environment.

Environmentalists could point to other recent major environmental disasters, such as what occurred at the Summitville mine in southern Colorado, owned by another Canadian mining company, Galactic Resources. In 1995, the US District Court in Montana ruled that Crown Butte was in violation of the federal Clean Water Act for failing to obtain water discharge permits with respect to water flowing from an historic mine adit and two open pits (Noranda 1996a: 11). The whole process became politicized, as then President Bill Clinton went so far as to visit the site in late August 1995, while he was vacationing in Wyoming. He subsequently announced a moratorium on the mining of 4,500 acres of federally owned land on the perimeter of Yellowstone. Meanwhile, at the behest of a coalition of fourteen US environmental advocacy groups, the International Union for Conservation of Nature (IUCN) was invited to visit the proposed mine site and in December 1995, with the environmental impact study (EIS) still pending, the IUCN declared Yellowstone a World Heritage Site in Danger (Benedetto 1999: 5).

In 1995, the then CEO David Kerr acknowledged that proposing a gold mine near Yellowstone National Park was a "public affairs problem for both Crown Butte and Noranda" (Noranda 1996a: 3). He further added that "Noranda . . . will not support the development of a mine if we believe it will damage the environment" (Noranda 1996a: 3). Noranda received a great deal of negative publicity over the issue, with extensive media coverage in Canada and the US. In the aftermath of the ICUN designation, and with the Administration actively working to derail the EPA process and prevent the EIS from being released, Noranda decided to abandon the New World project.

The New World mine experience led management to realize that it had to do more to stay on top of growing public expectations about environmental protection. The dilemma for Noranda was that it had met all environmental requirements, yet had seen the EIS process side-tracked. As David Kerr noted, "it is no longer good enough to simply comply with the law . . . [as] formerly 'acceptable' levels of pollution are increasingly less acceptable, legal or not" (Noranda 1997: 3). As such, Noranda and other mining companies would have to voluntarily move beyond compliance to "pre-emptive" and "preventive" planning and action. Kerr spoke of the need for a "cultural shift," entailing the total integration of environment, health, and safety into business thinking.

Appreciation of the need for a social license to operate set the stage for Noranda's *Environment 2000 Plus* environmental strategy. The learning from both the Tasmania and New World examples were explicitly acknowledged in the *Environment 2000 Plus* document:

The importance of the outside perception of Noranda as a leader and the resulting political capital is significant in light of events such as the Tasmanian Pulp Mill and New World projects. These are bold reminders that science and technology on their own are not enough for a project to move forward; political capital and an excellent environmental track record are essential. (Noranda 1996b: 6)

The impact of the New World mine was to strengthen the determination of management to respond to environmental concerns (Executive 1, February 16, 2006).

Noranda also faced its share of challenges in terms of access to markets. In the 1990s, metals came under increasing scrutiny in terms of their safety, with some metals banned outright under the Basel Convention (see Chapter 7). As a result, Noranda came under pressure from the automotive and electronics sectors to demonstrate that use of its products was safe, and that information it provided to customers was accurate, in order to maintain a presence in the marketplace in these sectors (Five Winds 2000: 72). Another major concern was the adoption of what Noranda considered to be non-tariff barriers to trade in consumer products that contain metals, especially in Europe. Noranda was concerned that measures implemented were more trade restrictive than necessary, that the risks associated with potential substitutes were not being considered (such as Bisphenol A in plastic bottles), and that there was inadequate information available for the evaluation of metals (Five Winds 2000: 81).

In the 1990s, Noranda and other companies also found that their potential access to finance was restricted by growing concerns on the part of banks about exposure to political risks surrounding mining. Noranda encountered this situation over attempts in 1998 to secure financing for the Antamina copper–zinc mine in Peru. Noranda owned a 33.75% share in the mine, together with two other Canadian companies, including Teck Cominco (22.5%) (at the time, Teck Corporation), Rio Algom (33.75%), and Mitsubishi Corp. (10%). (Rio Algom subsequently pulled out due to lack of finances, and BHP-Billiton stepped in.) Located in the Andes Mountains, 285 kilometers north of Lima, Antamina at the time was considered to be one of the largest undeveloped copper/zinc ore bodies in the world.

Securing financing for the project proved challenging, because of concerns about environmental risks in a context of bad environmental legacies, weak environmental laws in Peru, and weak capacity for environmental oversight. In 1999, a private banking consortium consisting of over twenty banks was arranged, which provided US$650 million in commercial lending, and another US$689 million came from export credit agencies, including US$135 million from the Export Development Corporation (EDC) of Canada (UNEP 2001: 45).

As a condition for their financing, the German banks insisted on changes to the original plans for getting the metal concentrate to port. Originally, the plan had been to truck the mine materials overland through the Huascaran National Park, a designated World Heritage Site, located beside the mine. Given the high volumes involved, transporting the material overland would have required a truck leaving every seven minutes, twenty-four hours a day, seven days a week (Executive 2, August 26, 2008). The German banks demanded, instead, that a 300-kilometer pipeline be built under the road to the port at Punta Lobitos, in the District of Huarmey. Up to that date, such a massive pipeline had never been undertaken, and the cost to build it was

US$180 million, driving the cost of the project up by about 7 per cent. Ultimately, the pipeline proved to be a good solution, both from an environmental perspective, as well as from a cost perspective, due to savings on labor and fuel.

The World Bank also played an important role in attaching environmental conditions to its lending for the project, through the Multilateral Investment Guarantee Agency (MIGA). There were government environmental standards in place in Peru, but there was weak capacity for environmental oversight. Furthermore, as noted in a World Bank report on Peru, in the mid-to-late 1990s, there was weak commitment on the part of the government to addressing environmental issues (World Bank 2002: 21). As a condition for the US$67.5 million of coverage for equity investments of the three Canadian mining companies, the MIGA imposed lending criteria that included the World Bank Group's elaborate procedures for environmental screening, disclosure, and public consultation. The World Bank became the de facto world standard, and private commercial banks came to insist on Bank standards in providing loans for such projects.

The above examples illustrate the barriers in access to land, markets, and finance experienced increasingly from the 1990s by Noranda and other mining companies.

In addition to the problem of weak capacity and/or non-existent environmental protections in developing countries, mining companies encountered corruption. Noranda contended with this problem when it considered investing in Zambia's copper industry in the mid-1990s (Executive 1, December 9, 2011). Noranda ultimately walked away because environmental assessments revealed that millions would have to be spent in order to clean up the operations, and billions more would be needed to invest in new equipment (Executive 2, August 26, 2008; McNeil 1998: 1). A tailings spill that occurred during one of Noranda's visits resulted in no remedial action being taken, even though local people were using water from a stream that in all likelihood had been contaminated by the spill (Executive 4, August 28, 2008).

The experience with corruption in Zambia was a factor influencing Noranda's decision to adopt a Code of Ethics in 1999 (Noranda 1999b: 25). The Code of Ethics was an explicit response to Noranda's strategic decision to expand its operations globally, and recognition of the need for ethical principles to guide Noranda's operations around the world (Noranda 1999b: 12).

As criticism of the mining industry intensified in the 1990s, Noranda executives came to recognize that a new strategy was needed to manage negative public perceptions about mining. As Noranda COO, David Goldman noted, "while the industry was responding to criticism with facts and figures, the public was seeing big holes, altered landscapes and huge smelters" (McGovern 1998: F3). Growing road-blocks to new projects led Noranda to recognize that environmental and social issues are interdependent, and that a new approach was needed to address this reality.

External engagement

One of Noranda's strategies to address reputational issues was to expand its external relations, both within Canada and globally. Starting in 1990, the start of the "era of action," Noranda came to recognize the growing political importance of environmental NGOs. In 1990, Noranda participated in an NGO conference organized in advance of the 1992 Rio Conference. There was real concern over the "venom" coming from NGOs, yet Noranda felt it was necessary to work with them to build trust between business and NGOs (Executive 1, February 13, 2006). Noranda budgeted US$150,000 per year in support of environmental groups, including Pollution Probe and the World Wildlife Fund (WWF).

After the 1990 NGO conference, Noranda proposed to the organizer that a regular mechanism be established for corporate–NGO dialogue, so that both sets of actors might work together to solve problems. In 1990, the New Directions Group was created, consisting of leaders of twelve Canadian environmental groups and twelve CEOs of major Canadian corporations with large environmental footprints. The New Directions Group sought to overcome the traditionally polarized nature of interactions between business and environmental communities (New Directions Group: 1).

NGOs who participated in the New Directions Group in the early years included the Pembina Institute, the WWF, Friends of the Earth, the Canadian Nature Federation, and Pollution Probe. The goal of the New Directions Group was to build consensus between business and environmental groups on how to move forward on environmental issues involving high-polluting sectors. The thinking was to create an informal space where the various stakeholders could learn together, to address key environmental policy issues which could contribute to a more informed and constructive policy debate on the environment in Canada.

Noranda also systematically worked to develop its relations with the Canadian government at the federal and provincial levels. Noranda was a major advocate of voluntary approaches to improving the environmental performance of industry as a whole. As a company that took its environmental performance seriously, this was not motivated by a desire to forestall environmental regulation so as to avoid its responsibilities. Rather, Noranda felt that governments tended to respond quickly to meet public pressure, without adequate consultation with industry (Executive 1, March 2, 2006). New requirements introduced by government are very costly for companies to implement. For example, when the Canadian government moved quickly to regulate the use of dioxins, the cost to industry of adjustment was about CAN$5 billion (Executive 1, December 9, 2011). The cost of adjusting to pending regulation would have been only 10 per cent of this amount. This realization motivated companies such as Noranda to attempt to be ahead of the group, to anticipate pending regulation, and to engage in long-term planning, a key early mover consideration.

In 1990, Frantisak initiated the "Friday Group," made up of environmentally minded Canadian businesses, to meet and maintain dialogue with the government (Vietor 2002: 8). The Friday Group serves as a forum where industry members, politicians, and bureaucrats can bounce ideas and provide feedback. The immediate impetus behind the Friday Group was the then Minister for the Environment's effort to develop a "Green Plan" without consulting industry (Executive 1, March 2, 2006). The Green Plan was a major environmental commitment of the government of the then PM, Brian Mulroney, and involved a range of environmental initiatives. There was concern on the part of industry and even other government departments (most notably Natural Resources Canada) that the development of the Green Plan had not been a sufficiently transparent process.

Frantisak, and a few other senior executives, recognized the importance of cooperating with government, and participating in the development of national environmental policies. As Frantisak put it in a 1990 address to Ontario Hydro:

Environmental issues will be deciding factors in the future of our businesses. We had better take it seriously. You, as senior officers, can slow down this process, you can accelerate it, but you cannot stop it. (Frantisak 1990: 11)

120	*Noranda Inc.*

One initiative that grew out of the Friday Group is the Greenhouse Gas Registry, now known as the Canada Climate Change Voluntary Challenge and Registry (VCR). Under the Registry, companies are required to report on the emissions from each of their Canadian operations, although they are not yet required to meet specific targets. Noranda established its own goal in 1991 to reduce energy consumption by 10 per cent from 1990 levels by 1995, a target which the majority of Noranda's operations had met by the end of 1995 (Noranda 1996a: 10). In 2000 and 2001, the VCR awarded Noranda gold-level champion status for its reports submitted in those years (Noranda 2002: 2).

The voluntary basis of the initiative further suggests that it was designed to anticipate or forestall harsh regulation. However, Noranda felt it was important to demonstrate that industry could take steps to reduce pollutants on a voluntary basis (Executive 1, February 13, 2006). As such, Noranda was a consistent advocate for non-regulatory approaches that allow businesses to deal proactively with the environment as a strategic priority, anticipating and responding to concerns in a way that enhances environmental performance and competitiveness, rather than reacting to regulatory pressures that increase competitive burdens. Certainly, Noranda's substantial investment in research and technology reveals its strategy to enhance competitiveness through the design and marketing of green technologies.

The New Directions Group worked to develop a series of recommendations to reduce and/or eliminate toxic substance emissions (Noranda 1992: 20; Vietor 2002: 8). In 1991, the New Directions Group proposed the voluntary Accelerated Reduction/Elimination of Toxics (ARET) program. Administered by Environment Canada, the program involved the identification of a list of toxic substances that were to be reduced or eliminated. Noranda represented the mining and smelting industry of the multistakeholder group that was set up to develop the ARET program. The government created an ARET stakeholders committee, which evaluated toxicity of 2,000 substances and identified a list of 117 for immediate action. Of these 117 potentially toxic substances identified, twelve were metal substances. The overall goal was to reduce the use of such substances by 50 per cent by the year 2000 (Noranda 1995: 18). Noranda's goal was to reduce metals emissions into air and water by 83 per cent by 2002, from the base year 1998. Some activist groups were opposed to the idea that toxic substances be reduced, rather than eliminated, and withdrew from ARET (Vietor 2002: 8).

The attraction for Noranda of promoting such voluntary programs as ARET is that it was felt they would garner more support for industry from government and environmental NGOs. Such efforts were deemed to help Noranda in obtaining permits, and earn it softer treatment in the event of regulatory infractions. While the ARET program could be seen as a means to forestall regulation, there was, in fact, no regulatory backstop to it when it came into effect (Executive 1 (Falconbridge), February 22, 2006).

Other government/industry action programs supported by Noranda included the Mine Environment Neutral Drainage Program (MEND), the Assessment of Aquatic Effects of Mining in Canada program (AQUAMIN), and the Aquatic Effects Technology Evaluation program. The MEND program was a major initiative based at Noranda's Technology Centre in Montreal on how to manage tailings from old mines. The provinces faced a huge environmental liability around the fact that a large number of acid-generating old mines revert back to the Crown once they are closed. Noranda felt it alone should not be footing the bill for this initiative, and was able to persuade the federal and provincial governments to contribute (Executive 1, December 9, 2011). MEND received CAN\$5 million from industry, CAN\$5 million from the Federal government, and CAN\$25 million from the Ontario provincial government, and the program proved to be very successful.

Noranda was active in the Mining Association of Canada, and wrote the draft of MAC's first Environmental Policy Statement (released 1989). It served on a committee that worked together with the Canadian Dam Safety Association to develop a guide to the management of tailings facilities. Noranda/Falconbridge supported a significant new initiative on the part of MAC, the Towards Sustainable Mining (TSM) initiative. In 2004, mining companies began reporting on the indicators developed under the TSM. The first progress report was published in 2005: *Towards Sustainable Mining Progress Report: 2004* (MAC 2005). Derek Pannell, CEO of Noranda, and then the merged Noranda/Falconbridge, served as Chair of the TSM Governance Team, a position he continued to hold until 2008.

At the global level, Noranda cooperated with such organizations as the United Nations Environment Program (UNEP) and the World Industry Council on the Environment (WICE), now the World Business Council for Sustainable Development (WBCSD). Noranda was a founding member of WICE, sitting on the Executive Committee of that organization and later, the WBCSD. Senior management recognized the opportunity these organizations provided for industry to address environmental challenges. Senior management ensured Noranda's Chair and CEO, David Kerr, understood the importance of Noranda's involvement in these initiatives (Executive 1, March 2, 2006).

The wide-ranging external activities outlined above illustrate management's orientation towards environmental challenges. The willingness to engage with external critics, and the institutionalization of ongoing dialogue with NGOs, as well as government, through the New Directions Group and the Friday Group, reflects an openness to external engagement which is essential to learning (especially deutero learning).

The path to sustainable development

As Noranda's EHS policies evolved over the 1980s, developments happening outside of Canada came to have growing salience. Sustainable development first appeared on Noranda's radar screen in the late 1980s, after the publication of the Brundtland Commission Report in 1988. The lead-up to the 1992 Rio Conference on Environment and Development, and the conference itself, was an important influence on Noranda. Frantisak led the Canadian business delegation that sought to address the implications of sustainable development for industry. Noranda realized that it needed to enlarge its understanding of its responsibility towards society, and to look at issues from a global perspective, not just from the perspective of local plants (Executive 4, August 28, 2008).

Noranda's first reference to sustainable development came early on, in its 1991 environmental report (Noranda 1992). In that report, the work of the Brundtland Commission in developing the concept is acknowledged. Indeed, the publication of the WCED's *Our Common Future* (1987) marked Noranda's first exposure to the concept (Executive 1, February 16, 2006). Frantisak spoke of the impression made upon him of meeting Gro Brundtland at the NGO conference held in Vancouver in 1990. After the release of the report, Canadian Prime Minister, Brian Mulroney convened a taskforce to decide on next steps, on which the CEO of Noranda sat. The taskforce identified sustainable development as an important Canadian objective, and recommended the launch of the National Round Table on the Environment and Economy. Noranda's involvement in this process reinforced the importance of sustainable development, an objective to be pursued at the highest level of the Canadian government (Executive 1, December 9, 2011).

The growing awareness of the concept coincided with the expansion of Noranda's global operations. Slowly, over the course of the 1990s, Noranda sought to come to terms with the concept in a manner that made sense to its operations. Having learned through its experiences in northern Canada the importance of factoring economic, environmental, and social considerations into its mining operations, Noranda encountered this reality anew as it moved to significantly expand its operations around the globe.

Sustainable development fit with the conviction of Noranda's senior management that business should be a catalyst for the promotion of environmental responsibility and achieving sustainable development (Executive 1, August 20, 2008). Senior executives were convinced that governments acting on their own would not be able to solve the global-scale political and social problems presented by environmental devastation. There was a felt need for companies such as Noranda to take a lead in promoting environmental responsibility and sustainable development. Understood in this context, sustainable development fit with Noranda's perception that it needed to look at the bigger picture beyond its own corporation (Executive 4, August 28, 2008).

Consistent with Noranda's approach to environmental performance, the promotion of sustainable development was seen to be in Noranda's best interest. As Trevor Eyton, Senior Chairman, EdperBrascan, put it in an address in 1997: "I don't want to put too much of a moral tone to this [sustainable development], ... Noranda's performance is really a matter of obligation"(Eyton 1997: 6). Eyton went on to say: "As the world chemical industry has demonstrated convincingly since the disaster at Bhopal, environmental obligation is commensurate with environmental imposition" (ibid.: 7). In order to flourish in global markets, business would have to contribute to the sort of stable political, economic, and social conditions that would allow business to survive.

Noranda executives understood that taking a business-as-usual approach, without concern for sustainability, would damage business interests in the long run. Frantisak likened the consequences of the business-as-usual approach to the reaction of a frog placed in hot water. If the water is hot, the frog will leap out of danger, but if it is placed in a pot of cold water that is gradually heated, the frog is boiled to death. Frantisak predicted that businesses that ignored sustainability issues would face the fate of the frog that discovers too late that it is in hot water (Frantisak 1998: 14). Instead, Frantisak argued for the need for sustainable growth that factors in environmental and social issues.

Sustainable development was consistent with Noranda's win–win approach to environmental improvement, as reflected in its investment in technologies to promote energy efficiency and reduce sulfur dioxide emissions through sulfur fixation. With environmental regulations becoming more stringent, Noranda saw the advantage of investing in environmentally smart technology to avoid having to reinvest at far greater cost in the future. Noranda had also responded to pressure from its customers, who were increasingly looking for assurance that Noranda's metals and forest products were being produced in a sustainable manner (Eyton 1997: 32).

Yet, although philosophically Noranda executives were prepared to adapt to the growing momentum behind sustainable development, Noranda had trouble grappling with sustainable development on the operational side. Noranda was initially not keen on the term, as it was considered to have no substance (Executive 1, February 16, 2006). Since Noranda had a very broad definition of the environment, it felt that the company was already practicing many elements of sustainable development. For example, executives felt that Noranda's recycling business contributed to sustainable development, by reducing waste disposal, providing energy savings, and extending the use of valuable commodities. Noranda was already anticipating future environmental requirements and building them into its operations. Noranda had been promoting environmentally cleaner and more energy-efficient techno-logies, which were seen to be good both for the environment, and the bottom line. For example, Noranda had invested in technologies that convert sulfur dioxide at its smelters. So in many respects, sustainable development was seen to be a good fit with Noranda's existing EHS policies and practices.

While Noranda had a good grasp of the economic and environmental side of sustainable development, learning on addressing the social side proved challenging. This did not appear to be due to a lack of appreci-ation of the social side; Frantisak had long understood the need to address this aspect of CSR. As Frantisak noted in a 2008 interview with Dr Blair Feltmate (Ontario Power Generation):

We came to the realization that we operate with the public's consent. We were convinced that our investments in new mines, smelters, refineries, etc. must be designed with environmental and social issues of the day in mind, as well as with an anticipation of future issues. (Feltmate, Interview with Frantisak 2008: 31)

Other senior executives also seemed to appreciate the social implications of sustainable development, as the following comments by Eyton suggest:

We are living in a time when values are beginning to determine the rules to a far greater degree than ever before. And not just the values of the people who run the companies or the politicians who run the government of the day. We must also take into consideration the values of the people who work with us and the people who live in the communities and countries where we operate. And not just this generation, but also those that follow. (Eyton 1997: 34)

An early example of Noranda's attempt to deal with the social side of sustainable development came in the early 1980s, when Noranda organized a series of press conferences across the country. The CEO was present, and people were invited to ask him questions on any issue of concern to them, including acid rain, which was a topical issue at the time. Although press conferences are not a sufficient way of dealing with image issues, it was justified by management on the grounds that the company was seeking to be open and transparent about what it was trying to do (Executive 1, December 9, 2011).

The first sign that Noranda was prepared to seriously embrace the concept was the announcement in its 1995 report of six sustainable development principles for the company. At that time, very few companies had stepped forward to give meaning to sustainable development. These principles were the result of a task force that was struck in 1995. Environmental managers from all the various business units (copper, zinc, etc.) were consulted and invited to comment on drafts of the sustainable development principles (Executive 4, August 28, 2008). Two outside consultants were hired for expert advice, and external stakeholders were also consulted. The principles included a commitment to:

Environment

- minimize the physical, chemical and biological effects of our activities on the environment
- nurture excellence by promoting environmental education, training and research programs within our workforce and communities

Social

- foster constructive dialogue with interested parties in the conduct of our activities
- ensure that our activities are sensitive to cultural considerations, employee and public health and the needs of future generations

Economic

- ensure that our activities maintain the long-term sustainability of resources; and
- strengthen the financial and competitive position of the Noranda group of companies.

(Noranda 1996a: 4)

Consistent with its approach to environmental improvement, these principles were understood to have a direct positive impact on Noranda's capital and operating costs.

Signs of continued grappling with the concept of sustainable development was evident in the 1996 report, where the *Environment 2000 Plus* EHS management system was announced. In the 1996 report, the challenge of communicating what such a vague concept means to employees was alluded to: "Sustainable development is a popular phrase that is not well defined around the world" (Noranda 1997: 3). As a result, Noranda set out in 1997 to develop a list of indicators of sustainable development, against which performance could be tracked.

The 1997 report revealed the difficulty Noranda encountered in defining indicators, suggesting considerable push-back within the company. As was candidly noted:

When trying to define sustainable development, it is difficult to claim that the mining part of our business is sustainable ... For a mining company, therefore, sustainability has to mean something different, if it is to mean anything at all. (Noranda 1998: 2)

This led the company in 1998 to seek outside advice from others both inside and outside the mining industry to come up with a list of indicators. Frantisak attempted to consult with members of the financial community in the development of the sustainable development indicators that would be meaningful to them, but there was little interest. Indeed, opinion surveys that Noranda conducted of mutual fund managers and banks worldwide revealed very little awareness of sustainable development, or even environmental issues (Feltmate, Interview with Frantisak 2008: 31).

After extensive consultation with the financial sector and academic experts, a set of eight indicators covering environmental, social, and economic aspects of sustainable development was developed, including:

1. reduction of SO_2 emissions in Noranda's copper business (with a target of 90% capture by 2002 and a 57% reduction from 1985 levels);
2. reduction of metal emissions to the air from copper and zinc operations, including smelters and refineries (with a target of reducing metals emissions by 80% of 1988 levels by 2008, while striving to achieve that by 2002);
3. reduce energy consumption and greenhouse gas emissions (to improve energy efficiency by 1% annually between 1990 and 2000);
4. minimize Noranda's "footprint" on the land through land-use tracking and reclamation;
5. community dialogue through community liaison committees (with transparency and openness);
6. safety (for both employees and public health);
7. profitable growth (with a target of 15% return on equity by end 2002);
8. environmental capital expenditures (Noranda will continue to make environmental capital expenditures, but they will decrease as Noranda allocates capital to investments that create value).

(Noranda 1999a: 10)

In 1999, the name of Noranda's stand-alone reports changed from "EHS" reports to "sustainable development" reports. Notwithstanding the announcement of these indicators, the reporting format remained the same as it had previously for 1998 and 1999. This changed with the 2000 report, where Noranda's sustainable development targets and objectives were more clearly laid out. A rather narrow definition was provided as to what sustainable development meant to Noranda: sustainable development entailed "economic sustainability, environmental protection and corporate social responsibility."

Starting with the 2001 report, a sustainability index was included which provided environmental, social, and economic data in one table, comparing 2001 data with 2000 and 1995. In 2001, Noranda revised its environmental policy to reflect its commitment to sustainable development, including the need to consider the long-term sustainability of communities, and ongoing improvements to its EMS (specifically the assurance aspect of EHS). Labeled the Environment, Health and Safety Policy, it was renamed again in 2002, the year Noranda and Falconbridge produced their first combined report, as the Sustainable Development Policy. Although the wording changed slightly, the substance remained largely the same. The following definition of sustainable development was provided: "Sustainable development is the implementation of practices and policies that contribute to the well-being of the environment, economy and society to address the needs of customers, suppliers, shareholders, employees, government, the general public and the communities in which we operate, without compromising the ability of future generations to meet their own needs" (Noranda/Falconbridge 2003: 2).

By 2003, Noranda/Falconbridge had developed a comprehensive sustainable development framework. It covered policies and codes, management systems, standards of performance, product stewardship, performance objectives, external dialogue, research and development, and financial viability (Noranda/Falconbridge 2004: 6–7).

Learning and sustainable development

The experience of mining was an important influence on the evolution of Noranda's CSR policies and practices, and on the eventual adoption of sustainable development. As one executive put it, Noranda had learned some "difficult lessons," which it sought to apply to its new investments, many of which were in the developing world (Executive 2, April 22, 2003). It was in the context of its global operations that the social side of sustainable development became important, since Noranda had invested heavily in developing countries such as Chile and Peru. Noranda sought to apply the difficult lessons it had learned to new investments in Chile and Peru, with mixed results.

One example of a reasonably successful application of sustainable development was at the Altonorte smelter. In 1998, Noranda acquired the Altonorte copper smelter in Antofagasta, Chile, and sought permission to expand the facility. At the time, the Chilean government was still developing its environmental policies, which were being modeled after the US EPA. Noranda agreed to conduct an environmental impact study, and sought public input before finalizing it. It was recognized that it was crucial to build and maintain community support (Manager 1, April 3, 2003).

As part of its public consultations, Noranda contracted local universities to provide input. It also held public meetings and talked to neighborhood associations close to the smelter. Although there was some NGO opposition, Noranda was able to establish that the level of public concern was low. The public consultations provided Noranda with a means of gauging the degree of public support before submitting the EIS, increasing the chances that it would be approved. As the Managing Director for Altonorte explained, Noranda took the lessons it had learned from the Yellowstone experience, and sought to apply them in Chile (Manager 1, April 3, 2003).

Noranda took further steps to help maintain public support. It suggested that a Citizens' Oversight Committee be established to monitor the smelter's environmental impact. Noranda agreed to give the Committee water samples that could be analyzed by independent labs. With respect to the biggest issue, air quality, the Committee was provided with ongoing air-quality data, and an independent agency was contracted to interpret the results. Noranda provided social assistance to the local community by providing internship training and funding teacher training.

Two other new projects, the Alumysa aluminum smelter in Chile, and the Antamina copper mine in Peru, met with considerably less success in terms of obtaining a social license to operate. These two projects reveal several reasons for problems in implementing Noranda's sustainable development strategies. One factor identified by executives is that Noranda lacked early mover advantages in Chile. For example, Noranda divested from Chile in the 1970s after Pinochet came to power, under pressure from church groups, which had begun to regularly attend annual board meetings (Executive 2, August 26, 2008). Noranda reinvested in Chile in the early 1990s, after the return to democracy. The decision to divest from Chile was seen as a mistake from a business point of view, because Noranda lost important contacts, and it came back in too late, after other companies had already invested (Executive 2, August 26, 2008). The loss of early mover advantages and key contacts was relevant for the failure of the Alumysa project to get off the ground.

The second reason for the failure of these projects from the social side is due to Noranda's decentralized organizational structure, which made it challenging for corporate office to exert control over the separate divisions. The third reason is that the managers hired to move these projects forward had a mining mindset/geology background, and were not sufficiently sensitive to and/or did not care about, the social side (Executive 1, December 9, 2011).

The proposed Alumysa aluminum smelter was a major new project to be located in Chacabuco Bay in the Aysen region of southern Chile. In contrast to Altonorte, the outcome with Alumysa was targeting by large NGOs, very bad publicity, and the ultimate abandonment of the project, in a manner reminiscent of the New World mine. In fact, although the Chilean government at the time had not acted to protect the Aysen region, it was similar to Yellowstone in terms of its beauty and attraction as an ecotourism destination, and its ecological significance.

The Alumysa project required the construction of a large dam, which by the mid-1990s had become a bit of a red flag for environmental groups. Although Frantisak was involved with the project from the early 1990s when it was first proposed, the project had been put on the back burner for most of the 1990s due to financial considerations. Although Chilean environmental laws did not come into force until 1997, Noranda nevertheless went ahead and hired Canadian consultants to conduct an extensive EIA.

According to the General Manager of the Alumysa project, the majority of people living in the near-by communities of Coihaique and Aisen supported the project, as they stood to benefit from the electricity generation (Manager 2, April 1, 2003). Noranda proposed to sell electricity from the project for rates lower than were currently available. Noranda was prepared to support training programs and curriculum development in schools, recreation, and the construction of new schools and housing.

However, there was some opposition to the project from the local salmon industry. Salmon farming is an important source of income in the region (and is an important Chilean export), and farmers would have had to be relocated from Chacabuco Bay to make way for the smelter and the attendant traffic. In addition to the Salmon and Trout Producers Association, there were a number of other small associations opposed to the project (Manager 2, April 1, 2003). Roughly twenty environmental, community, and law groups formed the Aysen Life Reserve Alliance to protest the project. They were joined by the tourism chambers of Coihaique and Puyuhuapi (Halifax Initiative 2003: 6).

Noranda did try to engage with the Salmon Association to work out a way to compensate those farmers who would be affected. However, momentum was lost when the whole project was put on the back burner for a number of years. There was inadequate effort made to sustain relations with the salmon farmers. Failure to maintain relations with the local community during this time led to the souring of relations (Executive 2, December 2, 2011).

When Noranda was ready to reactivate the project in the early 2000s, local NGOs built links with international NGOs. Chilean activists also sought to build "solidarity" with Canadian unions representing Noranda workers (Mining Watch Canada 2003: 1). In 2003–4, Noranda became the target of a sustained attack from Greenpeace over Alumysa, which formed an alliance with the salmon farmers (although fish farming is itself a polluting industry). Citing evidence from the World Commission on Dams, Greenpeace argued that the project would result in the flooding of rainforests and threaten the survival of rare and endemic species (Greenpeace 2003: 7–10). In December, 2003, Greenpeace staged a demonstration outside Noranda's headquarters in Toronto.

On August 1, 2003, the then Chilean President, Ricardo Lagos Escobar, publicly stated that the project should be relocated to another site in Chile, while also noting the benefits to the region of reducing the high energy costs. This led Noranda to announce on August 19, 2003 that the project would be temporarily suspended.

The decentralized structure of Noranda, and the lack of sensitivity to community concerns on the part of senior management responsible for the project, were major factors in explaining why NGOs gained the upper hand. The Alumysa project was left to the senior management of Noranda Aluminum, and due to a shortage of senior management, Noranda Aluminum hired someone from Alcoa (Executive 1, December 9, 2011). The management failed to understand the need for full and ongoing community engagement. As one executive put it, Noranda "blew it," in that it never really managed to get the community onside, and not enough was spent on community relations (Executive 2, April 22, 2003; August 26, 2008).

At the Antamina copper project, the problem was less to do with senior management, as the CEO set the tone on environment and safety (Executive 2, August 26, 2008). However, he left the management of the project to Peruvians, who did not share the same culture of commitment to community engagement (Executive 1, December 9,

2011). The Peruvian management had no real attachment to the community (Executive 2, August 26, 2008). The company had built what was in effect a gated community near the mine, for managerial staff and their families, complete with an international school for those who could afford it. Yet, the staff did not want to live there, preferring to live in Lima. This complicated the ability of the company to keep lines of communication open with people in surrounding communities, and it did not take long for community resentment to surface over issues of compensation for displaced families and environmental concerns (Greenpeace 2003: 25).

This situation, and allegations of environmental degradation, led to growing distrust on the part of the local community. Problems in the port area where the metal concentrate is piped proved to be especially serious. Community relations got off to a rocky (literally) start, when during the construction of the port, nearby homes were damaged. In order to accommodate ships arriving to take on the concentrate, a huge jetty was constructed, which interfered with fishermen in the nearby fishing village, who had to boat around it. There was inadequate consultation with the local communities, setting the stage for poor relations and mistrust. In 2005, the Federation of Peruvian Fishermen and the organization Life and Environmental Impacts, lodged a complaint with the Compliance Advisor/Ombudsman (CAO), an independent recourse mechanism for projects funded by the International Finance Corporation (IFC) and the Multilateral Investment Guarantee Agency (MIGA) (CAO 2006).

In the final report prepared by the CAO, the legacy of negative interactions between large-scale mining projects (not just Antamina), and how this has poisoned mine-community relations, was noted (CAO 2006: 4). The level of mistrust was found to be affecting communications between the mine and communities, as well as the credibility of Antamina's environmental monitoring and reporting (CAO 2006: 9–12).

While poor community relations cannot be entirely attributed to Noranda (Noranda was not responsible for managing Antamina), the overall pattern of Noranda's experiences in Chile and Peru point to ongoing difficulties in seeing the social side of sustainable development implemented at the operational level. When Falconbridge and Noranda merged their business functions in 2002, best practices from their combined operations were identified in the subsequent development of sustainable development policies (Noranda on the environment side, and Falconbridge on the social side). The acquisition by Xstrata of Falconbridge in 2006 meant that there was insufficient time for these efforts to be realized at the operational level.

Conclusion

This chapter has demonstrated that strong and supportive leadership is an essential part of the explanation for Noranda's early mover status in CSR adoption. Whereas many mining companies chose a defensive and reactive approach to environmental challenges, senior management recognized early on the need to maintain social acceptance and the potential opportunities in strengthening environmental performance. Early major developments, such as the Mississauga train derailment, the Bhopal chemical disaster, and the Exxon Valdez chemical spill sensitized management to potential vulnerabilities for the company. These developments prompted Noranda to be an early mover in establishing CSR policies and management systems in response to growing public awareness and concerns about environmental issues.

Senior management might have avoided its environmental responsibilities, or denied the implications of serious environmental disasters. Rather, with support from the Board, senior management sought to instill a values-based approach to EHS policies, and later to sustainable development. Through leadership, organizational change, extensive external engagement, a willingness to learn, and employee incentives, Noranda exhibited a culture of commitment to CSR. Senior management adopted a proactive stance to environmental improvement, moving beyond a compliance-based approach to one focused on long-term value. Management also sought to position the company in such a way that the considerable investments in green technology and processes would result in a "win–win" outcome for Noranda, in the form of greater efficiency, decreased energy costs, and a stronger competitive position.

Early experiences of mining in northern Canada were also identified by senior management to have been critical in influencing Noranda's approach to the environment and community engagement. Lessons learned from dealing with the Cree in northern Quebec in the early years, together with the New World mine, and experiences with mining in countries such as Peru and Chile in later years, shaped management's approach to CSR. Institutional context in Canada, the US, and developing countries clearly influenced CSR adoption. The examples cited in this chapter illustrate the growing barriers to access to land, finance, and markets which Noranda and other mining companies were facing. As an early mover, management adopted a leadership role in terms of its own CSR practices, as well as in terms of promoting global industry collaboration (see also Chapter 7).

Noranda was clearly motivated by potential early mover advantages, as evidenced in its investment in technological innovation, its decision to grow its recycling business, its adoption of standards that other companies would then feel pressured to adopt, and its efforts to anticipate future government regulation by setting the standard for best practices. Noranda sought to engage with its external critics as well as government, and institutionalized means for doing so through the New Directions Group and the Friday Group. By instituting its own CSR practices on a voluntary basis, Noranda demonstrated to government that command-and-control-style regulation was not necessarily the best path to improved environmental performance.

Noranda was influenced by global normative developments, but also was active in shaping global public policy affecting mining and minerals. Relevant developments included the strengthening of global environmental regulation through such treaties as the Basel Convention on the Transboundary Transport of Hazardous Wastes, the rise of management systems through global organizations such as the ISO, and participation in milestone events such as the 1992 Rio Conference, which entrenched sustainable development as the normative framework for environmental protection.

Participation in national and international industry associations was found to be an important influence on Noranda, but management also saw participation as an opportunity to show leadership in improving industry practices. Membership in the CCPA because of the chemical side of Noranda's business was an important early influence because it gave Noranda a taste of public outreach and management systems for EHS, especially in the aftermath of the Bhopal tragedy. Membership in many international metals associations, such as the International Copper Association (ICA) and the International Zinc Association (IZA), promoted learning as they were all confronting increasing regulation and scrutiny. Later, Noranda's membership in the WBCSD from its founding influenced Noranda's receptiveness to the appropriateness of framing its CSR in terms of sustainable development.

In responding to the growing significance of the norm of sustainable development, Noranda sought to reconcile the concept with its existing EHS practices. Although professional background (the mining mindset) was not found to be of huge significance, management did find the concept to be ill-defined. To make sustainable development meaningful to the mine managers who would have to implement it at the operational level, Noranda demonstrated leadership in developing measurable sustainable development indicators. The negative experience of the New World mine served to strengthen the determination of management to overcome doubts about what sustainable development means in the context of mining.

The actual implementation of the social side of sustainable development proved difficult, as the examples from Peru and Chile illustrate, a reflection of the mining mindset in one instance, but also of the highly decentralized organizational structure of Noranda. Although senior management was able to maintain strong support at the highest levels of the organization in the corporate office for CSR, it was less effective in overcoming the strong independent culture of the many separate business units (Executive 2, December 2, 2011). Reaching down to the operational level was less of a problem with long-established mines and smelters, but proved more of a challenge with new projects (Executive 1, December 9, 2011). Leadership from the top, while very important, nevertheless brushed up against structural determinants in the implementation of CSR at the operational level.

5 | Placer Dome Inc.

Introduction

Placer Dome Inc. (PDI) is the product of a merger between Placer and Dome in 1987, two old companies that had been operating for over fifty years. The analysis of the evolution of Placer Dome's CSR policies begins at that time. In contrast to Noranda, which by the late 1980s had already developed CSR policies, had managerial practices to implement them, and was working towards publishing its first EHS report in 1990, Placer Dome was at the beginning of the process of developing its CSR policies. Placer Dome can nevertheless be considered an early mover compared to the majority of major mining companies in terms of the development of CSR policies and practices, the adoption of sustainable development as a normative frame for its CSR, and the commencement of stand-alone CSR reporting. As was the case with Noranda, it is argued here that internal leadership is a critical part of the explanation for CSR adoption at Placer Dome. Senior management was responsive to global normative developments, and Placer Dome was one of the first companies to adopt sustainable development as an integrative framework for its CSR.

The need to manage the serious environmental and associated social risks inherent in gold mining provides the setting in which Placer Dome's policies evolved. The original Placer company had experience in dealing with challenging social issues stemming from its operations in Papua New Guinea (PNG) dating back to the 1920s. As stakeholder theory predicts, over time Placer Dome came to respond to these environmental and social risks as part of a strategic effort to address reputational concerns, and to ensure the company's long-term viability. In embracing sustainable development, Placer Dome sought to weave its thinking about sustainable development together with the company's core values. The implication of this effort is that, as much as the framing of CSR in terms of sustainable development was a strategic response to external

136

stakeholder pressures, management sought to align Placer Dome's core values with sustainable development. The adoption of CSR framed in terms of sustainable development was driven by both interest-based and norms-based considerations.

Placer Dome had a range of environmental challenges to manage associated with the gold-mining process. One of the most difficult problems is what to do with the crushed rock (tailings) left over after the mineral has been extracted from the ore. How tailings are stored is a technical problem whose solution is dependent on geological conditions in the vicinity of the mine. At Placer Dome's Marcopper mine in the Philippines, tailings were kept in a mined-out pit. On March 24, 1996, the plug to the tailings drainage tunnel gave way, causing chemical-laced tailings to pour into nearby rivers. This event led to Placer Dome becoming the subject of sustained attack from NGOs, and served as an impetus for moving forward with sustainable development.

Tailings disposal was an issue at other PDI mines, such as Porgera and Misima in PNG, where the company had to resort to controversial riverine and submarine tailings disposal methods, respectively. The Porgera mine is located in steep mountainous terrain, where the risk of building tailings dams was judged to be too great, due to difficult geography, earthquake potential, and high rainfall. Tailings were there-fore discharged into the Strickland River, after they had been treated to remove cyanide and other contaminants. In the case of the Misima mine on Misima Island, there was very limited land available, so the tailings were piped to a holding tank, where they were mixed with seawater before being deposited into a deep underwater basin in the sea.

Another serious environmental challenge confronting Placer Dome was acid-rock drainage (ARD), which occurs when sulfide rock is exposed to water and air, causing the formation of sulfuric acid. Acidic water moving through waste rock piles, tailings, or old mine workings will dissolve metals contained in the rock. If not contained, contamination of surface and groundwater then occurs, seeping into lakes and rivers, causing harm to animals and humans. Placer Dome had a severe problem with acid-rock drainage at its Equity Silver mine in northern British Columbia, which closed in 1994.

As a gold-mining company, Placer Dome had to contend with the management and use of cyanide, which is used to extract gold. After the ore has been crushed and ground, the cyanide dissolves the gold into a solution, which is further processed to recover gold. After processing, the cyanide appears either in tailings ponds or on heap leach pads, posing a threat to local waterways and groundwater if spills occur before the cyanide has decomposed or been treated. Cyanide handling is a serious safety issue for mine workers.

Institutional setting: external pressures (global and domestic)

Placer Dome's external environment, operating at the local, provincial, national, regional, and global levels, exerted a range of pressures to which senior management had to respond. At the global level, sustainable development became, in the 1990s, the key normative framework for pushing ahead both globally and nationally with environmental protection. At the same time, governments in countries such as Canada and Australia, where Placer Dome had major investments, had adopted sustainable development as an overarching normative frame for their environmental policy initiatives. As outlined in Chapter 3, these countries, along with the other major industrialized countries, began to tighten existing legislation in the 1990s, and introduce new regulations respecting the environment. The changes to taxation and foreign ownership regimes in developing countries opened up new opportunities for Placer Dome to expand its global operations.

In the province of British Columbia (BC), where PDI was headquartered, a very strong and politicized environmental movement, coupled with the left-leaning New Democratic Party (NDP) government, resulted in significant uncertainty over access to land and with respect to the permitting process. British Columbia was a hotbed of the environmental movement, and the home of Greenpeace. Much earlier than other provinces, a culture of respect for the environment grew in BC, a reflection of its rich native culture, rich salmon resources, and love of the outdoors. The legacy of the many large, open-pit mines built in the 1960s in northern BC was brought to the public's attention by activists years later. The provincial government was under political pressure to respond to growing public demands for greater environmental protection. Placer Dome was undeniably influenced by this setting (Executive 3, January 26, 2006).

In 1993, the provincial government denied the Windy Craggy proposal to build a large copper and gold mine in the province's northwestern corner. Instead, the government created a vast provincial park in the area of the proposed mine, the Tatshenshini-Alsek Provincial

Park, and declared the area a World Heritage site. The move permanently barred development of one of the province's richest mineral reserves.[1] Opportunities for developing new mining projects were effectively closed off to mining companies in British Columbia and North America as a whole (as Noranda's New World mine experience demonstrated). In BC, the government approvals process became very lengthy, and targets set by the provincial government were deemed by Placer Dome to be unrealistic (Executive 2, January 25, 2006). As CEO John Willson put it in a 1997 address to the Canadian Club:

Part of the reason for a Canada-based mining company going global is that our governments make us feel unwelcome. How else can one interpret the tax laws that bind us, the environmental approval processes that delay us beyond reason and the uncertainties that restrict our land use and investment prospects? (Cooney and Willson 1997: 1)

The province was effectively closed off to new mining investment by the early 1990s.

The provincial context influenced the shift in thinking within Placer Dome on the importance of sustainable development for the mining industry. In 1991, the provincial government set up the BC Round Table on the Environment and Economy, with the mandate to develop a sustainable development strategy for the province (Hansen 1991). Placer Dome represented the mining-industry perspective on developing sectorial strategies, and three-day meetings took place on a quarterly basis. The Placer Dome executive who participated in the process found it to be a hugely important education, which helped crystallize his understanding on the implications of sustainable development (Executive 2, December 6, 2011). This executive pushed for the establishment of guidelines for the mining industry in BC, but encountered resistance to this idea from mining companies at that time (Executive 2, January 25, 2006). When the provincial government disbanded the Round Table in 1995, the executive applied his thinking on sustainable development to Placer Dome.

---

[1] Since the mid-2000s, the BC government has again been encouraging mining, by streamlining the approvals process and moving forward on aboriginal land claims. After lengthy negotiation with affected aboriginal communities, a mixed-use agreement was reached for the Tatshenshini-Alsek Park, which will allow some areas of the Park to be developed for mining.

Developments at the national level which influenced thinking within Placer Dome include the Whitehorse Mining Initiative (WMI) (see Chapter 3). The impetus behind the WMI was the rising tide of stakeholder pressures, and Placer Dome was at the meeting in 1992 in Whitehorse that endorsed the launch of the WMI. The common view in the industry at the time was that mining faced a communications challenge, but the WMI demonstrated that mining companies had to better understand the different perspectives of stakeholders, including indigenous communities (Executive 2, December 6, 2011). The WMI was a path-finding initiative in which Placer Dome was very active, and it further reinforced corporate learning about the importance of coming to terms with sustainable development.

The evolving global context, in turn, influenced thinking within Placer Dome and the BC mining industry as a whole. In 1998, the environmental Mining Council of BC, created by the mining industry in that province to address environmental challenges, released a code of environmental conduct for mining operators (Environmental Mining Council of BC 1998). The code of conduct drew upon extensive work on principles and codes of conduct for mining operations carried out by a variety of Australian NGOs in 1997. The Environmental Mining Council of BC also drew on discussions with the Washington, DC-based Mineral Policy Center, the Western Mining Activist Network and with BC-based environmental mining experts. The code called for much greater transparency and accountability than was generally the practice amongst major mining companies operating in BC at the time.

Developments in Australia were significant to Placer Dome, because of its extensive operations in the Pacific region. As in Canada, pressure was growing on the mining industry in Australia. In the mid-1990s, the Australian Labor government contemplated the application of extraterritorial legislation for its mining companies operating abroad. To forestall government action, in 1995 the Minerals Council of Australia (MCA) was established, which worked to develop a code of conduct for the mining industry (MCA 1996). In 1996, the MCA developed a Code for Environmental Management, which committed signatories to continual improvement and public reporting of code implementation and environmental performance. Placer Pacific was a signatory to the Code, which was revised in 2000, following a review and consultation with the Australian government and NGOs. Placer Pacific's early engagement with the Australian mining industry's attempt to promote environmental excellence and to be more open and accountable to the community was to influence PDI's subsequent progress on sustainable development.

The tailings failure at Marcopper brought home forcefully to Placer Dome the role of global communications, and in particular, the internet, in disseminating information about the company. CEO John Willson expressed unease about the deluge of news about Marcopper, and the ease with which what he considered misinformation about Placer Dome and mining in general could be spread (Willson 1997: 7). Placer Dome sought in 1997 to counteract that by setting up a company web page to disseminate information about the company. Clearly, however, senior management recognized that a public relations exercise would not suffice to remedy the reputational issues facing Placer Dome and the mining industry generally.

Even before the disastrous tailings accident at its Marcopper mine in the Phillipines, Placer Dome was sensitive to the impact of environmental accidents involving other mining companies on its own operations. The 1995 Omai tailings dam failure in Guyana, for example, was seen to have a potential impact on Placer Dome's Las Cristinas project under development at the time in Venezuela. On August 20, approximately 3.5 million cubic metres of tailing water was released into the Omai River, and from there, on into the Essequibo River. The concentration of cyanide in the tailings was enough to kill fish in a section of the Omai River, but concentrations further downstream were determined to be insignificant.

The manner in which this accident was reported points to the difficulty of ascertaining the veracity of claims made by different stakeholders. The environmental community, for example, termed the event an "environmental catastrophe." Engineering, consulting, and mining communities termed the event an "environmental incident," as it was determined that there were short-term and limited environmental impacts (Executive 6 (Placer Dome) 1995: 1). Whatever the facts, the legitimacy enjoyed by environmental NGOs lent greater weight to their claims in the public eye. It is also the case that the response to an incident may be more dramatic than the incident itself. Placer Dome anticipated that the Las Cristinas project would come under greater scrutiny as a result of the accident. Indeed, Venezuelan officials had expressed concerns about the parallels between the Omai and Las Cristinas projects, especially around the type of tailings dam proposed (ibid.: 7).[2] The lesson here was that an approach consistent with sustainable development might give Placer Dome an edge in obtaining permits for its projects.

Placer Dome had received its share of negative publicity around the operations of its mines. Prominent examples include the Porgera and Misima gold mines in Papua New Guinea. Local communities raised concerns about possible poisoning from water contaminated by arsenic, mercury, and other pollutants. A number of NGOs drew international attention to these concerns, including allegations that the environmental standards set by the PNG government (which has a 25 per cent stake in Porgera) were more lenient than Australian standards on such matters as heavy metals concentrations (Kennedy 1996: 1). Many of these NGOs were based in Australia, where they trained their eyes not just on mining in Australia, but in the Pacific region, including PNG. Both Las Cristinas and Porgera demonstrated the negative spill-over effects of mining in the information age.

A combination of external developments shaped the operational challenges and institutional environment to which senior management felt compelled to respond. These external developments included the tightening and expansion of regulations in Canada, Australia, and the US, the hostile environment to new mining projects in BC by the early 1990s, the emergence of concerns about the impact of mining on indigenous peoples in Canada and other countries (addressed at the WMI), and the public relations disaster arising from the Marcopper tailings failure. The negative publicity about the mining industry generally, and the central role played by NGOs in disseminating negative information about mining, led to the targeting of individual mines for exposure of damaging environmental practices. In 1999, a new NGO was established in Canada, Mining Watch Canada, which, as the name implies, had as its mandate to scrutinize the activities of Canadian mining companies at home and abroad. Placer Dome was a prime target of Mining Watch Canada, because of Marcopper and its operations in PNG.

---

[2] Placer Dome ultimately sold in 2001 its interest in the Las Cristinas project, after having written off its investment in the property in 2000. The reason cited was that the deposit was low-grade in nature, and was deemed not to be sufficiently viable under market conditions at the time.

Organizational and managerial response

The institutional context outlined above helps to explain why Placer Dome came to adopt CSR policies. In order to understand how the firm responded to external pressures, organizational and managerial factors need to be brought into the analysis. By the early 1990s, the evidence suggests that Placer Dome was seeking to bring the organization into alignment with shifting societal expectations. While all mining companies were attempting to do so by the early 2000s because of external pressures, the external environment alone cannot explain how senior management chose to approach the challenges it faced, or why the company sought to play a leadership role in moving towards sustainable development. This section begins with a brief look at the arrangements in place at Placer Dome before the changes to policy and procedures took place, to serve as a baseline for comparison to subsequent measures implemented in support of CSR.

By the late 1980s, there is some evidence to suggest that Placer Dome had begun to give serious attention to its social and environmental responsibilities. Subsequent to the merger of Dome mining with Placer in 1987, two key people were transplanted from Dome to the headquarters of Placer Dome. These people took up key positions: Placer Dome's first Senior Vice-President, Environment position in 1991, and Director, International and Public Affairs, for Placer Dome. After the appointment in 1992 of John Willson as CEO, there were a number of key people in senior management who were well-placed to serve as policy entrepreneurs for CSR and later, sustainable development.

Willson's leadership was crucial in moving Placer Dome forward on CSR, and in shaping its approach to sustainable development. Willson, whose father was a mining engineer, is a self-described "mining brat" (Executive 1, July 31, 2002). Exposed to dirty coal mining from an early age, Willson developed a consciousness of environmental and safety issues, and his early experiences imprinted how mining should *not* be done. As Willson moved up in the industry, as CEO of Western Canadian Steel (a subsidiary of Cominco, now Teck Cominco) in the 1980s, and then CEO of Pegasus Gold in the US in the late 1980s to early 1990s, he acquired extensive experience on environmental issues.

Willson's concern for mining's reputation is revealed in his response to the situation at the Summitville mine, Colorado, owned until 1992 by Galactic Resources Ltd. In 1992, the American EPA took over supervision of the site, after Galactic Resources declared bankruptcy and walked away from the threat of a massive spill of cyanide-laden water. Willson convened a meeting in Denver to deal with the problem. He proposed that a number of mining companies get together and take over the mess, and help fund the clean-up, which was estimated to cost over US$100 million. Willson's proposal did not get a good reception from other mining CEOs, and he was told that he was acting like a "boyscout" (Executive 1, July 31, 2002). Willson can be considered to have been ahead of his time, and brought his experiences and approach to the environment with him to Placer Dome.

Prior to Willson's appointment, Placer Dome had taken a number of steps to strengthen its environmental policies. In this regard, leadership was provided with a view to avoid liability through environmental failure (Executive 2, December 6, 2011). In 1990, the company released a broadly worded policy statement on the environment, which simply stated broad principles to which Placer Dome would adhere (Placer Dome 1990a). The 1990 *Environmental Policy Statement* identified ten steps the company would take to meet its stated commitment to the "integration of good stewardship in the protection of the natural environment with efficient management in the extraction of mineral resources" (Placer Dome 1990a). The policy statement also referred to the establishment of environmental-monitoring programs and audits, and to the introduction of reporting to its Board of Directors on these programs on a quarterly basis. These policies, together with a commitment to engage in research on environmental technologies, suggest that at the hortatory level, at least, Placer Dome was displaying commitment to CSR as it relates to the environment. Together with the environmental policy statement, Placer Dome released an *Environmental Management* document, which was intended to raise awareness among employees about the company's environmental policy and management goals (Placer Dome 1990b).

In addition to the annual review, in 1990 a Corporate Environmental Group was established, which reported to the Board on a quarterly basis on any non-compliant events, progress on issues of special concern, audit results, and emerging issues. The Corporate Environmental Group was headed by the Senior VP, Environment, and was responsible for ensuring that auditing and monitoring activities were carried out, and for reporting to the Board and CEO. The Group also provided support to the project development and operating groups, including the mine managers, in the form of expertise and assistance in dealing with individual issues. A further step, taken in 1990, was the establishment of an environmental Management Review Committee, comprised of all Senior Operating Officers, as well as the officers responsible for Project Developments, Exploration, Legal, and the Corporate Environmental Group. Those at the COO level were accorded special responsibility for ensuring that performance standards were achieved and all major issues were identified.

In 1989, Placer Dome arranged for its environmental management systems to be examined by an outside consultant. Ernst and Young was contracted to review its systems, in order to transform Placer Dome's environmental policy and concerns into a comprehensive program. Using the Campbell Mine in northern Ontario as the guinea pig, the review led to roles being more clearly defined, and provided a clearer idea of what steps had to be taken next. One such step was the development of Environmental Operating Plans, a process which was completed in 1993. All of these initiatives point to early efforts to improve Placer Dome's environmental performance.

Management attitudes in the late 1980s to early 1990s point to the recognition of the need to take environmental issues seriously, largely for strategic reasons. A presentation given in 1991 by Henry Brehaut on improving environmental performance reveals that key considerations driving Placer Dome's policies at this early stage were risk prevention and minimizing environmental liability (Brehaut 1991). Brehaut declared that while having an environmental policy is a good start, what matters is how a company interprets and communicates its environmental obligations. This includes having employees who can establish specific operating procedures, ensuring that employees are sufficiently trained in their duties, and working towards establishing a proactive environmental culture throughout the company. In effect, he was saying that simply having an environmental policy provides little guidance for action.

Brehaut's presentation provides an interesting glimpse into the state of thinking about the environment at the time, from the perspective of a mining executive. He demonstrates that companies go through different stages in their degree of environmental awareness, as revealed in Table 5.1.

The "redneck" phase is self-evident, and in the early 1990s there remained a significant number of mining companies that were at this stage. The "lip service" stage refers to companies that have endorsed the Mining Associations of Canada's (MAC) *Environmental Policy*

Table 5.1 *Corporate attitudes towards the environment*

Stage	Policy	Employees
Clean and green	Management system	Committed
Proactive	Codes of conduct	Involved
Concerned	Company policy	Brochure
Lip service	MAC policy[3]	Unaware
Redneck	No policy	Unaware

Source: Brehaut, 1991.

Statement, but which do not have internal environmental policies of their own in place (MAC 1989).[3] Endorsement of such policies would have little impact, as they offered no guidance as to how companies should improve their environmental performance. At the "concerned" stage, the consciousness level of senior executives on environmental issues is raised, and the company produces an environmental policy. At this stage, the policy is understood at the corporate office level, but is likely to end up as "another framed policy on the wall at the mine site" (Brehaut 1991).

At the time Brehaut presented his paper, he felt that Placer Dome was approaching the "proactive" stage. At this stage, the company has developed codes of conduct, standard designs and procedures, and is trying to get ahead of the environmental agenda. At this point, employees become involved in the design and implementation of individual programs. In the "clean and green" stage, the environment moves from being a technical issue, to a management issue as well. As Brehaut put it, "by management I mean more than systems to ensure individual issues are assessed, responsibilities assigned and performance monitored ... it also means that a corporate culture has been established whereby consistent actions and responses are the primary keys to success." Important to fostering a corporate culture of commitment to CSR was the introduction of annual President's Awards (made of gold and silver) for the PDI operation with the best safety and environmental record (Executive 1, July 3, 2002).

In 1994, Placer Dome released a revised environmental policy statement (Placer Dome 1994). The updated policy reflected the company's intention to broaden the involvement of employees and stakeholders in

[3] In 1989, the Mining Association of Canada (MAC) released a six-point Environmental Policy Statement, which all members of MAC had to endorse.

Table 5.2 *Timeline of organizational and policy changes: Placer Dome,*
1989–94

1989: External environmental audits commissioned
1990: Environmental Policy Statement released
1990: Environmental Management Review Committee established
1990: Corporate Environmental Group established
1991: Senior Vice-President, Environment appointed
1992: Environmental Policy established by Board of Directors
1993: Environmental operating plans developed throughout Placer Dome Group
1994: Environmental Policy revised
1994: Environment and Safety Committee of the Board established

environmental issues. In the same year, an Environmental and Safety Committee of the Board was established, with members selected from the Placer Dome Board. As of 1994, Placer Dome had forty-eight people working in environmental control across the company. Table 5.2 provides a timeline of the major organizational and policy changes instituted by Placer Dome in the early years.

These developments in the areas of policy, management, and organizational change reflected a deepening commitment to the environment on the part of Placer Dome. At this early stage, environmental issues were still perceived as costs to be avoided, although reputational concerns were becoming salient. Environmental policies were conceived as a strategic response to risk prevention, and minimizing environmental liability.

Shift in thinking

By the mid-1990s, there was evidence that internal company thinking had begun to evolve towards a more comprehensive view of its environmental responsibilities. A paper presented in 1994 by officials in the Environmental Group in Caracas attested to the need to consider environmental impacts through the entire life cycle of the mine, from claims staking to exploration, to mine operation and post-closure (Billette and Robertson 1994). In 1995, PDI released an Environmental Management Framework for implementation. The company had also begun to participate in research on such difficult environmental issues as acid drainage prevention and control, in the form of on-site, in-house research, joint research with universities involving graduate students, and in joint industry/government task forces on environmental issues. As of 1998, for example, Placer Dome had invested US$325,000 at the University of Saskatchewan in research funding for cover-design technologies to control acid-rock drainage (Executive 6 (Placer Dome) 1999: 33).

Placer Dome's expansion into developing countries was a further impetus behind a more comprehensive approach to environmental issues. Indeed, by 1994, internal documents reveal the recognition that not just environmental, but also social issues, needed to be better handled. Although Placer Dome had experience working with local populations in its North American and Asia Pacific operations, the complexity of working in foreign locales was acknowledged. Managers were becoming attuned to the growing attention of the international media and human and environmental rights groups, and the impact of their activities on the ability of a project to move forward: "Our performance in all aspects of exploration and development in any country is quickly communicated to other countries targeted for exploration and possibly used in decisions regarding a general willingness to have [Placer Dome] investment" (Executive 6 (Placer Dome) 1994: 1).

The need for people with specialized skills to respond to the greater complexity of communicating with stakeholders in foreign countries was recognized. As one valuable member of the Corporate Environmental Group noted, historically, geologists had been assigned all tasks associated with environmental and social communications on a new project. Increased demands on geologists in these areas had diluted their ability to focus on exploration tasks for new projects, and required them to manage difficult issues without the necessary skills or resources (Executive 6 (Placer Dome) 1994: 1). A multi-skilled team was proposed for new exploration projects, which would bring together exploration staff, corporate and regional environmental staff, and corporate and regional "political/socio-economic" staff (ibid.: 2). Placer Dome was an early mover in recognizing the limitations of having people trained in geology and engineering responsible for handling delicate community-relations issues.

Together with the need for people with specialized skills beyond geology and mining engineering, came the recognition that potential environmental and social issues had to be recognized and adequately addressed at the preliminary exploration stage, so as to avoid projects being excessively delayed or derailed at the mine development stage.

A proposal was made that certain generic issue areas be identified, with team leaders responsible for each area. Four areas needing coverage were identified, including: 1. government relations/environmental; 2. environmental technical programs; 3. technical transfer to developing countries; and 4. government relations/social (Executive 6 (Placer Dome) 1994: 2). Government relations/environmental refers to the need for persons with "human" interaction skills to initiate dialogue with government agencies involved with exploration permits, and in later phases, additional permits and environmental impact statement documents. Government relations/social refers to the need for people capable of communicating with environmental or social activist groups and local communities, with a view to early detection of problem areas, and to establishing long-term relationships (Executive 6 (Placer Dome) 1994: 4–5).

Concurrent with this evolution in thinking on environmental issues, a major, company-wide discussion was initiated under the leadership of CEO Willson. The purpose of this discussion was to encourage employees to ponder how they perceived Placer Dome, and what core values they felt should inform the company's activities. This process of corporate "navel gazing" (as it was referred to by one person involved with the process), influenced the evolving approach to environmental/social issues. Through the identification of underlying ethical norms guiding individual behavior, Willson sought to inculcate a collective corporate identity, where the company would see itself as a community, or in the words of one executive, a "collective moral agent" (Executive 2, January 25, 2006). The intent was partly strategic, in that Willson hoped to develop stronger corporate cohesion, but also values-based, in that he wanted Placer Dome's stated values to resonate with those of employees.

In the company's mission statement, released in 1995, the first core value listed was ethics, defined as "governing our actions with integrity, honesty, fairness and respect" (Placer Dome 1995: 4). The focus of the document was on the quality of interactions amongst employees within the entire corporation, and with core values including trust, teamwork, recognition, and continuous improvement through ongoing learning. The final core value was to be stewards of the environment, understood as "living the ethic of environmental responsibility in our business practices" (Placer Dome 1995: 5). The push to define the company's CSR was thus both interest and norms-based.

Willson came to believe that sustainable development should be embedded in the corporate culture, as an expression of the company's value system. The extended process of identifying the company's core values fed into evolving thinking on sustainable development. By aligning the values of the company with the personal values of employees, the foundation was laid for people to commit to sustainable development (Executive 4, July 31, 2002). In some respects, sustainable development was a way of framing some aspects of CSR which the company had already been doing in places such as PNG. It was also a conceptual structure for encouraging integrative thinking about what the company was doing, and what still needed to be done (Executive 2, July 30, 2002). To embed sustainable development in the corporate culture, the position of Vice-President, Sustainable Development was created in 1997 (replacing the VP, Environment position). The executive appointed to this position spent eight years as mine manager at Porgera. He brought his knowledge of sustainability initiatives on the operational side at Placer Pacific, and took on the responsibility of coordinating the formulation of policy, providing leadership for implementation, and developing an understanding of emerging issues.

As the company moved forward on sustainable development, Willson sought to integrate CSR into the company's strategic business plan. In 1998, sustainability was designated an element of the 1998 Corporate Strategic Plan by the Executive Council, consisting of the CEO, CFO, the Executive VPs for Strategic Development, Exploration, and for the three geographic regions (at the time North America, Latin America, and Asia Pacific). As such, Willson recognized the need to emphasize the business case for sustainable development, while also seeking to align the norm with the company's core values.

Lessons from the experience of mining

As noted earlier, global, national, and provincial developments had an impact on thinking in Placer Dome, and learning was taking place on sustainable development norms. The available documentation and interview material make it clear that the experience of operating mines in Canada and the Asia Pacific region is central in explaining Placer Dome's approach to sustainable development. In the 1960s and 1970s, mine managers cut their teeth in remote communities in Canada. These people grew up there, and developed awareness of living in these small communities. Mine managers moved up in the company as it expanded throughout the globe. This progression influenced the culture of Placer Dome, and set the foundation for the adoption of sustainable development policies (Executive 3, January 26, 2006). The role of leadership can also be seen as the projection of learnings from operational challenges which management faced at specific mine sites to the development of corporate-wide policy and practices.

Lessons learned from the operation of the Campbell (Ontario) and Equity (BC) mines in Canada, and the Porgera and Misima mines in PNG fed into the evolving thinking on CSR policies and practices. Placer Dome had managed social as well as environmental issues at these mines, which were to inform subsequent approaches to CSR. Existing practices at socially challenging sites such as Porgera were later formalized in policies on sustainable development.

One key lesson that emerged out of Equity and Porgera was the value of having community-oversight committees (Executive 2, December 6, 2011). These committees were initially set up at Equity and Porgera to address extreme circumstances, but later evolved into being best practices at many of Placer's socially challenging operations.

In 1980, Placer opened the Equity Silver mine in northern BC. Shortly after, in 1981, acid-rock drainage was found originating from the mined waste rock, and from 1982, the mine became a severe producer of ARD. The situation posed a technical challenge for Placer in managing the environmental problem, as well as a social challenge in dealing with the concerns of the downstream communities (Aziz et al. 1998). Downstream communities impressed upon Placer Dome the need for structures to promote accountability on the part of the mining company, and to provide accurate information to the public. At Equity, this need led to the establishment of the Equity Mine Technical Monitoring Committee, which meets regularly. An annual report for the Equity site is distributed, and monthly effluent discharge records are available for review upon request (ibid.: 8).

At Porgera, a stakeholder-monitoring committee was established in 1996 to monitor Placer's management of environmental issues around riverine tailings disposal (Togolo 1999: 8). Established in 1996, the Porgera Environmental Advisory Komiti (Peak) was the first of its kind in PNG. In addition to government representatives from the PNG Office of Environment and Conservation and the PNG Department of Mineral Resources, the "Komiti" consisted of NGOs representing indigenous peoples (Conservation Melanesia), the churches (Melanesian Institute), the PNG Institute of Medical Research, and the World Wide Fund for Nature (Australia). Independent experts were also made available to NGOs, to assist in their understanding of the technical issues surrounding environmental management at Porgera.

Placer Dome eventually established permanent community-liaison committees at the Campbell, Equity, Musselwhite, and Porcupine mines in Canada, the Golden Sunlight mine in the US, the Misima and Porgera mines in PNG, and at Zaldivar in Chile. Where permanent committees were not in place, ongoing stakeholder engagement was maintained through site-specific reports, newsletters, regional reports, and informal engagement.

The experience of operating mines also taught valuable lessons about how being responsive to community concerns translates into success at the permitting, building, and operational stages of a mine's life. In 1997, Doug Fraser (newly appointed VP, Sustainability) met with a group of shareholders in Toronto, to explain Placer Dome's emerging sustainability policy. In describing his years from 1987 to 1990 as site manager on the Porgera project in PNG, Fraser described the huge learning process he and those working with him underwent in dealing with social issues. In working on final feasibility for the mine, it was necessary to prepare a social/economic impact study and an environmentalist from Australia was hired to do the work. Very candidly, Fraser noted that the environmentalist "wore an earring," and was not the sort of person he would naturally gravitate to, given his engineering training, which at the time, "held little regard for non-tech issues" (Fraser 1997).

The project required that over 230 families be relocated, and once project approval was obtained, the company attempted to move forward with relocating the families. As Fraser noted, "after several months of frustration, we realized we had to change our approach" (Fraser 1997). The relocation effort was continually being stopped by irate landowners who had unsettled issues to discuss. Nothing moved until the issues were resolved, leading to the realization that the company would have to work together with the affected families and land staff in order to address the social issues satisfactorily. As Fraser put it, "the lesson we learned here is that to be successful in permitting, building and operating mines today, we needed to get beyond our personal biases and judgments about people, and get creative about dealing with the issues" (1997). In other words, it was necessary to listen to the local community, learn about the issues affecting them, and find creative solutions to solving them.

The Musselwhite mine in northern Ontario, which opened in 1997, is an example of how engaging with the local community helped facilitate and speed up the permitting process. Specific issues affecting local First Nations (indigenous) communities were identified before the mine was developed. An agreement was signed with First Nation representatives and two levels of government, detailing how the local community would benefit from the mine (the Musselwhite Agreement). The agreement included provisions for employment, training, and scholarship opportunities and social, cultural, and community support, recognized the traditional activities of indigenous communities, and created a planning board to review issues on an ongoing basis. Fraser claimed that by dealing with stakeholders up-front, a strong relationship was fostered, which sped up the environmental approval process for the mine, thereby avoiding costly delays (Fraser 1997).

Early lessons about the challenges of operating in developing countries influenced the development of Placer Dome's CSR policies. In a developing-country context, where the reach of government into remote communities is tenuous at best, Placer Dome found it beneficial and appropriate to step in to deliver social services. In 1992, Placer Pacific introduced a tax credit scheme that was inspired by the concern that the tax benefits of resource development were not returning to the local communities affected by the mines in PNG. Under Placer's initiative, government approval was obtained to allow mining and petroleum companies in PNG to spend up to 2 per cent of their taxable income on approved infrastructure and social projects in their immediate impact areas (Togolo 1999: 7). Considered to be very successful, the scheme allowed private corporations to support education and health facilities, physical infrastructure, water supplies, community development projects, and sporting facilities (ibid.). This same thinking was later echoed in PDI's approach to dealing with the HIV/AIDS problem at its South Deep mine in South Africa.

In seeking to apply best practices to its operations around the world, Placer Dome learned that applying the same standards was not the answer, as circumstances in individual communities were not identical, so that different strategies and tactics had to be devised (Executive 3, January 26, 2006). Specific policies needed to be applied on a site-specific basis, tailored to meet the specific conditions in mine sites. For example, in PNG, closure guidelines emphasize the social aspects, as there is little in the way of basic social services. In North America, closure guidelines emphasize mostly environmental aspects.

As had been the case at Porgera, Placer Dome conducted a social impact assessment (SIA), in addition to the EIA, at its new mine developments. The conduct of an SIA in South Africa before opening its South Deep mine enabled Placer Dome to anticipate serious social problems surrounding the mine development and operation (Placer Dome owned 50 per cent of South Deep and formed the Placer Dome Western Areas Joint Venture (PDWAJV)). Placer Dome introduced an innovative and highly regarded program to address the high incidence of HIV/AIDS amongst its workers. In partnership with organized labor, the provincial government, local NGOs, and two other mining companies, the Tshwaragano Project sought to assist those in surrounding communities suffering from HIV/AIDS, as well as raise awareness about prevention. The program included the provision of home-based care and support to medically incapacitated workers and their families, as well as income support. The home-based care program won a Development Innovation Award and a People's Choice Award at the World Bank's 2002 Development Marketplace competition. The South Deep mine introduced wide-ranging prevention and treatment programs at the mine site, in the surrounding communities, and in the mineworkers' home communities (including migrant workers from Lesotho, Mozambique, Botswana, and Swaziland).

The path to sustainable development

The lessons learned and various activities around Placer Dome's operational challenges would eventually be integrated and formalized as part of the company's sustainable development approach to CSR. The experiences of mining were understood to be part of the company's political risk-management strategy, in keeping with the risk mitigation culture of mining companies. To make sustainable development relevant to the corporation, it was necessary to link the elements of sustainable development with political risk management (Executive 2, July 30, 2002). This fact highlights the importance of relating change to existing cultural frames.

It took considerably more effort to move the company to a point where sustainable development would serve as a conceptual glue for integrating all the initiatives on the environmental and social side. Sustainable development played a very important role in integrating and broadening thinking within the company, not just at the HQ level, but at the mine level as well (Executive 4, July 31, 2002). Existing corporate practice ultimately integrated into conceptions of sustainable development, included risk management, reputational concerns (the business case), and the core values of the company.

Three important factors combined to propel Placer Dome towards integrated thinking around sustainable development. First, leadership from senior management was critical in allowing the initiative to move forward. Leadership was also provided by those who had worked with Placer Pacific, and who had hands-on experience. Second, the historic practice and experience of operating mines in remote communities in Canada and abroad was key in shaping the implementation of Placer Dome's sustainable development policies. Third, the leadership became persuaded of the business case for sustainable development. The Marcopper tailings spill in 1996 forcefully drove home some important lessons that people in the field, as well as at HQ, could relate to (Executive 4, July 31, 2002).

In the mid-1990s, senior management began to pull together the various strands of these different influences in the form of an explicit policy formulation on sustainable development. Key individuals played the role of policy entrepreneurs in moving the idea of sustainable development forward. In a speech delivered in 1995 to the Northwest Mining Association (US), Jim Cooney spelled out the direction he felt mining companies should take in order to confront the political challenges of operating in the developing world. The speech proved to be a reliable indicator of the strategic vision Cooney and others were pushing for within Placer Dome.

Given the fact Cooney's professional background was in philosophy, not in engineering, he was quick to understand the significance of sustainable development for the company. His position gave him a strong mandate to engage in the international public policy arena, participating in frequent dialogue with NGOs and international governmental organizations. Leadership in this sense was his role in transmitting perspectives on sustainable development to Placer Dome, and using that experience to promote change from within.

In his 1995 speech, Cooney spelled out three priorities for mining companies seeking to expand their operations in the developing world:

1. gain access to the world's mineralized jurisdictions; 2. establish security and predictability in the governmental treatment of mining; and 3. sustain the welcome of mining companies in developing countries over the long term (Cooney 1995: 11). Put another way, the third priority addressed the need to reduce and contain the long-term political risk exposure of mining companies in developing countries. To address these political risk and reputational issues, Cooney pointed to the need for an evolution in the thinking and practices of mining companies. To accomplish these goals, he called for mining companies to define their activities in the framework of sustainable development (ibid: 12).

Cooney's views were echoed by the Senior VP, Environment. In a revised speech originally given in March 1996, Brehaut noted that mining companies are now expected to justify their activities, not just on economic grounds, but on social and environmental grounds as well (1996: 6). In a similar vein to Cooney, he observed that most governments had adopted sustainable development as a key part of their national agenda, and that the mining industry "must talk the language of the audiences it must convince" (Brehaut 1996: 6). Brehaut called for a comprehensive framework focused on sustainable development, which would provide the basis for individual project decisions in the "real world" (as opposed to the world of academic debates on the meaning of sustainable development) (ibid.: 7). He recognized that a key component of this was the need to consult with "civil society," that building a good relationship with governments was not enough (ibid.: 10).

The speeches by Cooney and Brehaut reveal that internal thinking about sustainable development preceded the Marcopper disaster. In essence, Cooney and Brehaut were selling sustainable development to their own company, as much as to the industry as a whole. Their speeches demonstrate the view that the mining industry had to engage in some "unlearning," in order to broaden understanding about mining's role and responsibilities in the economy and society. In the mid-1990s, much of the mining industry remained uncomfortable with the terminology of sustainable development (Executive 2, July 30, 2002). Sustainable development was seen to veer away from a market-oriented understanding of the operating environment. It would take time to recognize that it was not enough to think that the provision of jobs in local communities would foster lasting socio-economic development.

In 1996, the decision was made to develop a formal sustainable development policy. In that same year, on March 24, the disastrous tailings spill happened at the Marcopper mine in the Philippines, in which PDI had a 39 per cent interest. The fall-out from this accident was huge, and it brought PDI under critical scrutiny from NGOs and even prompted an investigation by the United Nations (UN 1996). As one executive noted, before Marcopper, few in the company knew what "NGO" stood for, but after Marcopper, everyone understood what the term referred to (Executive 2, January 25, 2006). Although Marcopper did not cause PDI to adopt a sustainable development strategy, the incident helped to catalyze the change in thinking within the company. Marcopper clearly provided added impetus and urgency to the decision to move forward with a sustainable development strategy.

Marcopper proved to be very costly to the company in both tangible and intangible ways. PDI was a minority shareholder in Marcopper, a publicly listed company in the Philippines, with the Philippine government having the majority stake. Although Placer Dome was not responsible for the management of the company, two PDI employees had been seconded as Chair of the Board and as Mine Manager. To save money in a context of low commodity prices, Marcopper tended to use local engineers and construction personnel for the building of the tailings tunnel (Executive 2, January 25, 2006). PDI assumed responsibility for the environmental clean-up, and by 1998, close to US$100 million had been expended on repair work, clean-up, divestiture, and compensation costs (Sloan 1999: Part 1). Less tangible costs were those to PDI's reputation. The company learned at its Las Cristinas mine in Venezuela, for example, that critics and competitors would invoke Marcopper to oppose PDI's involvement in new mine projects (ibid.: Part 1).

Willson's earlier reaction to the Summitville disaster informed his response to Marcopper, in that walking away was not an option. Placer Dome actually had a lot of difficulty getting permits to do the clean-up, and Willson had to appeal to then President Ramos to help get permits issued. Extraordinarily, Ramos later asked Willson why he was spending so much to clean up Marcopper, as the majority owner was not prepared to spend money (Executive 1, July 31, 2002). In addition to feeling it was the right thing to do, Willson saw it as pragmatic, as the company was looking for permits elsewhere.

The experience of Marcopper provided momentum behind the decision to move forward with sustainable development but the impetus did not merely come from the corporate office. Placer Pacific, in part because of its experience with social and environmental issues in

Australia and PNG, played a leading role, as it was ahead of the game on many issues. In fact, the first sustainable development report actually came out of PPI for the 1997 reporting year (Placer Pacific 1998). It reflected the decision that Placer Dome should not only revise its policies, but should also report on its performance in the environmental and social domains (as well as the economic one).

In moving forward on sustainable development, extensive internal consultations took place, as a means for building consensus. Consensus building was not merely a top-down process, although Willson set the tone in terms of corporate culture, and provided leadership (Executive 2, January 25, 2006). Placer Dome was not a strongly hierarchical organization, so there were two parallel processes taking place, one through Placer's regional operations in the Pacific and the other through corporate headquarters in Vancouver. In both instances, in addition to the company-wide consultations, external stakeholders were invited in to provide feedback. That feedback was then considered by company officials, with a view to determining what could be incorporated into the company's sustainable development policy and first report.

Sustainable development appeared on the agenda of the company's "Public Affairs Round-Up" meetings, an annual gathering of company officials from all of the regional operations. At the April 1997 Public Affairs Round-Up held in Vancouver, issues surrounding sustainable development were given a prominent place on the agenda. Thirty-five key individuals from PDI's worldwide operations were brought together, along with ten outside academics and mining consultants. At the workshop held on sustainable development, discussion was organized around three key questions: 1. What are the key aspects of sustainable development?; 2. What internal obstacles limit Placer Dome's capacity to support sustainable development?; and 3. What actions can Placer Dome take over the next ten years to implement sustainable development? (Resource Futures International 1997: 1; also cited in Sloan 1999: Part II).

Documentation on the Round-Up reveals that questions were raised about how to define sustainable development, how to operationalize the concept within the context of mining, and how to contend with organizational and financial constraints within Placer Dome. On financial constraints, concern was raised about how to reconcile the interests of shareholders, who are driven primarily by short-term returns, and the fairly significant expenditures needed to promote a sustainable development agenda (Placer Dome, Manager 3, 1997: 2). The need to secure shareholder support was identified as a key imperative. In a related vein, it was noted that most people within Placer Dome, whether financial or engineering based, are used to the concept of trying to maximize near-term performance, and that Placer Dome at the time lacked a framework for incorporating the longer-term "softer elements" into the equation (Placer Dome, Manager 4, 1997: 4).

On the organizational side, the following point was made:

Most of our organization is focused on the actual mining process. We talk about ourselves as being a company whose objective it is to grow over time and to expand globally, but for the vast majority of people in this organization the real focus is on running mines today, on getting the mills fed. We have to recognize this fact as we try to move and communicate these visions (sustainable development) throughout the organization. We really have to bring that group into the process more, and that is going to be a very substantial challenge. I think that will be very well accepted, because as has also been pointed out we do fundamentally share core values. (Placer Dome, Manager 4, 1997: 1)

The significance of this point was that the challenge of getting middle management to understand and implement corporate sustainable development initiatives was acknowledged. It was recognized that senior management would need to communicate with the operators who make the daily decisions.

There was some internal push-back from within Placer Dome to sustainable development. The company's senior lawyers, for example, were concerned about risk exposure, and the sort of commitments the company might make. Still, they saw the idea of sustainable development as a business necessity. Concerns were also expressed that Placer Dome would become a lightning rod for environmental activists and that a policy would be used as a platform for spreading misinformation about the company. Doubts were expressed about the utility of the concept itself, as had been the case at Noranda (Executive 2, July 30, 2002). Some within Placer Dome saw sustainable development as a Trojan horse, allowing the arguments of those critical of mining to be implanted within the company.

Compelling business reasons were essential in persuading the company's mine managers, who did not want to hear about more expenditures and time-consuming procedures (Executive 4, July 31, 2002).

Industry needed to participate in decision-making about global public policy affecting mining, or risk regulation that was unreasonable from an industry perspective (Executive 2, July 30, 2002). Furthermore, national governments, the EU, and the World Bank were all placing their policy initiatives in the context of sustainable development. Sustainable development, it was argued, would address deficiencies in developing countries where regulations were weak or non-existent. Change agents within Placer Dome thus argued that the only practical approach was to place Placer Dome's strategy within the context of sustainable development. The Board of Directors proved to be very supportive of a sustainable development policy, which was helpful. The appointment in 1997 of the position of VP, Sustainable Development, was seen as a key means to contend with push-back from within the company.

Notwithstanding the rather significant challenges that were identified on a variety of fronts, a consensus was reached that Placer Dome should go ahead with sustainable development, and a strategy was worked out to plan the way forward. External consultants recommended that Placer Dome consider engaging in annual sustainable development reporting and auditing of performance. Three stages of action to implement sustainable development were identified. The first stage was the creation of a realistic sustainable development policy framework, involving the development of a company sustainable development policy, the education of shareholders, and the cultivation of relationships with external stakeholders, in order to integrate external perspectives into the development of policy. The second stage was the evaluation of Placer Dome's position against the sustainable development policy, involving gap analyses of its current practices, the development of an audit mechanism of existing operations, to compile an inventory of where the company now is on sustainable development, and to establish a plan of action for implementing the sustainable development policy. The third stage involved the systematic integration of sustainable development into company practices, through a comprehensive training program, the hiring of personnel trained in sustainable development, and the development of internal performance standards related to sustainable development (Resource Futures International 1997: 7–9).

In 1997, Placer Dome proceeded to develop a draft discussion paper on sustainable development. That same year, the Sustainable Development Group was formed, to assist in the dissemination of a sustainability policy at all business units within the company. Placer Dome followed through on the decision to consult external stakeholders, and a number of NGOs were sent drafts of the policy. A great deal of effort was devoted at this formative stage to securing input from leading-edge thinkers. At the same time as this was occurring at the corporate office, a similar process of policy development and consultation took place out of the Placer Pacific regional office in Sydney. In September 1997, Placer Pacific held a workshop with NGOs in Sydney, which included participants from NGOs, academia, and Placer Pacific employees. The purpose of this workshop was to discuss sustainable development in general, and to review Placer Dome's initial discussion paper on sustainable development.

In February 1998, a second workshop was held in Sydney involving external stakeholders, with a view to discussing Placer Pacific's draft 1997 Sustainable Development Progress Report, and the difficult task of developing sustainable development performance indicators. Placer Dome acknowledged the need for a cultural change, moving away from "Decide–Announce–Defend," to "Listen–Learn–Engage" (an explicit intent to learn from others), on operational matters requiring consultation with external stakeholders, including local communities (Placer Pacific 1998a: 3). From external participants, comments ranged from: "Placer's ability to handle the process to date is impressive – progress is being achieved," to "Sustainability is about people's lives and mining is social engineering that causes genocide" (ibid.: 6–7).

The corporate office also consulted with various external stakeholders, including NGOs, academic experts, and consultants. Among the NGOs consulted were the World Resources Institute (WRI), the Taskforce on the Churches and Corporate Responsibility (TCCR), and the North–South Institute. The TCCR had been formed to address the issue of corporate responsibility in apartheid-era South Africa, and developed important benchmarks for measuring CSR performance (Kairos 2002). In March 1998, James Cooney met with members of the TCCR involved with mining to discuss at length Placer Dome's draft Sustainability Policy (TCCR 1998). In 1998, the North–South Institute released its Annual Development Report, which focused on Canadian corporate responsibility (North–South Institute 1998). These NGOs were responsive to Placer Dome's request for feedback. Not surprisingly, a common theme in all of their responses was the need to move beyond policy towards implementation, calling for verifiable performance indicators.

The extraordinary nature of Placer Dome's consultations with external stakeholders cannot be over-emphasized. To consult with external groups, who are often hostile to the company, represents a loss of control over the agenda that few companies are prepared to entertain. Even ten years after Placer Dome began this process, very few companies in the extractive sector are prepared to engage in the way Placer Dome did. As CEO Willson and Cooney explained:

The sustainable development model is different. The paternalistic role which a large well-endowed multinational corporation has traditionally practiced is exchanged for a partnership role. The multinational corporation sacrifices some autonomy and efficiency for greater long term effectiveness. (Cooney and Willson 1997: 16; also cited in Sloan 1999: Part III)

NGOs willing to participate in the process were also taking risks, and were concerned they not be seen to be endorsing Placer Dome's policies or reports.

As Cooney and others had recommended, Placer Dome began to build strategic relationships with internationally based NGOs, including the World Resources Institute (WRI), the Worldwide Fund for Nature (WWF), Conservation International (CI), the International Union for Conservation of Nature (IUCN), the International Institute for Sustainable Development (IISD), the Task Force on the Churches and Corporate Responsibility (TCCR), and the Mineral Policy Center (MPC). Links were established, and information sought from, international organizations, such as the World Bank and the United Nations and its various agencies (WHO, UNCTAD, UNDP, UNEP, UNCHR).

In February 1998, the Placer Dome Board approved a "sustainability" policy. Critical to this "buy-in" from the Board was the need to inform and generate support from shareholders. Part of management's strategy to accomplish this was to appeal to the values the company wished to adhere to. Management also stressed the strategic importance of sustainable development, by presenting it as a core business issue directly related to the company's future ability to access new resources and grow (Sloan 1999: Part II). Embracing sustainable development was portrayed as a strategic calculation to enable the company to gain access to new gold reserves, by, for example, obtaining support from local inhabitants, thereby ensuring its long-term survival. The policy was also justified on the grounds that it would reduce the social, economic, and environmental risks of mining development. As CEO

Willson put it: "It is difficult when others, your shareholders for example, are more concerned about risks than the future rewards ... but
going global requires long-term vision" (Willson 1997: 10).

Table 5.3 provides a timeline of the major organizational and sustainable development policy initiatives from 1995 to 1998.

Table 5.3 *Timeline of major organizational and policy initiatives:
Placer Dome, 1995–8*

1995: Environmental Management Framework released (Placer Pacific)
1996: Placer Pacific commits to Australian Minerals Industry Code for
       Environmental Management
1996: Decision to develop sustainable development policy
1997: Vice-President, sustainable development appointed
1997: Environmental Management Framework adopted (PDI)
1998: Sustainability Policy established by Board
1998: First Sustainability Report published by Placer Pacific: *Taking on the
       Challenge: Towards Sustainability, 1997*
1998: Code of Business Conduct updated

Sustainable development policy

In the course of developing its new policy, Placer Dome adopted the
term "sustainability" to define its CSR initiatives. In Placer Pacific's
1997 Progress Report, the company's understanding of the difference
between sustainability and sustainable development was described:

At its simplest level, we view sustainability as meaning that we must add
economic, social and environmental value to society through our activities.
Sustainable development, on the other hand, describes society's goal and therefore is the broader framework in which we operate. (Placer Pacific 1998b)

The corporate *Sustainability Policy* defined Placer Dome's approach to
sustainability as follows:

For Placer Dome, sustainability means the exploration, design, construction,
operation and closure of mines in a manner that respects and responds to the
social, economic and environmental needs of present generations and antici-
pates those of future generations in the communities and countries where we
work. (Placer Dome 1998a: 2)

The evolved thinking on the company's place and role in the larger project of sustainable development is reflected in the vision Placer Dome ultimately adopted. A distinction was made between corporate citizenship, CSR, and sustainability (Executive 2, July 30, 2002). Corporate citizenship was understood as a set of minimalist obligations a company has towards its stakeholders, reflecting a compliance-based approach, as set out by regulations. CSR is understood as a set of obligations that corporations should recognize, not just by virtue of what is fundamentally required, but by a desire to go beyond that. As determined by management, the corporation moves beyond the idea of doing no harm, to doing "good." With sustainability, the corporation sees itself as one actor in a complex scheme of many actors with which it must interact and work. As reflected in the company's extensive consultations with external stakeholders, sustainability entails moving towards collective action for a common goal (Executive 2, July 30, 2002). As will be seen in the next chapter, Placer Dome and Barrick differ quite significantly in their understanding of CSR and sustainable development/sustainability.

Two policy developments reflected PDI's efforts to realize its commitment to sustainability; the first was the 1998 release of the *Sustainability Policy* (Placer Dome 1998a), and the second was the release in 1999 of the first *Sustainability Report* (for the year 1998 – Placer Dome 1999). The main elements of the *Sustainability Policy* were as follows:

- Corporate Commitment: establish an effective management system based on ethical conduct and a commitment to continuously improve performance; integrate sustainability as an essential element in the duties of all employees; and encourage the adoption of our sustainability principles by our joint venture partners.
- Public Responsibility: communicate with stakeholders and work towards consensus based on honest discussion and a mutual understanding of concerns and needs.
- Social Progress: contribute to the quality of life of employees, local communities and host countries, while respecting their cultures, needs and priorities.
- Environmental Stewardship: protect human health, reduce our impact on the ecosystem and return sites to a state compatible with a healthy environment.
- Economic Benefits: integrate our activities with the economic development objectives of local communities and host countries in which we operate.

(Placer Dome 1998a: 2–4)

To align the new policy with its management and accountability systems, all aspects of sustainability, economic, social, and environmental, were integrated into the company's general management systems. This action was a significant break from the past, when economic and financial aspects of performance were handled through the general management systems, and a separate system was used for safety and environmental management (Sloan 1999: Part III). Placer Dome also took steps to improve competencies, through employee training, and the acquisition of new skills through the hiring of new people.

Mine General Managers were delegated responsibility for achieving sustainability objectives at the mines and exploration sites, with support and guidance from the Executive VPs of the North America, Latin America, and Asia Pacific regions. The mine managers were expected to translate corporate sustainability policies, and apply them to the local circumstances in their specific operations. By the early 2000s, many mines were releasing their own sustainability reports, in addition to the corporate sustainability report.

Senior executives recognized that merely publishing a list of sustainability policies would not suffice to cement Placer Dome's credibility and commitment to sustainable development. The company therefore decided to report annually on its economic, social, and environmental activities. As already noted, the first annual report, *Towards Sustainability*, came from Placer Pacific, covering the period October 1996 to September 1997 (Placer Pacific 1998b). It provided economic, social, and environmental details on Placer Pacific's operations, covering Marcopper in the Philippines, Porgera and Misima in PNG, and Kidston, Osborne, and Granny Smith in Australia. It reflected a first attempt to incorporate sustainability performance indicators, a challenging task, as endeavors such as building trust are not easily measured. Importantly, the report included targets for improved performance in a range of areas, from improving environmental management systems to frequency of community consultations, to rectification of identifiable health and safety risks.

In preparation for the publication of PDI's first annual sustainability report, head office grappled, together with Placer Pacific, to develop sustainable development indicators for the company-wide report. A consulting firm was contracted to present the various options for sustainable development reporting, based on work in this area available at that time. The consultants' report hints at the possibility of learning from Noranda, which was developing sustainable development indicators around the same time (Ecos Corporation 1998: 4). The main challenge identified for mining companies developing sustainable development indicators was to translate the concept of sustainability into business language and processes (i.e. as measurable outcomes) (ibid.: 4). Placer Dome also had to consider that its performance would be judged against any indicators or targets it set for itself, potentially exposing itself to further attack.

In 1999, Placer Dome released its first company-wide sustainability report, covering the year 1998 (Placer Dome 1999). As was the case with the Placer Pacific report, it reported on a range of economic, social, and environmental indicators, now on a company-wide basis. Data on such aspects as contribution to the local economy, water consumption, safety, and cyanide use was provided for each mine site. Five "sustainability priorities" were identified, including surface and groundwater quality, acid-rock drainage and metal leaching, tailings management, cyanide management, and closure (ibid.: 29). Environmental incidents, including cases of non-compliance due to ground or surface water contamination or an uncontrolled release onto land outside the operational mining lease were reported for each mine.

Documentation on the sheer magnitude of preparing the first report is testament to the steep learning curve the company was undergoing. The company was experiencing transformative change, for not only did it institute a new policy that in itself represented a substantial shift in thinking, it also commenced annual reporting on its performance, which required a major mobilization of personnel across the entire company. In a summary prepared by a member of the Sustainability Group on the development of the 1998 report, a number of challenges encountered by the sustainable development team were identified.

One major problem arose out of trying to meet the expectations of NGOs that had been consulted on the report, while at the same time ensuring adequate consultation with company personnel. The VP, Sustainable Development conducted tours of the mines, to help communicate the project to site personnel and to get their input. This was important, as having senior personnel visit the mines demonstrated the seriousness with which head office viewed the project. Yet, it was determined that more time was needed to get buy-in from the bottom up, in order to get consensus around commitments to be made. It was deemed especially critical to get this right before attempting to incorporate the expectations of external stakeholders, in order to prevent hostility from Placer Dome employees over being committed to someone else's agenda with inadequate consultation (Executive 6, Placer Dome, 1998: 4).

The process of collecting environmental indicators revealed significant lacunae in Placer Dome's environmental systems. The report noted that the company had overstated its environmental systems, and a major lesson was that it did not have its act together on major environmental questions. Areas identified for improvement included consistency of closure plans and programs, consistency of tailing management systems, and EMS completeness at sites and at head offices (Executive 6, Placer Dome, 1998: 3). It was observed that Placer Dome was "nowhere near ready for external reviews in some areas."

As early as 1995, PDI had recognized that its existing environmental management systems needed improvement. After a review of international environmental management standards, Placer Dome decided to develop a customized approach, which led to the adoption in 1997 of the Environmental Management Framework. In assessing environmental risks, PDI sought to move away from the tendency to equate priorities with those issues requiring immediate attention, to identifying potential risks and taking steps to eliminate or mitigate them. Such an approach requires enhanced monitoring and verification programs, to allow early detection and mitigation activities, as well as the implementation of contingency and emergency preparedness programs. By December 2005, Placer Dome's sustainability leadership team had well-established accountability through the line structure, as depicted in Figure 5.1 below.

Circling this line management configuration was the Board's Safety and Sustainability Committee (to which the Executive Leadership Team reported), Government Relations, and the Projects, Communications, Finance, Legal, and Systems departments. In 2002, a Corporate Safety Group separate from the Sustainability Group was established, reporting to the Executive Leadership Team, and the Safety and Sustainability Committee of the Board. Operational management at the mining sites had ultimate responsibility for sustainable development implementation.

PDI sought to apply the example of initiatives in the Asia Pacific region to its company-wide operations. In Australia, the Australian Minerals Council (AMC) developed a Code for Environmental Management (1996), which Placer Pacific adopted. Placer Pacific led the way in adopting, in 1997, the International Safety/Environmental

CEO Executive Leadership Team
(CEO, CFO, COO, regional VPs)

VP, Sustainability

Corporate Sustainability Group (3.5 persons)

Country Sustainability Managers (6 persons)

Site and project sustainability staff – environmental and community relations (60+ persons)

Figure 5.1 Sustainability leadership structure: Placer Dome (as of December 2005).

Rating System (ISRS/IERS) developed by Det Norske Veritas (DNV), a European auditing firm. In 2002, PDI began to use DNV's system in order to commence environmental and safety audits at all its sites, with a plan to commence environmental audits at ten sites between 2002 and 2004 (Placer Dome 2004a). The results of these audits revealed that, although Placer Dome attained high scores for emergency preparedness and regulations, permits, and operations control, it received low scores for environmental aspects and impacts (Placer Dome 2004a: 10). These score results revealed that PDI was still grappling with weaknesses in its environmental performance, as had been acknowledged at the start of the reporting process in 1999.

Placer Dome's first company-wide sustainability report attracted much attention, including from the NGO community. The Mineral Policy Center, for example, published a "report card" on Placer Dome's 1998 report. Assigning a grade of "incomplete," it noted that inadequate performance targets made it difficult to judge what Placer Dome would consider to be "success" in terms of specific objectives or benchmarks (Mineral Policy Center 1999: 8). In its subsequent sustainability reports, Placer Dome responded to these and other comments provided by external stakeholders. Goals and targets were more clearly articulated, and the company worked towards continual improvement in its environmental management systems. Supplemental to the company-wide reports, some of the individual mines began to provide their own sustainability reports, including Misima (PNG) and Zaldivar (Chile).

Willson retired in 1999, and Jay Taylor became the new CEO. Taylor continued to push sustainable development forward, and established the goal that Placer Dome take on a leadership role in implementing sustainability policies. In 1999, a Sustainability Committee of the Board was established. In 2001, Taylor announced a three-point strategic plan for the company (Placer Dome 2002: 11). The third goal was to invest significantly in research and technology, with a view to reducing costs, PDI's "footprint" on the land, and to improving the company's social acceptance.

Taylor's vision regarding technological innovation reflected the importance he attached to research and development to attain sustainability, by employing technological breakthroughs to minimize harmful environmental impacts (Placer Dome 2002: 4). In 1999, PDI committed US$24 million over two years to conduct research into five key priority areas: alternatives to cyanide and recovery methods, prevention of ARD, improved effluent treatment and discharge systems, and best practices approach to integrating community development and mining (Placer Dome 2000: 8). In 2001, PDI increased its research and development budget to US$29 million (Placer Dome 2002: 11). In addition to reducing the amount of land disturbed, Taylor hoped that technological innovation would reduce costs, by, for example, developing machinery that could target the vein deposits more efficiently, reducing the tonnage of rock needing to be processed. In this respect, Placer Dome attempted to develop the "win–win" strategy which had been central to Noranda's approach to CSR.

Under Taylor's leadership, Placer Dome also sought to improve its health and safety management systems, and from the late 1990s, serious efforts were made to improve PDI's safety record, and promote a culture of commitment to safety. As part of its effort to promote safety as a corporate value, Placer Dome added in 2000 "safety" to the title of the position, VP, Sustainability, to become VP, Safety and Sustainability. In effect, "safety" was separated from "sustainability," with a view to making safety Placer Dome's highest and core value (Placer Dome 2005c). When PDI acquired the South Deep mine in South Africa in 1999, the issue of safety became even more pressing, with ten fatalities recorded in 2001 and 2002 (out of a total of thirteen for the company's entire operations) (Placer Dome

2003: 2). From 1996 to 2000, Placer Dome operations recorded 1,648 critical incidents, of which twenty-seven were fatal, a rate deemed unacceptable by Placer Dome (Placer Dome 2001: 8). In response to this bad record, and in light of evolving legislation involving workplace accidents, in 2001, PDI launched the Critical Incident Initiative, which identified a number of issues that were to inform the company's evolving policy on safety. In 2002, PDI appointed three Corporate Safety Directors, creating the Corporate Safety Group, to facilitate safety systems deployment through the DNV system.

PDI also launched in 2001 the PlacerSMART process, in order to promote engineering safety and behavioral safety. The PlacerSMART program emphasized training of supervisors and employees, workshops, and training for contractors not in the direct employ of Placer Dome (Placer Dome 2005c: 5). In the same year, a Health and Safety Charter was released, to promote uniformity and standardization at all mine sites. The "triple zero" safety goal was established; zero medical injuries, zero lost-time injuries, and zero fatalities. Unfortunately, PDI continued to experience fatalities at its South Africa mine, with three fatalities in 2003 and two fatalities in 2004 (Placer Dome 2004a, 2005b). In 2003, a Safety, Sustainability, and Environment Committee of the Board was established, to provide oversight in the development of a comprehensive strategic approach to safety (Placer Dome 2005b).

Efforts to continually improve Placer Dome's performance are evident in its policy initiatives and management practices. In 2003, for the first time, Placer Dome began to report against the 2002 GRI Sustainability Reporting Framework, a clear effort to identify indicators against which PDI's performance could be gauged. Starting in 2004, Placer Dome began incorporating indicators from the GRI's Mining and Metals supplement, with a commitment to report against all of these indicators for the 2006 Sustainability Report (which was never released) (Placer Dome 2005b: 3). In October 2005, Placer Dome signed onto the International Cyanide Management Code (ICMC). The ICMC was an industry initiative to promote the safe transport, handling, use, and containment of cyanide in the gold-mining process, and to work towards reducing the amount used.

Placer Dome sought to incorporate indicators that would be relevant to the local communities, in addition to site indicators, and indicators

relevant to the country or region as a whole. Overall, senior management felt that the longest list of indicators should apply to the local level,
with a smaller list of standards from the national level, and the smallest
list of standards from the global level. The view was that global
prescriptions for behavior were generally unhelpful, because of the
need for site-specific indicators in the face of considerable variation in
social situations and geological conditions from one site to the next
(Executive 3, January 26, 2006).

By the time the last sustainability report was released for the year
2004, considerable progress had been made in developing and
reporting on sustainable development indicators. Beginning in
2003, it included a supplement to its sustainability reports, consisting
of additional detailed sustainability information and technical data.
In this regard, Placer Dome sought to align itself with evolving global
standards relevant to mining, a process in which it played a leading
role.

From "sustainable development" to "sustainability"

In the early 2000s, there was still some internal resistance to the drive
to promote sustainable development. One problem was that by
2001, sustainable development had ceased to be as useful a means
of differentiating Placer Dome from other mining companies, as
more major mining companies came to adopt the norm. This made
it harder to sell Placer Dome as a leader in this area, and to win out
over competitors for permits in countries where sustainable development was a priority. Head office costs grew substantially, and when
Peter Tomsett became CEO in 2004, he took steps to reduce them.
Noteworthy among these was the disbandment of PDI's research and
development unit. Cutbacks at head office did not affect the implementation of sustainability policies, however, as these were integrated throughout the operation, and absorbed as part of
operational costs (Executive 3, January 26, 2006). Closure costs
were running at around US$20 million per year in the mid-2000s,
as reported to the Canadian Securities and Exchange Commission
(SEC) (Placer Dome 2005a).

Overall, Placer Dome remained committed to sustainable development, both as an intrinsic value, and as part of its risk-management
strategy. In addition to immediate concerns about cost, however, was a

philosophical questioning of what the extent of Placer Dome's role should be, especially in the developing country context where the need was so great. One dimension of the problem is that local communities develop a relationship of dependency on the mine, which creates problems (in the absence of effective government) when the time comes to close the mine. CEO Willson called for a "new model" for structuring the responsibilities of mines, governments, and local communities to achieve long-term social and economic development, in the form of a multi-institutional approach (Willson 1997: 3–5). This led Willson to declare that:

> Our experience in PNG, Venezuela and elsewhere is convincing us that market forces alone are unlikely to make mining succeed as a contributor to development . . . [rather] . . . sustainable development directs the mining company, the host government, aid agencies and non-governmental organizations to work collaboratively to plan for integrated economic, social and environmental progress. (1997: 8–9)

The need to constantly evaluate and re-evaluate PDI's proper role in developing societies was reflected in its evolving understanding on CSR. Initially framing its policies in terms of sustainable development, the company moved to the concept of sustainability (as reflected in its reporting), to capture the idea that it was but one player in a larger, complex process. The drift towards increasing social intervention in communities, such as in South Africa, led to escalating costs and concerns about how far the company should properly go in stepping in where governments were not necessarily able or willing. These concerns led to the introduction in the mid-2000s of CSR into Placer Dome's understanding of its sustainability policies, to reinforce the reality that the company could only be one of many actors seeking to assist in the larger goal of sustainable development.

Ongoing initiatives reveal that overall, PDI's commitment to sustainable development was becoming institutionalized through specific practices consistent with the norm, but its thinking on sustainable development continued to evolve. In 2004, under Tomsett's leadership, a Sustainability Charter was released, reiterating PDI's core values and beliefs, and commitment to sustainability (Placer Dome 2004b). The Sustainability Charter reflected Placer Dome's evolving view that sustainability is a dynamic process involving ongoing learning. The Charter also incorporated the concept of CSR, to better reflect the understanding that the corporation is only one of many partners involved in the ultimate goal of sustainable development. Placer Dome's CSR policies were understood to be an integrated framework through which goals in the areas of the environment, society, the economy, and governance could be realized (Executive 2, January 25, 2006).

A stated goal of the Charter was to enhance buy-in throughout the organization, especially from senior management and the Board (Placer Dome 2004b: 20). This suggests that concerns lingered about just how much Placer Dome could do on its own, or should be doing on its own. One executive saw sustainability as a means for the company to change its orientation in terms of how to make decisions to meet its interests (Executive 2, January 25, 2006). In order to counter the results-oriented "mining mindset," a system was needed that would emphasize process rather than outcomes or results. From the company's perspective, sustainability would not be an end result, but an ongoing process. To make sustainable development attractive to the corporate mindset, it was proposed that there could be trade-offs between the economic, social, and environmental dimensions of "sustainability" (Executive 2, December 6, 2011). By the mid-2000s, there was no more internal push-back to sustainable development/sustainability policies (Executive 2, January 25, 2006).

The evolution of thinking on sustainable development within Placer Dome over the course of a decade shows that there was not a simple linear progression towards acceptance of the norm, and adoption of practices consistent with it. Thinking about the nature of Placer Dome's obligation to society continued to evolve, although lingering internal pushback and concerns about costs suggest a degree of backtracking. However, the company continued to undertake organizational changes and introduce new practices consistent with sustainable development, pointing to the need to look at organizational attributes in determining the extent of commitment to the norm. Table 5.4 outlines the major organizational and policy changes undertaken up to the time of Placer Dome's acquisition by Barrick Gold.

Conclusion

The case study of Placer Dome confirms the importance of external institutional context, and internal managerial leadership in explaining CSR adoption. The global momentum behind sustainable development

Table 5.4 *Timeline of major organizational and policy initiatives:
Placer Dome, 1999–2005*

1999: First Sustainability Report published by PDI: *It's About Our Future: 1998*
1999: Sustainability Committee of the Board established
2000: VP, Sustainability position became VP, Safety and Sustainability
2001: Critical Incident Initiative launched
2002: Corporate Safety Group established
2002: Health and Safety Charter released
2003: Safety, Sustainability and Environmental Committee of the Board established
2003: Reporting against GRI Sustainability Reporting Framework commenced
2004: Sustainability Charter released
2005: Signed International Cyanide Management Code

informed the evolution of Placer Dome's CSR policies and practices. Senior management was heavily engaged with global NGOs and international governmental organizations, to make sure the company's perspective was represented in global decision-making bodies. Through the course of dialogue with these actors, senior management was in turn influenced by their perspectives on sustainable development. Management also learned from engagement in national and provincial processes, including the BC Round Table on the Environment and the Whitehorse Mining Initiative. Placer Dome's openness to learning from external actors such as NGOs in the process of developing its sustainability policies taught the value of learning how to learn (deutero learning) from external actors.

The support of senior management from the CEO on down was essential to bringing about transformative change. This case study shows that leadership took on different forms, and combined to produce a very effective group for bringing about change. Leadership from the top is always essential, and when CEO Willson joined Placer Dome in 1992, he brought with him a lifetime of experience and a strong understanding of how mining should be done in a manner consistent with respect for the environment.

Strategic motivations were paramount, but Willson also sought to instill a values-based approach to its new policies. This he did by engaging in a corporate-wide discussion on what the company's core values should be, and then working to integrate those core values into Placer Dome's sustainable development strategy. While the need to establish the business case for sustainable development was ever present, Willson used the norm to promote integrated thinking about the company's economic, social, and environmental responsibilities, as well as to foster cohesion amongst employees around common, values-based goals. His successors sought to inculcate a culture of commitment to sustainability and later, safety, by institutionalizing practices consistent with the norm. In short, management was driven both by norms and interest-based considerations.

Another form of leadership was provided by policy entrepreneurs, who moved thinking forward on sustainable development. One senior manager's specific mandate was to engage with public institutions at the global, national, and provincial levels, and his background in philosophy facilitated his ability to comprehend the relevance and applicability of sustainable development to mining. At the senior management level, others, including those with engineering backgrounds, quickly grasped the significance for mining of the emerging norm of sustainable development. Professional background was a factor, but not decisive in explaining sustainable development adoption (Executive 2, December 6, 2011). It was anticipated that resistance to sustainable development would be especially acute at the level of the mine site, as mine managers were responsible for implementing corporate policies. Positive steps were taken to counteract resistance and encourage buy-in, including extensive consultations throughout the organization.

As senior officials attested, the experience of operating mines in remote parts of Canada and the Asia Pacific provided vital lessons that were incorporated into the development of Placer Dome's CSR policies. Crucial leadership was provided in the form of projecting learnings from operational challenges in specific locales into specific policies and practices. The VP, Sustainable Development, who had prior extensive experience as a mine manager at Porgera, was tasked with the job of selling sustainable development to the mine managers. At the same time, management recognized that practices appropriate in one developing country location might not be completely transferable to other locations due to variation in local community dynamics. It was the responsibility of mine managers to institute specific practices relevant to their operational challenges. Placer Dome worked proactively to counteract the problem of sub-cultures at specific mine sites undermining corporate CSR initiatives.

In making the case for sustainable development, Placer Dome was driven in the development of its policies by instrumental considerations, including reputational concerns, the need to manage social and environmental risks, and the need to maintain a social license to operate. Leadership also took the form of spelling out the need to avoid liability through environmental failure, and demonstrating the direct correlation between avoiding costly delays and/or disruptions to its operations, and the profitability and long-term viability of the firm. By selling sustainable development as a risk avoidance/mitigation strategy, norms entrepreneurs were able to relate the concept to the dominant cultural frame within the company.

The combination of internal leadership, receptiveness to global normative developments and learning from experiences in specific institutional settings explains why Placer Dome was an early mover in CSR adoption framed around the norm of sustainable development.

6 | *Barrick Gold Corporation*

Introduction

The purpose of this chapter is to highlight the similarities and differences between Barrick Gold's approach and response to corporate social responsibility and sustainable development, as compared to Noranda and Placer Dome. In some respects, the trajectory of Barrick is not all that different from Placer Dome and Noranda. Barrick undertook EHS initiatives in the 1990s to meet its regulatory responsibilities, and by the early 2000s, came to recognize that the social dimension of CSR would have to be addressed as well. There are differences, however, that relate to the timing of adoption of CSR initiatives and external reporting, the approach to sustainable development, and the role and importance of global CSR standards in shaping Barrick's CSR practices. As with the Noranda and Placer Dome case studies, this chapter analyzes the role of leadership, learning, and the influence of global CSR standards in shaping the evolution of Barrick's CSR policies and practices.

The role of senior management was a significant factor influencing the trajectory of Barrick's CSR, as was the case with Noranda and Placer Dome. Differences in approach and timing of CSR adoption can in part be explained by the fact that until the late 1990s, Barrick's operations were concentrated in North America. In the early 2000s, the company experienced rapid expansion into Central America, Australia, and Africa. The experience of operating mines in less developed countries (LDCs) was clearly a major impetus behind the racheting up in the early-to-mid-2000s of CSR policies and practices, and internal organizational changes. Upon assuming the position of CEO in 2003, the late Greg Wilkins provided crucial leadership to the drive to build upon the company's existing CSR practices, to championing policy innovation and instituting organizational changes to implement them. Both structure (the changes in Barrick's mining portfolio) and agency (the role of leadership) work together in this case to explain CSR adoption.

There was not a simple linear progression towards improvement in Barrick's CSR. CSR policies in the 1990s were within industry norms, and Barrick undertook a number of initiatives that reflected the context of the times, and the various levels of awareness and categorization of CSR. The passing of a senior executive in the late 1990s, who had spearheaded Barrick's CSR initiatives, left the company without clear direction in this regard. Upon becoming CEO in 2003, Wilkins' leadership played an important catalytic role in formalizing the range of CSR intiatives already undertaken, in promoting substantial internal organizational change and making a major push to align Barrick's CSR with emerging global CSR standards. When Aaron Regent became CEO in 2009, the major changes, with new staff and management, began to produce a cultural shift that is beginning to see results.

Barrick differs markedly from Placer Dome, and to a lesser extent Noranda, in terms of its approach to sustainable development. In contrast to Placer Dome, Barrick chose not to use sustainable development as a conceptual frame to integrate its various CSR initiatives. Noranda, although ambivalent about sustainable development, was an early mover in terms of incorporating sustainable development indicators into its CSR reporting and practices. Barrick has incorporated many initiatives that fall under the rubric of sustainable development, and rejoined the ICMM in late 2005 after leaving the organization in 2002, where adherence to sustainable development principles is a condition of membership. As will be elaborated, the resumption of membership in the ICMM and other CSR initiatives are understood to reflect the need to catch up with rapidly evolving global CSR standards, which in turn reflect changing societal expectations. Barrick's efforts to align its CSR and sustainable development policies with global standards confirm the global norms dissemination literature in terms of the growing influence and weight, by the mid-2000s, of global CSR norms and standards.

Environmental/social challenges

As a mining company whose business is almost exclusively about gold, Barrick's EHS challenges are similar to those faced by Placer Dome. The major environmental challenges associated with gold mining include tailings disposal (which at Porgera in Papua New Guinea entails the controversial riverine disposal method), handling of cyanide, acid-rock drainage, metal leaching, and the major displacement caused by surface mining.

The global industry trend of reverting to surface mining in the 1990s brought with it social challenges, in addition to the environmental ones, as mining operations came increasingly into conflict with surface users. Barrick also inherited the social challenges and complexities of the operations it acquired from the merger with Homestake in 2001, and the acquisition of Placer Dome in 2006. Most challenging have arguably been the North Mara and Porgera mines in Tanzania and PNG, respectively. North Mara is located near an impoverished town, where residents have engaged in artisanal mining for decades, causing conflict when large-scale mining commenced. Porgera, in addition to its controversial riverine tailings disposal method, is situated amongst indigenous peoples who have fought vigorously over land claims and other issues.

Institutional setting: external pressures

Barrick is headquartered in Canada, with one operation in Hemlo in Northern Ontario as of July 2011. (It previously had an operation in Quebec.) Its flagship operation is the Goldstrike property in Nevada. Until Barrick expanded from its North American base, most of its operations were in the United States. This legacy is reflected in the fact that the VP, Environment position was until the early 2000s based in Salt Lake City, not corporate headquarters in Toronto. (A small group of corporate staff remain based in Salt Lake City.) The regulatory context affecting mining in Canada and the United States is broadly similar, albeit with different government departments and jurisdictional reach in the two countries. Having outlined the regulatory context in Canada in earlier chapters, the focus here is on the United States.

Mining in the US is regulated by the General Mining Law of 1872, which was designed to encourage mining development. The law grants free access to individuals and corporations to prospect for minerals in public domain lands, and allows them, on discovery, to stake a claim on that deposit. Most metal deposits (gold, silver, copper, iron) are located in the western part of the United States. Starting in the 1960s, with the awakening of public consciousness about environmental concerns, there was growing pressure to regulate polluting industries, including mining. In 1976, the Federal Land Policy and Management Act (FLPMA) was introduced, which gave the Bureau of Land Management (BLM), under the Department of the Interior, the authority to regulate mining claim operations in public domain lands. The Act requires bond posting for reclamation after the mine closes and requires mining operations that involve cyanide leaching to meet specific standards.

The United States Environmental Protection Agency (EPA) (created in 1970), and the Department of the Interior both have regulatory oversight over the mining sector. The Clean Water Act (1977) is the most directly significant to mining, with permits governing the release of mining effluent under the National Pollution Discharge Elimination System (NPDES). Other laws relevant to mining include the Mining and Minerals Policy Act, Resource Conservation and Recovery Act (solid waste disposal) (1976), the Clean Air Act (1963, most recent amendment, 1990), the Toxic Substances Control Act, the National Environmental Policy Act (Environmental Impact Statements) (1969), the Comprehensive Environmental Response, Compensation and Liability Act ("Superfund") (1980), under which mining companies may be liable for the release or threat of release of hazardous substances, covering releases to air, surface water, groundwater, and soils), and the Emergency Planning and Community Right to Know Act (1986). In addition, the Forest Service (FS) regulates mining activities on Forest Service land, with a similar mandate to minimize adverse environmental impacts. The National Forest Management Act of 1976 provides the Forest Service with authorities and responsibilities similar to those provided to BLM by FLPMA (EPA 1995).

In the 1990s, and under a receptive Clinton administration, there was renewed pressure to tighten up existing legislation affecting mining. The disaster at the Summitville mine (1991) in Colorado, involving a Canadian company, was an important development that drew public attention to continued irresponsibility on the part of the mining industry. As was the case in Canada, stricter regulations governing exploration, strong opposition to new mining projects, and no-go areas set aside for environmental preservation limited opportunities for expanding operations in the US. The liberalization of mining laws in most developing countries, together with a new pro-foreign investment stance on the part of developing country governments (and as NGOs claim, the lure of less regulation), pushed Barrick to look for opportunities outside North America, as had been the case with Noranda and Placer Dome before it.

Coupled with the stricter regulatory context in North America was an increasingly effective and influential national environmental movement, aided by information technologies. Publicity-generating activities such as the People's Gold Summit, held in 1999 in California, called for a moratorium on exploration of gold, adding to the pressure on the gold-mining industry (People's Gold Summit 1999). As one of the largest gold-mining companies in the US, environmental NGOs, such as Earthworks in the US and Mining Watch Canada, began to target Barrick in their campaigns. Such targeting intensified in the 2000s, as Barrick became the world's largest gold producer, surpassing Newmont in 2006.

In the period when Barrick was rapidly expanding its global operations in the early-to-mid-2000s (see Table 1.7), the stakeholder terrain was becoming ever more challenging. In 2004, for example, Earthworks and Oxfam America jointly launched the "No Dirty Gold" campaign, fashioned along the lines of what at the time was considered to be the successful "conflict diamond" campaign (Kimberley Process). The No Dirty Gold campaign is directed at encouraging a consumer boycott against buying jewelry sourced from companies engaged in irresponsible practices (www.nodirtygold.com). Major jewellers, such as Tiffany's, Signet, and Cartier, anxious to forestall public-relations disasters (such as over furs and diamonds), signed on, expressing their commitment to ethical gold sourcing (Patterson 2006: 1). From the perspective of the mid-2000s, gold-mining companies appeared quite vulnerable to such activism, in a context where it was understood to be a non-essential commodity, and at a time when gold was less important as an investment hedge than became the case after the 2008 financial crisis.

As the world's largest gold-mining company, Barrick has come to be specifically targeted by NGOs critical of mining. CorpWatch, for example, issued a detailed report in 2007 alleging serious environmental harm and human rights abuses at a number of Barrick's operations around the world. "Protest Barrick" is a dedicated portal that, as the name implies, was set up to specifically target Barrick. It provides links to news articles, testimonies, and backgrounders to Barrick's organizations worldwide (www.Protestbarrick.net). It partners with other NGOs, such as Mining Watch Canada, the Mineral Policy Institute, and Mines and Communities, among others. Global and local NGOs have used social networking technology to coordinate activities in opposition to mining, such as the coordinated demonstrations that took place around Barrick's AGM in April 2011.

In addition to the risk of consumer pressure campaigns and critical NGOs, major mining companies face growing pressures from institutional investors. As socially responsible investing (SRI) gained traction, companies such as Barrick encountered effective shareholder pressure to improve their environmental and social practices. In advance of Barrick's 2009 AGM, for example, the Ethical Funds Company (now Northwest Ethical Investments) put forward a share-holder proposal asking that Barrick convene an independent third party to review the company's community engagement practices and performance to provide assurance to investors that it is adequately handling risks related to community opposition (Ethical Funds Company 2009). The proposal argued that Barrick was not adequately mitigating risks associated with community opposition to its operations in the US, Australia, PNG, Tanzania, and Chile.

By the mid-2000s, collaborative efforts at industry self-regulation, such as through the ICMM, meant that major mining companies had to report according to a range of indicators in order to maintain or gain credibility with external stakeholders. For the ICMM, a require-ment of membership includes supporting its Sustainable Development Framework, and reporting according to the GRI indicators under the Mining and Metals Sector Supplement (MMSS). Beyond the ICMM, adherence to a range of other global CSR voluntary initiatives became an accepted norm of business practice in mining and other sectors. Global initiatives most relevant to the mining sector include the ISO 14001 EMS, the IFC Performance Standards, the International Cyanide Management Code (ICM), the Extractive Industries Transparency Initiative (EITI), and the Voluntary Principles on Security and Human Rights. Respect for human rights is the most recent normative development, as reflected in global con-sensus around the "Ruggie Framework" (Ruggie 2008). A key chal-lenge for Barrick (as with most major mining companies) has been to anticipate, interpret the appropriateness of, learn from, and in some cases, catch up to, these various global standards and norms. How this process has evolved at Barrick will now be elucidated.

Organizational and managerial response

Shift in thinking and role of leadership

There is every indication that, so long as it was operating projects in North America, Barrick was able to manage its environmental and social responsibilities quite well, relative to other mining companies. In the view of senior management, and as reflected in company documents, Barrick considers itself to have had good CSR policies and practices, starting from the "early days" of its operations (Executive 1, May 6, 2003; Executive 2, May 28, 2003; Executive 3, May 5, 2011). The early development of Barrick's CSR policies and practices is associated with Robert (Bob) Smith, who joined the company in 1984, and served as President from 1987 to 1996. Smith became Vice Chairman in 1997, but passed away in 1998. Smith was clearly held in very high regard, and was the one who spearheaded Barrick's early CSR initiatives, as reflected in the following statement in the 2007 Responsibility Report:

Bob created a team that excelled not only in mining expertise but also in the human qualities of trust and respect. For Bob, operating excellence extended beyond production results to include a strong sense of responsibility to the environment, local communities and Company employees. Bob's sense of integrity was most evident in programs established in Elko Nevada, the community located closest to Barrick's Goldstrike mine. (Barrick 2008)

The Goldstrike operation in Nevada is considered to be Barrick's flagship operation, and an exemplar of its commitment to community building (Executive 1, May 6, 2003; Barrick 2002a). Referred to as the "Goldstrike Model," Barrick's initiatives at Goldstrike are considered the best early example of the company's CSR activities (Executive 1, May 6, 2003).

From the late 1990s, Barrick's policy was to give 1 per cent of annual pre-tax earnings to charitable endeavors, through its "Heart of Gold" Fund. In 1999, 1 per cent of pre-tax earnings amounted to US$4 million (Barrick 2000: 28). Barrick gave over US$ 11 million between 1992 and 2002 to Nevada communities and charities. The Fund provided assistance in the categories of health/hospitals, education, arts and culture, and environmental groups/projects. Barrick's statements also refer to a sizeable number of major environmental awards won over the years (seven between 1997 and 1999) (Barrick 2000: 29).

The philosophical approach of senior executives to CSR in the 1990s focused on the environmental, health, and safety aspects of CSR, all driven by ever-stricter regulations in Canada and the US. The social side of CSR was seen more as charity and hence, discretionary, as reflected in statements from the 1999 Annual Report, where generous donations to "community causes and charities," such as schools and children's camps, are described, and as reflected in the Heart of Gold Fund (Barrick 2000: 28). Reflecting its charitable origins, the Heart of Gold Fund supports Barrick's philanthropic endeavors, as opposed to its community initiatives under its CSR commitments. Today, the Heart of Gold Fund is now only for corporate donations and scholarships in Canada. The Fund does not cover community initiatives on a global basis, as community initiatives are managed at the regional and site level according to local priorities. By 2010, Barrick's overall community initiatives amounted to over US$42 million (Barrick 2011a).

CSR was also understood in terms of the economic development Barrick's operations provide. At Barrick's flagship Goldstrike property in Nevada (Betze-Post and Meikle mines), a "Buy Nevada First" policy was instituted with annual purchases of more than US$200 million in goods and services. Barrick's contribution is understood in terms of the jobs created and overall contribution to Nevada's economy. Over 14,000 direct and indirect jobs have been generated from its Goldstrike operations at Betze-Post and Meikle (Barrick 2002a). At the Elko community near Goldstrike, Barrick built seven hundred houses for workers at its mines for a cost of US$44 million, providing them with mortgage guarantees (Barrick 2003a: 34).

Recognition of some of the limitations in Barrick's approach to CSR became apparent to management by the early 2000s, when the company began to encounter complex community issues affecting existing and new projects under development. Barrick's "Responsibility Reports" from the early 2000s reflect management's recognition that the social side of CSR is about much more than charitable giving or initiatives to benefit the communities where Barrick employees live. By 2004, Barrick had clearly recognized the importance of community engagement, as reflected in the CEO's comments in the 2004 Responsibility Report: "We have an obligation to ensure that neighboring communities share in the lasting benefits of mineral resource development" (Barrick 2005: 2). In this statement, the social side of CSR is seen as an obligation, not as merely discretionary, and the thinking about benefits to local communities is recognized as needing to be long term in nature.

There was also a shift in thinking with respect to the relationship of the social side of CSR to the company's business. Maintaining high social standards came to be recognized as a core part of the business, with a clear distinction between the discretionary or philanthropic side of CSR, and CSR as necessary to the success of doing business. Although senior management believes that CSR is "the right thing to do" (Executive 1, May 6, 2003), there is also the strategic recognition that good CSR on the social side reduces risks by ensuring there are no disruptions to operations through community opposition. Management believes that this business objective also contributes to socio-economic development, assuming that the two objectives are compatible (Executive 3, May 5, 2011).

After Greg Wilkins became CEO in 2003, there was a strong push to improve Barrick's CSR policies, with the requisite organizational structure and competency to implement them effectively. As Wilkins stated: "Leadership at the executive and Board level is fundamental to our efforts to achieve company-wide excellence in EHSS (environment, health, safety, society) performance" (Barrick 2004a: 2). In 2004, to provide greater corporate guidance to Barrick's social responsibility programs, Wilkins established a Corporate CSR Steering Committee, chaired by then Vice-Chairman, John Carrington (Barrick 2004a). Carrington chaired the Mining Association of Canada when it launched its Towards Sustainable Mining initiative, and was considered the right person to move Barrick forward in terms of formalizing its CSR activities and communications.

In the mid-2000s, the support of top leadership was crucial in the major push to develop the community relations side of Barrick's CSR. When a new position was created with responsibility for community relations in 2005, the new Director, CSR, was not pushed to the side, on the periphery of the core business function. Rather, the CSR Director was in high demand, as the company was facing community issues that no one knew how to deal with (Executive 3, May 5, 2011). This was especially so as the new CSR Director was hired just as Placer Dome was acquired, and was tasked with dealing with problematic legacy issues involving North Mara and Porgera at a time when the company lacked experience with the complex social realities at these operations (Manager 2, August 18, 2011). The CSR Group quickly grew from one person to almost ten people, in order to deal with the demand.

Greg Wilkins served as a catalyst for formalizing Barrick's existing CSR practices, and provided the leadership necessary to bring about organizational changes and adopt new CSR initiatives. After the passing of Greg Wilkins in 2009, Aaron Regent took over as CEO, and has continued to provide the strong leadership and support from the top for the full range of CSR functions, including community relations (Executive 3, May 5, 2011). Regent brings with him his earlier experience at Falconbridge, which instituted innovative polices and practices around working with indigenous peoples in Canada. Regent is clearly seen to be in the "driver's seat on CSR" (Northwest Ethical Investments, Official 2, August 30, 2011; see Table 1.5 for full list of supplemental interviews).

Barrick can be considered to be a late mover compared to Placer and Noranda in terms of the release of stand-alone CSR reports, which commenced in 2003 for the 2002 reporting year (although Barrick was within range of the mining industry norm). In the early 2000s, Barrick began to provide information on corporate responsibility on its website, and from the mid-1990s, a brief section (two pages in 1999) dedicated to CSR appeared in the annual reports. Senior executives expressed the view that Barrick's CSR actions should "speak for themselves" (Executive 1, May 6, 2003; Executive 3, May 5, 2011), implying that Barrick should be judged on its actions. In the early 2000s, management began to appreciate the value of communication with external stakeholders, and the CSR reports became one important means of doing this. By packaging Barrick's CSR initiatives appropriately, the reputational pay-off could be more effectively realized. From 2002 to 2009, the Environmental Group was responsible for CSR reports, after which, the CSR Group assumed responsibility for reporting.

In the extensive organizational and policy improvements to its approach to community relations undertaken since 2005, already established global CSR standards are acknowledged as an important source of information and best practices for Barrick (Executive 3, May 5, 2011). At the same time, Wilkins anticipated the centrality of effective EHSS policies and practices as the company embarked on a growth phase involving the completion of four new mines: Veladero in Argentina, Cowal in Australia, Lagunas Norte in Peru, and Tulawaka in Tanzania (Barrick 2004a). As stated in the company's Responsibility Reports, "Barrick's vision is to be the world's best gold company by finding, developing and producing quality reserves in a profitable and socially responsible manner" (Barrick 2005).

Organizational and policy changes

In terms of the environmental side of its responsibilities, Barrick is on par with other industry members with respect to when it began to build up organizational capacity around environmental issues. In 1994, an Environmental Committee of the Board was established, and the position VP, Environment created. In 1995, a Corporate Environmental Policy Statement was approved by the Board. On the occupational health and safety side, a corporate-wide OHS policy was approved by the Board in 1998 and a corporate-wide internal auditing program for OHS was established in 2002 (Barrick 2003a: 4). CEO Wilkins expressed disappointment with Barrick's safety and health performance, citing fatalities (Barrick 2004a: 2). After extensive review of Barrick's existing practices, and of best practices of other companies, Barrick revised its approach to safety and health, by introducing the Barrick Health and Safety System in 2003. The OHS function lagged behind the environment in terms of leadership, in the sense that the position VP, Health and Safety was not created until 2005. These changes marked the beginning of significant expansion of organizational attributes necessary for enhanced CSR competency and performance.

The 2001 merger with Homestake provided Barrick with the opportunity to increase its competency across the board. Barrick inherited Homestake's Environment and Health and Safety Groups, and internal environmental management system audits were expanded (thirteen were conducted in 2002) (Barrick 2003a:11). Health and safety programs and staffing also expanded during 2002 following the Homestake merger. To promote a zero incident culture, awards for superior health and safety performance were introduced (Barrick 2003b: 23). In terms of CSR staffing, Barrick had environmental and health and safety staff at all its operations, but typically only one community relations specialist at its North American operations. Recognizing the need for greater expertise in community relations at its developing country operations, there were twelve community relations specialists at Bulyanhulu and eight community relations specialists at Pierina in 2002 (Barrick 2003a: 36). The size of Barrick's community relations staff increased dramatically in the 2000s, and now total over 250 throughout sites on five continents.

In 2003, under Wilkins' leadership, there was a push to codify the company's responsibilities across the EHSS spectrum. In 2003, a new Code of Business Conduct and Ethics was introduced, setting out standards of behavior for all Barrick employees as well as the Board, covering issues pertaining to corporate governance (conflict of interest, conduct of business abroad, insider trading, etc.), as well as expectations regarding environmental, health, and safety performance (amended in 2006)

(Barrick 2003c). Among the policies embedded within the code are Barrick's Safety and Health Policy (Barrick 2003d), and Barrick's Environmental Policy Statement (Barrick 2003e).

Among the functions of the Executive Environmental, Health and Safety and Social Steering Committee (created 2004) was to review performance trends and issues, ensure that corrective actions are completed, and approve EHS strategic plans. Policy innovation included the approval in 2004 of the CSR Charter, with a view to integrate thinking and action on CSR throughout the organization. The CSR Charter frames Barrick's approach to CSR and includes four key pillars:

1. Ethics
2. Employees
3. Community
4. Environment, Health and Safety

(Barrick 2004b)

The organization of the CSR Charter, with community relations as a discrete function, is reflected in the organizational structure of CSR within the company. CSR is generally understood to refer to community relations, as reflected in the responsibilities of the VP, CSR, with a separate reporting structure. Environment has its own group, as does Safety and Health. When the Security Group was created in 2005, it was separate from the EHS functions.

In 2003, Barrick implemented a new organization design using Regional Business Units in keeping with its growing global footprint. Barrick now has regional headquarters in Australia Pacific, South America, North America, and Africa (Barrick spun off its African operations as African Barrick Gold (ABG) in 2010, maintaining a 73.9 per cent controlling interest). Wilkins envisaged that EHSS performance would benefit from the reorganization, as each region was to have increased accountability and responsibility for EHSS functions.

In 2002, Barrick had Directors/Managers for Environmental Services for Canada, the US, South America, and Australia, one Manager, EHS Assurance, and one Director, Safety and Health, all reporting to the VP, Environment (based in Barrick's US office in Salt Lake City) and the VP, Regulatory Affairs (based in Toronto) (Barrick 2003a). The governance structure included no executive-level position for the social side of its operations, with environmental, health, safety, and community-relations managers at mine sites reporting to the General Managers,

Operations, who in turn reported up the line to the VPs, Operations, and on to the COO. The lack of executive-level leadership dedicated to the social side of CSR presented difficulties in responding to community issues as the company began to expand its operations.

By the mid-2000s, it had become clear to senior management that Barrick needed greater competency to address the challenges it faced in the communities where it operated. Prior to 2005, the practice had been to hire consultants to address specific issues/initiatives, as well as to work with NGOs with a focus on specific aspects of development, such as water and sanitation (Executive 3, May 5, 2011). In early 2005, a consultant had been hired to prepare guidelines on community engagement, and after the job was completed, senior management recognized the enormity of the task ahead, leading to the decision to create the position Director, CSR (Executive 3, May 5, 2011). The Director, CSR has responsibility for community relations, to address weakness in managerial leadership in this regard, and a CSR Group with responsibility for community relations was created in the same year. The position was upgraded to Senior Director, and then Vice President in 2009, a reflection of internal recognition of the importance of good community relations to the company. In 2006, the position Manager, CSR was created, to support the work of the Director, CSR.

The timing of the decision to create the Director, CSR position reflects three factors: 1. recognition by senior management of the need to significantly improve competency to address community engagement needs; 2. the need to address the lack of internal institutional infrastructure for dealing with CSR; and 3. the need to incorporate new international standards and codes into Barrick's practices (Executive 3, May 5, 2011). Although the CSR position would have been created anyway, the finalization of the acquisition of Placer Dome in November 2005 cemented the decision (Executive 3, May 5, 2011). The timing reflects a combination of internal demand, due to the recognized need for competence in dealing with community relations, and external demand from stakeholders for greater responsiveness to community concerns (Executive 3, May 5, 2011).

The consultant, who ultimately became Director, CSR, was tasked to develop a Community Relations Strategy, and Community Engagement and Sustainable Development Guidelines (CE&SD Guidelines). The CE&SD Guidelines spell out Community Management Standards, key principles informing community engagement, and a set of guidelines for managing community engagement, social impacts, and sustainable community development. The key objective of the Guidelines is to "improve the effectiveness and consistency of Barrick's community engagement and sustainable development activities globally" (Barrick 2006a). The CSR Group is responsible for social impact assessments, compliance with the IFC Performance Standard 5 on resettlement, indigenous relations, community engagement, local procurement and employment, social due diligence, and a new community-relations management system that is being rolled out in 2011 (Executive 3, May 5, 2011).

In 2007, Community Engagement and Sustainable Development Plans were launched, to be implemented at all mine sites (Barrick 2008). The Community Relations Strategy was launched in December 2008, in order to strengthen the community relations function across the company, including the management of social risks, and to secure a social license to operate (Barrick 2011a: 54). In 2008, Barrick formalized a Community Relations Vision strategy. The Community Relations Vision is intended to capture the key elements of Barrick's community relations approach:

- Strong collaboration with the community
- Mutual benefits for the company and the community
- A positive sustainable legacy

(Barrick 2011a: 57)

As a general rule, corporate standards and policy are set by the corporate office, and the regional and country offices are responsible for implementing them. There was a real need for corporate-level policies, as individual mines were traditionally very independent, run almost as "fiefdoms" (Northwest Ethical Investments, Official 2, August 30, 2011). There was therefore a real need to standardize practices across the organization. The decision-making process is not entirely top down, however. Regular meetings and workshops are held on an ongoing basis, and once a year, the regional/country leaders for Community Relations and CSR are brought together for a week-long conference to discuss policies, tools, and social risk management (Executive 3, May 5, 2011; Manager 2, August 18, 2011).

In seeking to address the social side of CSR, Barrick instituted significant organizational changes in the mid-2000s. Although the various CSR functions were understood to be interdependent, the growing extent and complexity of Barrick's CSR activities presented challenges of coordination and efficient delivery and tracking of activities. An

Executive Committee integrating the CSR, EHS, and Security functions was created in 2008. Referred to as CHESS (Community, Health, Environment, Safety and Security), the committee reviews CSR performance, trends, and issues, and approves CHESS policies and business plans (Barrick 2010). The VP, CSR, however, continues to report to the Executive VP, Corporate Affairs, so at the organizational level, there is still a separation of functions. The Legal and Communications departments (which used to be completely separate) were also rearranged to report to the EVP, Corporate Affairs (above paragraph drawn from interview with Executive 3, May 5, 2011).

The creation of a separate security group reflects the growing security concerns encountered by Barrick at its operations in developing countries, where issues such as the security of expatriate personnel and local employees, the protection of property, trespassing by artisanal miners, and large anti-mining demonstrations are of particular concern. The joining of human rights to the security group reflects acknowledgment on the part of Barrick of evolving global norms around business and human rights. In mid-2011, Barrick launched its Human Rights policy, which is informed by the Ruggie Framework and the Voluntary Principles on Security and Human Rights (recent developments at North Mara and Porgera gave added impetus to this initiative) (Barrick 2011a: 65). Barrick became the first Canadian mining company to gain membership in the Voluntary Principles in late 2010. Barrick's CSR Charter also affirms its commitment to human rights. In light of the challenging security situation at some of its mines, and the attendant human rights dimensions, Barrick developed a Security Policy and a Security Management System (Barrick 2011a: 65). Table 6.1 itemizes the major policy and organizational changes undertaken that are of relevance to CSR.

The organizational changes and policy initiatives outlined above demonstrate a clear trend line from the early 2000s towards increased commitment to addressing the complexities of CSR in Barrick's operations around the world.

Experiences shaping the learning process

In a manner similar to Placer Dome and Noranda, Barrick learned from the experience of managing its operations in developing its CSR policies and practices. In addition to the organizational attributes outlined above, learning is another indicator of commitment to CSR.

Table 6.1 *Major organizational and policy developments: Barrick*

1994	Environment, Health and Safety Committee of Board established
1994	VP, Environment appointed
1995	Corporate Environmental Policy Statement approved by Board
1998	Corporate Occupational Health and Safety Policy approved by Board
2002	Corporate-wide health and safety audit program introduced
2003	Release of first CSR report, *Responsibility*, for 2002 reporting year
2003	Code of Business Conduct adopted
2003	Health and Safety System approved
2004	CSR Charter adopted
2004	New Corporate Health and Safety Information System developed
2004	Courageous Leadership and Personal Commitment awards established
2004	Executive EHSS Committee formed
2005	Creation of Director, CSR (Community Relations) position
2005	VP, Safety and Occupational Health position created
2005	Environmental Management System Standard launched
2006	Community Engagement and Sustainable Development guidelines released
2007	Security Policy developed
2007	Security Management System adopted
2008	Community Relations Strategy launched
2008	Community Relations Vision launched
2008	CHESS Executive Committee created
2009	Position Director, CSR upgraded to VP, CSR (Community Relations)
2010	Community Relations Standard developed
2010/11	Community Relations Management System under development

Source: Barrick, Responsibility Reports, 2002–10.

The company explicitly sought to extend Smith's vision as its operations expanded in the late 1990s (Barrick 2008). Indicative of single loop learning, Barrick sought to improve on its existing CSR, and apply it to its expanding operations. Referred to as the "Goldstrike Model,"

Barrick drew upon best practices in the US and applied them to its operations around the world (Barrick 2002a). For example, Barrick provided housing for its employees at Pierina in Peru and Bulyanhulu in Tanzania, as it had for workers in Elko, Nevada. At the Pierina mine (production commenced 1998), a new school for children living near Pierina was built (named the Robert Smith school) (Barrick 2002a). The community focus is on the provision of new health care facilities, new roads, new drinking water and irrigation systems, and training programs for local farmers. At Bulyanhulu (acquired 1999, start operations 2001) houses were built for employees, and similar improvements were made to educational, health, and basic infrastructural facilities for the benefit of employees and the local communities.

Given the enormous contribution made by Bob Smith to Barrick's CSR activities, it does seem safe to say that a CSR leadership lacuna emerged after his passing in 1998. Those who have been with the company for a long time, and knew him well, found that it took the company some time to recover from the loss of the leadership he provided around CSR (Executive 4, August 23, 2011). In seeking to extend the Goldstrike Model to its expanding operations in Africa and South America, different conditions in developing countries would present new challenges (and risks). Key among these is the lack of (or inadequate) government structures, the failure to recognize fully who the other relevant stakeholders are, and the tendency to underestimate the full scope of what are often complex issues in local communities (Bird 2004; Borzel and Risse 2010; Dashwood and Puplampu 2010).

These challenges became apparent at the Pierina operation, where Barrick's efforts to hire people from the tight-knit local communities created "huge social problems" (Executive 2, May 28, 2003). These problems stemmed from the mode of social organization, where everyone had specific tasks within the community. When the men went to work in the mines, the women were left doing everything. To address the problem, Barrick hired a sociologist, who, in consultation with the elders in the community, worked out a solution. The elders were to decide who should work in the mine, and workers were hired on a three-month rotation, allowing the community to redistribute the work load (Executive 2, May 28, 2003).

One key learning point for Barrick was the need to move to an understanding of CSR that reflects a sense of obligation towards local communities, rather than a more discretionary approach. Replicating the more charity-oriented, benevolent approach to CSR characteristic of the Goldstrike operation would prove to be inadequate, especially in places where government does not adequately fulfill its social welfare functions. This point was acknowledged in the 2007 Responsibility Report:

> Historically there are many companies that have been generous in making donations to communities and Barrick is no exception. However in the developing countries where we operate, our Community Relations Teams are looking beyond philanthropy and determining new and innovative ways to proactively engage local community members, governments, and other stakeholders in community development initiatives. This participatory development increases a community's sense of ownership in the initiatives and leads to community capacity building. (Barrick 2008)

The limitations of the Goldstrike Model to the developing country context became apparent to management at the Bulyanhulu mine in Tanzania, which was acquired in 1999 from Sutton Resources (Executive 4, August 23, 2011). First among the challenges was establishing who Barrick should be engaging with, as the nearby community at Kakola was largely a transient one, made up of people who came to the area to engage in small-scale mining. In a country which at the time had little experience with large-scale mining, the mentality among locals was that they should try to get as much from Barrick as quickly as possible (Executive 4, August 23, 2011). Management realized that, in the first instance, meaningful community engagement would depend on communicating the fact that the company would be in the area for the long term.

Another important lesson learned from Bulyanhulu was that community engagement had to entail more than offering up good deeds. For example, Barrick built a local market where it expected that people would come to trade, but nobody came. Barrick had failed to ask whether or not the locals wanted the market. From this experience, management realized that community engagement had to be a shared responsibility, whereby the community needs to be consulted on its development needs and priorities, and in turn, needs to commit to contribute to community projects (Executive 4, August 23, 2011).

Inexperience with operating in developing countries aside, the challenge of fostering constructive community engagement was made more difficult by legacy issues before Barrick acquired the Bulyanhulu mine, surrounding the forcible eviction in 1996–8 of small-scale miners, who had been working in the area since the late 1970s (Manager 2, August 18, 2011; Compliance Advisor Ombudsman 2002). There had also been allegations that Sutton Resources' wholly owned subsidiary company, Kahama Mining Corporation, had been implicated, together with the Tanzanian police, in the deaths in 1996 of over fifty African small-scale miners on its property (Council of Canadians 2001). Barrick management was very disturbed and concerned by these allegations, and hired a Canadian legal team in 1999 to conduct an extensive investigation into the matter. The resulting report found no evidence to support the allegations (Executive 4, August 23, 2011). An independent investigation by the Compliance Advisor Ombudsman (CAO) of the World Bank, brought in because of a MIGA guarantee provided for the mine, substantiated Barrick's finding that the allegations were false (Compliance Advisor Ombudsman 2002). Although the allegations respecting the burying alive of artisanal miners were discredited, the issue continues to fester, prompting Barrick to provide a special link on its website about Bulyanhulu (Barrick 2002b).

Barrick's experiences with Pascua-Lama have provided important lessons about the centrality of community engagement and the need to communicate with external stakeholders (Executive 3, May 5, 2011). The Pascua-Lama exploration property was acquired from Lac Minerals in 1994. Ratification in 2000 of the Mining Integration Treaty between Chile and Argentina made development of the project feasible, although development was postponed because of low prices for gold in the early 2000s. In 2002, it was announced that the expected start-up date for Pascua-Lama would be 2008, however, the construction phase did not begin until 2009 (Business Wire 2002). Delays can be attributed to the unique, bi-national aspect of the mine, and the attendant complexities surrounding the need to negotiate such items as tax agreements with two independent governments (Manager 3, August 18, 2011).

At Pascua-Lama, Barrick has worked hard to secure a social license to operate. The Pascua-Lama project has been controversial from the start, given the ecologically sensitive nature of the remote Huasco Valley, adjacent to glaciers of the Andean mountains straddling the border between Chile and Argentina. In 2004, in an open letter from the agricultural communities of the Huasco Valley to the President of

Chile, concern was expressed about the negative impact of mining on agriculture in the area, as well as concerns about threats to the economic, social, cultural, and environmental sustainability of the valley (OLCA 2004).

Barrick's initial contacts with the local communities pre-dated the company's efforts in the mid-2000s to strengthen its community relations function, and management recognized that engagement at the local level would have to be improved (Executive 3, May 5, 2011). The 2005 Responsibility Report cites the strenuous efforts to respond to community concerns about the possible environmental effects of the mine (Barrick 2006b). The original environmental impact assessment was approved in 2001, but in light of subsequent environmental concerns, Barrick was asked to make modifications to the project. The modifications were approved in early 2006 by the Chilean environmental authorities, and later the same year by the Argentinean authorities (Barrick 2006b). Barrick has built many overlapping layers of environmental safeguards into its operations, in order to satisfy concerns of external stakeholders (Executive 3, May 5, 2011). The extra environmental safeguards are also seen as a necessity, to address perceptions about the environmental risks involved, as opposed to the actual reality of what is considered a world-class site (Executive 3, May 5, 2011). Barrick has a special link from the main page of its website devoted to dispelling misinformation about Pascua-Lama (Barrick 2006c).

Despite Barrick's community-engagement efforts, in 2009 the Huascoaltino agricultural community petitioned the Inter-American Commission on Human Rights on the infringement of their human rights by the Pascua-Lama mine. In February 2010, the Commission agreed to review the petition, with denial of free, prior, and informed consent being one of the main claims (Protest Barrick 2010). Furthermore, the passing in September 2010 by the Argentine Senate of a law to protect glaciers in Argentina arguably raises questions about how it could affect the Pascua-Lama project (Henao 2010). However, in November 2010, the Federal Court in the Province of San Juan suspended the application of the new federal glacier law in the province, after unions, trade organizations, and mining companies (including Barrick's subsidiaries in Argentina) challenged the constitutionality of the law. In December 2010, the province of San Juan joined this challenge and the case will now be decided by the Supreme Court of

Argentina (Barrick 2011b: 91). Among the grounds for challenging the constitutionality of the law is that in Argentina, the provinces have jurisdiction over natural resources, as is the case in Canada (Manager 3, August 18, 2011). Pascua-Lama is an excellent example of the challenges inherent in gaining community acceptance, challenges made more difficult by the fact that community expectations do not stay stagnant, but are dynamic and shifting.

Managing indigenous community relations is a difficult challenge that mining companies with operations in developed countries such as Canada and Australia, as well as in developing countries, must grapple with. Barrick has sought to give indigenous communities a stake in its operations, through the provision of employment and business opportunities, skills development, cultural preservation projects, and advancement of education. Consistent with its approach at Cowal through the Native Title Agreement with the Wiradjuri, Barrick signed in 2004 a Collaborative Agreement with the Tahltan First Nation at its Eskay Creek operations in northern BC (now closed). With funding from Barrick, the Tahltan Nation Development Corporation (TNDC) was established under the Collaborative Agreement, providing skills training and opportunities for local First Nations contractors (Barrick 2011b: 71). Barrick's Eskay Creek operation is rightly considered an early success story (Executive 2, May 28, 2003).

Barrick has learned to adapt its indigenous strategies to local contexts, in part because indigenous communities in developed countries such as Canada, the US, and Australia tend to have experience with natural resources development (and operations), and often have more capacity to engage with corporations than their counterparts in developing countries (Manager 2, August 18, 2011). Management came to recognize the need to customize its approach at each site to accommodate the different social conditions encountered (Executive 2, May 28, 2003). At Pascua-Lama, for example, Barrick has been responsive to the concerns of the indigenous Diaguita community to preserve their culture and engage in viable agriculture. In 2006, the Diaguita were recognized by the Chilean government as indigenous (not to be confused with the members of the agricultural Huascoaltino community, who have raised concerns about Pascua-Lama). Barrick played a role in that recognition, by explicitly identifying the Diaguita as a distinct ethnic group in its 2001 environmental impact assessment (Barrick 2009: 8). Barrick has developed a long-term, constructive relationship with the indigenous

Diaguita communities (Manager 2, August 18, 2011), by providing support to a range of activities to strengthen cultural traditions, and by providing assistance to agricultural practices upon which their livelihood depends (Barrick 2009: 7–9; Barrick 2011a).

Barrick's relations with the Western Shoshone tribes at its Cortez Hills project in Nevada is an interesting example of community engagement, because notwithstanding the company's longstanding efforts to foster constructive engagement, they have not entirely produced the desired results. There are five federally recognized tribes that are widely dispersed in the geographical region of rural Nevada, where Barrick operates. In 2001, Barrick began the permitting process on what was in 2005 to become the Cortez Hills project, after the discovery of additional deposits north of the original deposit at the base of Mount Tenabo. In 2005, the Bureau of Land Management (BLM) approved Barrick's request to explore an area on public lands claimed by the Western Shoshone.

Barrick was targeted by the NoDirtyGold campaign, which joined forces with elements of the Western Shoshone tribes in its bid to halt the Cortez Hills project, although none of the tribes live close to the mine, and many live as far as a hundred miles or more away from the site (Manager 2, August 25, 2011). In 2008, Barrick sought permission to expand the Cortez Hills project, incorporating the additional discoveries. In 2009, some members of the Western Shoshone and others not residing in the area (Western Shoshone Defence Project; Great Basin Resource Watch) sought an injunction to halt construction of Barrick's Cortez Hills project, claiming that the BLM had failed to consider all environmental impacts of the project (Schertow 2009). The judge, disagreeing with the full injunction request, granted a "tailored" injunction which allowed mining operations to continue while Barrick and the BLM prepared a Supplemental Environmental Impact Statement (SEIS) to address two specific environmental concerns raised by the claimants. The injunction restricted the mine from trucking certain ore types to be processed at the Goldstrike mine, and limited the amount of water the Cortez mine could pump from the open pit and underground. Neither of these restrictions affected mine operations because they related largely to future plans, not current production activities (Barrick 2011b: 88). Following the preparation of an SEIS, the BLM issued a Record of Decision in March 2011, which removed the tailored injunction at Cortez Hills (Barrick 2011b: 74–5).

Notwithstanding opposition from some Shoshone tribal members within and beyond Barrick's operational area, according to Barrick, the majority of Western Shoshone are supportive of Barrick's operations (Manager 2, August 25, 2011), as reflected in the signing in 2008 of a Collaborative Agreement with four of the five Western Shoshone tribes in Nevada. Since 2005, quarterly "Dialogue" meetings have been taking place with senior company managers and Western Shoshone tribal leaders and community representatives (Barrick 2011a). This structured dialogue has fostered learning about Western Shoshone priorities, including insights into how to promote cultural preservation, a key concern of the Western Shoshone (Manager 2, August 18, 2011). In 2010, under the Collaborative Agreement, Barrick established the Western Shoshone Cultural Advisory Group, comprised of elders and members of several Western Shoshone tribes, to provide input on early stage mining projects and operations (Barrick 2011a: 70). Among the lessons that have been learned from ongoing dialogue is the importance of the pine nut tree to Shoshone culture, resulting in an understanding on how to protect pine nut trees near the mine as part of environmental mitigation plans. Mine staff also work closely with Shoshone communities to organize groups of elders for traditional pine-nut picking and the associated ceremonies in remote areas on Barrick property and public lands (Manager 2, August 23, 2011).

A key challenge of learning around CSR is staying on top of dynamic intra-community relations. Efforts to engage with the Western Shoshone are reflective of deutero learning (learning how to learn), where Barrick recognizes that ongoing interaction is necessary to address changing and/or evolving stakeholder expectations. The widely dispersed geographic area of rural Nevada where the Shoshone reside has made the process of community engagement more challenging (Manager 2, August 25, 2011). There was no monolithic opposition to Cortez, but some members of the Te Moak tribe were opposed. Members of the Te Moak tribe, who opposed Cortez, nevertheless participate in the Dialogue meetings, and a recent Dialogue meeting was hosted by the Te Moak tribe. All Western Shoshone are welcome at the Dialogue meetings. Senior management at Barrick have had meetings (outside of Dialogue meetings) with Western Shoshone tribal members who oppose the mine, and continue to be available for meetings whenever these are requested. Indeed, according to Barrick, relations with members of the Te Moak who opposed Cortez have improved significantly over the past two years (Manager 2, August 25, 2011). The institutionalization of consultations through the quarterly Dialogue meetings and the Western Shoshone Cultural Advisory Group create spaces where ongoing learning can take place, and have helped improve community/company relations.

Early experiences of expansion into developing countries clearly influenced learning around community engagement. Lessons learned at Pascua-Lama, Periena, and Cowal in the early 2000s came to be applied at subsequent projects, such as Veladero and Cortez Hills, where the importance of initiating engagement long before the project begins is acknowledged (Barrick 2006b). The experience of operating mines in developing countries led Barrick to not just improve on existing ways of doing things, but to substantially change and transform its practices (reflective of double loop learning).

The need to communicate with external stakeholders before a new project is under development is another lesson learned from the experience of mining in developing countries. The expectation still prevalent in the early 2000s that good deeds would speak for themselves had given way by the mid-2000s to recognition of the need to communicate what is being done (Executive 1, October 14, 2011; Executive 3, May 5, 2011). To further enhance its communications efforts, Barrick in 2006 began to release separate responsibility reports for its regions, and later introduced its *Beyond Borders* newsletter to provide detailed information about CSR initiatives in all its regions.

Engagement with external stakeholders

A key indicator of learning around CSR is receptiveness to engaging with external stakeholders. Barrick has learned, as did Placer Dome and Noranda before it, that failure to earn and maintain a social license from local communities can cause serious disruptions to its operations, and cause lengthy delays in the permitting process. Barrick has institutionalized formal mechanisms for ongoing consultation with local communities, including the establishment of community liaison offices in local towns and communities, and the formation of local community advisory groups. Stakeholder oversight committees have been maintained or established at a number of mines, including the Porgera Environmental Advisory Komiti (PEAK) (set up in 2000 by Placer), the Citizens' Environmental Oversight Committee at Pascua-Lama, and the Community Environmental Monitoring Group at Cowal (Barrick 2011a: 59).

Receptiveness to concerns raised by external stakeholders, even those highly critical of Barrick's operations and the mining industry in general, such as NGOs, is also an important indicator of learning. The perception of NGOs expressing allegations respecting the previous operator at Bulyanhulu was that Barrick was not open to their concerns (Council of Canadians 2001). In the mid-2000s, Barrick's operations in the US were targeted by the NoDirtyGold campaign. In response to criticisms about the large amount of waste rock associated with gold mining, Barrick's Vince Borg (VP, Communications) was quoted as saying: "That's just a sound bite . . . intended to conjure up awful images of this very useful rock that's being destroyed" (Patterson 2006). In response to evidence that Barrick in 2004 produced approximately twenty-seven tons of waste rock per ounce of gold produced, Borg stated: "You've got to take the rock, crush it, and process the gold out of it . . . you cannot uncrush the rock" (quoted in Patterson). Borg was also quoted as saying: "If gold is 'dirty,' what does society do about using gold as the symbol of a union between two individuals?" (Patterson 2006). Notwithstanding the validity or not of the claims made by either side, Borg's comments are suggestive of a degree of arrogance and dismissiveness in responding to external critics.

Allegations of other NGOs opposed to Barrick include those of CorpWatch, whose 2007 report, *Barrick's Dirty Secret: Communities Worldwide Respond to Gold Mining's Impacts*, accompanied activities in advance of Barrick's 2007 AGM (CorpWatch 2007). The report drew a strongly worded rebuttal from Barrick, defending its relations with local communities as constructive and positive, and claiming that "CorpWatch falsely inflates community opposition to a number of Barrick operations" (Barrick 2007).

Claims that Barrick understates the seriousness of issues at some of its mines have persisted, however. Harder to dismiss, and more serious, have been concerns raised by investors. The injunction against the Cortez Hill project served as the impetus for The Ethical Funds Company (now Northwest Ethical Investments) to launch a shareholder proposal at Barrick's 2009 AGM (Ethical Funds Company 2009). The proposal called on Barrick to convene an independent third party with the mandate to review the company's community engagement practice and performance against the objectives of the existing Community Engagement and Sustainable Development Guidelines. In addition to the legal action over the Cortez Hills project, problems at Barrick's other operations, including Lake Cowal in Australia, North Mara and Bulyanhulu mines in Tanzania, the Pascua-Lama project in Chile/Argentina, and Porgera in PNG were cited. Northwest Ethical Investments claimed that Barrick understates the existence of "costly and problematic situations" at various mine sites, raising doubts for investors as to whether adequate risk mitigation measures are in place. The shareholder proposal was significant, because it received 17 per cent support at the AGM, a high number for such resolutions.

Northwest Ethical Investments chose Cortez as a proxy for community engagement at Barrick's other sites, the thinking being that if things are not going well in the relatively stable climate of Nevada, then what would that mean for how well community engagement was going at Barrick's far more difficult and problematic sites (Northwest Ethical Investments, Official 2, August 30, 2011)? The team sent by Northwest to Nevada met with representatives from about nine band councils covering a wide geographic area. The sentiment expressed by most council members was found to be one of dissatisfaction with the Dialogue process Barrick had set up (Official 2, August 30, 2011). The message conveyed was that the Dialogue process was not being conducted in a way which would foster ongoing relationships, taking on the form of information sessions, rather than two-way feedback.

As part of its mandate, Northwest had been in dialogue with Barrick for several years before the shareholder proposal was put forward in 2009. The proposal was seen as a means to address underlying issues at the corporate level by making concerns about community engagement public (Northwest Ethical Investments, Official 1, August 30, 2011). Senior management was not considered ready for what Northwest had been seeking through dialogue, and the shareholder proposal got people's attention at a very high level (Official 1, August 30, 2011).

More recently, there have been especially serious allegations about human rights abuses at Barrick's North Mara and Porgera operations. Both the North Mara and Porgera operations were obtained when Barrick acquired Placer Dome in 2006. The Porgera operation has a long history of difficult relations with the local indigenous communities, and Placer Dome also encountered challenges handling the situation. The Ipili people on whose land Porgera sits are renowned for their strong negotiating skills, and after lengthy bargaining with Placer prior to the mine's opening in 1990, are reputed to have said: "If you open a mine without our permission, we will kill you" (Taylor 2004: 24). In 2001, during national elections, power pylons leading to the mine were blown up, causing production at the mine to be cut off for several months. In 2005, Placer Dome admitted that eight people had been killed in self-defence by police and Porgera Joint Venture (PJV) security guards between 2000 and 2005 (Burton 2005).

At both Porgera and North Mara, Barrick inherited difficult and complex legacy issues, at a time in the mid-2000s when it was inexperienced with operating in areas with such high social risks. This new reality had significant implications for its capacity to adjust and manage these issues effectively (Manager 2, August 18, 2011). A key learning for Barrick has been the need to be more fully cognizant of the social risks inherent with new acquisitions, and of the broader social pressures beyond the immediate catchment area of the mine. At the time of the acquisition, Barrick's internal procedures for assessing social risks were not as robust as they are today. The company has since strengthened capacity at the corporate, regional, and site levels, and also from the perspective of policies and management systems (Manager 2, August 18, 2011).

Human rights NGOs have also raised questions about Barrick's willingness to engage with external stakeholders critical of its operations. In a report prepared by Human Rights Watch, serious allegations were made about the findings of an investigation involving incidents of gang rape by mine security personnel between 2008 and 2010 at Porgera (Human Rights Watch 2011: 9). Efforts on the part of community representatives from the Porgera area to raise these concerns with Barrick management have not, in the view of Human Rights Watch, led to sufficient efforts to address the situation. In its report of February 1, 2011, Human Rights Watch found that "*too often in the past, Barrick has responded to legitimate human rights and environmental criticisms of the Porgera mine with a 'shoot the messenger' approach, attacking the company's critics while failing to address important substantive concerns*" (Human Rights Watch 2011: 62). These alleged incidents were cited in a formal request for review of Barrick's operations submitted on March 1, 2011 to the Canadian National Contact Point under the OECD Guidelines for MNEs by Mining Watch Canada, the Porgera Landowners Association, and the Akali Tange Association (Mining Watch Canada 2011). Amnesty International has also claimed that Barrick is not responsive to community concerns (Amnesty International 2010: 17).

The claim that Barrick has not responded to ongoing concerns at its operations is not entirely accurate. Barrick has responded extensively to the concerns raised in the Human Rights Watch report, which is acknowledged in the request for review to the Canadian Contact point of the OECD (see Barrick Gold letter dated December 23, 2010 in Human Rights Watch 2011: 87–94). In June 2010, Human Rights Watch presented the findings of its investigation (which was subsequently released in the February 1 report) to Barrick officials, prompting the company to request that the PNG Commissioner of Police conduct a full criminal investigation. Barrick also brought in a fifteen-member investigative team of experts to conduct a comprehensive internal investigation, and asked a former Chief Ombudsman of PNG to conduct an independent inquiry into the allegations (Barrick 2011c: 34). These examples suggest that in the past few years, Barrick has become more responsive to, and willing to engage with, its external critics, reflective of a cultural change.

In November 2010, Barrick was admitted into the Voluntary Principles (VPs) on Security and Human Rights, following a process of consideration by parties representing the member constituencies that took close to a year. Admittance into the Voluntary Principles is dependent on the determination by a Steering Committee of NGOs and government and company representatives that an applicant has in place internal policies and procedures that demonstrate it has the capacity and commitment to adhere to the VPs. Barrick's decision to apply for admission to the VPs is an important signal of its commitment to human rights, and its admittance reflects the assessment of the Steering Committee (whose members include Human Rights Watch and Amnesty International), that Barrick can meet its commitments under the VPs. Admittance to the VPs aligns Barrick with the "Building the Canadian Advantage" strategy of the Canadian government, which formally endorses the VPs (Government of Canada 2009). Barrick already had systems in place to meet its human rights commitments, so was not merely reacting to pressures from human rights NGOs, but anticipating the need to strengthen its human rights commitments and organizational capacity (Manager 2, August 18, 2011).

In January 2011, following completion of the internal investigation, Barrick announced that employees found to have breached Barrick's policies were terminated, including those who had knowledge of, but did not report, assaults against women at Porgera (Barrick 2011c: 34). Following the February 2011 release of the report prepared by Human Rights Watch, Barrick announced further actions and indicated that further dismissals might occur, pending the outcome of the police investigation. Barrick also moved to develop a formal human rights policy and enhance its capacity to detect and prevent human rights abuses.

Barrick had also earlier responded to ongoing concerns about the riverine tailings disposal method at Porgera. Upon acquiring Porgera in 2006, Barrick commissioned a two-year study to investigate possible alternatives to the controversial riverine tailings disposal method and to explore ways to reduce the discharge of tailings. The US$5 million review confirmed earlier assessments that the terrain and high rainfall make the area highly unsuitable for a large tailings storage facility. Barrick has introduced modifications to reduce the amount of tailings disposed of in the river (Barrick 2010: 66–7). Nevertheless, in February 2009, Norway decided to exclude Barrick from its pension fund, citing specifically concerns about the riverine tailings disposal method at Porgera (Saunders 2009).

In light of the blow to its CSR reputation as a result of the release of the Human Rights Watch Report in February 2011, it was especially damaging when new reports surfaced in May 2011 about similar serious human rights abuses at Barrick's North Mara operation in Tanzania. On May 16, 2011, five people scavenging for gold from waste rock on Barrick property were allegedly shot dead by Tanzanian police. Although Barrick had an arrangement with the Tanzanian police that only the minimum force necessary be used to control violent situations, police had chosen to fire on the crowd of between 800 to 1,200 villagers that appeared at the mine that day (York 2011b).

Two weeks after this unfortunate incident, reports surfaced that Barrick is investigating allegations of sexual assault by police and company security guards at North Mara, including allegations of gang rape similar to what occurred at Porgera (York 2011a). Having signed on to the Voluntary Principles, with the Porgera incidents serving as the immediate catalyst, Barrick is obliged to investigate and report on credible allegations of human rights abuses at its operations. Indicating how "deeply distressed" Barrick is by the allegations, the company acknowledged that if these crimes are confirmed, they send a "clear message that we (Barrick) have not met the promises we have made to the community, and to ourselves to pursue responsible mining in every location where we and our affiliates operate" (Barrick 2011d).

In its statement on the North Mara allegations, Barrick posted a detailed list of ongoing and new initiatives to prevent human rights abuses in the future, covering steps to strengthen community conditions and relations, improve the security function, and strengthen its measures to ensure human rights are respected. Promised initiatives include the commissioning of a study by third-party experts to identify best practices in preventing and dealing with human rights abuses, and the institution of a new, global human rights compliance program, to be aligned with the human rights framework developed by the UN Special Representative on Business and Human Rights, John Ruggie (Barrick 2011d; Ruggie 2008).

These initiatives mark a significant improvement over Barrick's response to allegations about human rights abuses at other sites over the years (Northwest Ethical Investments, Official 2, August 30, 2011). As recently as the 2009 AGM, concerns raised by a community representative near Porgera had been dismissed by a senior company executive. In an important signal of the seriousness with which Barrick takes the situation at North Mara, its CEO, Aaron Regent, wrote a piece for the comments page of the *Globe and Mail*, where he indicated that, "Barrick's revulsion at discovering the evidence [of sexual assault] is deep," and noted the "enormous disappointment" felt by employees on the ground at the mine site, all the way up to the most senior levels of management (Regent 2011).

According to the Ethical Funds Company's 2009 shareholder proposal, Barrick was considered at the time to be lagging competitors in recognizing the value of comprehensive and independent reviews of community engagement policy and performance (Ethical Funds Company 2009). Starting in 2009, in accordance with the new ICMM Assurance Process, Barrick retained a new company, Bureau Veritas, to provide independent external assurance to stakeholders about the data provided in Barrick's reports. One of the criticisms of the 2009 shareholder proposal prepared by the Ethical Funds Company was that the ICMM Assurance Process was not comprehensive enough in scope to unearth the sorts of complex social issues Barrick was dealing with at some of its mines.

Barrick went over and above the ICMM's requirements, by expanding the scope of stakeholder engagement beyond what is called for

under the Assurance Process, by selecting the most challenging operations and projects for site visits and by arranging for interviews with a
range of stakeholders, including community members, local landowners, business owners, indigenous peoples, government officials,
and women's groups (Barrick Manager 2, August 18, 2011). Indeed,
without the expanded scope of the ICMM's Assurance Process, there
would not have been a sufficiently detailed assessment of community
engagement policy and performance (Northwest Ethical Investments,
Official 1, August 30, 2011). Although the timing of these activities
might make it appear that Barrick was responding directly to pressure
from The Ethical Funds Company, in fact, the scope of the independent
assurance process was identified in the Fall of 2008, well before the
shareholder proposal (Barrick Manager 2, August 18, 2011). The
shareholder proposal helped strengthen the internal momentum for
expanding the Assurance Process (Barrick Manager 2, August 18,
2011), and set the path for getting people in place at the corporate
level who were prepared to promote a culture of commitment to constructive community engagement (Northwest Ethical Investments,
Official 1, August 30, 2011). The shareholder proposal served to legit-
imize the efforts of those within Barrick seeking a more responsive
approach.

The independent assurance processes of the last two years have
included visits and stakeholder interviews at ten Barrick sites, including the more challenging sites at North Mara, Porgera, Cortez, Cowal,
and Pascua-Lama. Barrick remains in ongoing, constructive engagement with Northwest Ethical Investments (Barrick, Manager 2,
August 18, 2011) and Northwest has since confirmed it is satisfied
with Barrick's independent assessment process in Nevada (where the
injunction had prompted the 2009 shareholder resolution) (Northwest
Ethical Investments 2010). Barrick considers that engagement with
Northwest has had a positive influence on its CSR performance and
management of ongoing challenges (Barrick, Manager 2, August 18,
2011).

Significantly, the independent Assurance Report prepared by Bureau
Veritas noted that "the company is demonstrating more humility,
accountability and transparency," a noteworthy improvement over
concerns raised in various quarters earlier about Barrick's approach
to external stakeholders (Barrick 2011a: 9). Among the recommendations was that Barrick increase transparency for material issues at ABG

(a prescient observation), and that site-level stakeholder communications be improved to include more information about material issues, community support, and how Barrick uses stakeholder feedback in the planning, development, and operation of mining activities (Barrick 2011a: 9–10). The independent stakeholder surveys conducted for the past two years by Bureau Veritas have not been made public, and Northwest continues to feel that the one-page letter provided in Barrick's Responsibility Reports does not provide enough information (Northwest Ethical Investments, Official 1, August 30, 2011). What is disconcerting for Northwest is that although the independent stakeholder surveys revealed hints of significant problems at North Mara and Porgera, Bureau Veritas had no mandate to deal with the issues (Official 2, August 30, 2011). The extent and severity of human rights abuses at both these operations indicates a clear break-down in Barrick's internal systems, in the view of Northwest.

Evidence from Barrick's Responsibility Reports dating from the late 2000s shows that Barrick has sought to better disclose difficulties at its mines involving community relations. The 2008, 2009, and 2010 Responsibility Reports, for example, include a section under Community Relations detailing significant incidents affecting communities, as required under the GRI reporting indicators (Barrick 2010: 65–6, 2011a: 73–5). Furthermore, in response to the allegations at Porgera and North Mara, Barrick acknowledged the problems, and initiated independent investigations into the allegations at both sites.

Barrick has sought to respond to stakeholder concerns in other ways. In order to address concerns that Barrick was under-reporting the extent of controversies at its mine sites, the company has significantly increased the amount of information on its website about CSR challenges. Barrick has also taken steps at corporate level to improve its ability to identify and assess emerging stakeholder issues. In 2011, an independent member with a background in CSR was elected to the Board of Directors. Northwest Ethical Investments, in a shareholder resolution filed in April 2010, had requested that Barrick add a director to the Board with experience in CSR (Northwest Ethical Investments 2010). Barrick's decision to undertake this initiative preceded Northwest's proposal, but the proposal had the effect of reinforcing for management that Barrick was on the right path (Barrick, Manager 2, August 18, 2011). Ongoing internal discussions had confirmed for management the appropriateness of taking this step, as it reflected industry practice both within the mining sector, and across all sectors (Manager 1, August 18, 2011; Manager 2, August 18, 2011).

In 2012, Barrick established an external CSR Advisory Board. The Board is comprised of external experts and representatives of key stakeholder groups, who will provide advice on challenging social and environmental issues the company is facing (Barrick 2011c: 3). The establishment of an external advisory group is a clear indication of Barrick's commitment to listen to and learn from external stakeholders and experts. Barrick also commissioned GlobeScan in early 2011 to conduct a major stakeholder survey, to ascertain stakeholder perceptions of Barrick's CSR performance and the issues of most concern to stakeholders.

The continuous efforts on the part of Barrick to create spaces for stakeholder engagement, from the community level up to the corporate level, reflect the company's efforts to respond to, and ideally, stay ahead of, a constantly shifting stakeholder terrain. To manage these challenging realities, the ability to learn how to learn (deutero learning), through the experience of mining at the site level, and through interactions with stakeholders at the local, national, regional, and global levels, is critical to successful management of CSR in the twenty-first century. The casting away of old mindsets and practices (unlearning), for example, the notion that "good deeds should speak for themselves" is also a necessary part of the learning process around CSR (as was the case with Noranda and Placer Dome). Leadership and support from the top remains critical to this process, and fortunately, Barrick's CEO "gets it" (Executive 3, May 5, 2011). Indeed, Northwest believes the real turn-around has come since Regent became CEO in 2009, as he has been able to promote a cultural shift in respect of responding to external critics, stakeholders, and community concerns (Official 2, August 30, 2011). Certainly, the detailed and comprehensive response to the situations at both North Mara and Porgera speak to a cultural shift taking place.

Approach to sustainable development

Barrick's approach to sustainable development is interesting, in that the company appears to go against the norm within the industry, which is to wholeheartedly embrace the concept (at least, at the discursive level). The fact that its stand-alone reports are referred to as "responsibility" reports, as opposed to "sustainable development" or "sustainability" reports, is the first clue. The first stand-alone report for 2002 acknowledges the Brundtland Commission Report's definition of sustainable development, but also claims that Barrick has long been fostering sustainable development through its CSR practices (Barrick 2003a). In this respect, Barrick's CSR initiatives are consistent with sustainable development, but it has interpreted the concept differently from Noranda and Placer Dome.

In its 2004 Responsibility Report, Barrick explicitly endorsed the World Bank's definition of CSR, as opposed to sustainable development, as the approach informing its CSR policies, understood as "the commitment of business to contribute to sustainable economic development – working with employees, their families, the local community and society at large to improve the quality of life, in ways that are both good for business and good for development" (Barrick 2005). Noteworthy is Barrick's view that "responsibility means more than sustainable development" (Executive 3, May 5, 2011; Barrick 2006b), encompassing "a broad range of issues," including the maintenance of high ethical standards, operating in a safe and healthy manner, environmental protection and stewardship, developing the full potential of employees, and "making a positive difference in the communities in which we live and work" (Barrick 2006b).

This interpretation is interesting, because it goes against the grain of how most mining companies understand the concept. At a time when the mining industry had launched the MMSD initiative, and the ICMM was created to promote sustainable development, Barrick stepped back. In 2002, shortly after the ICMM was created, Barrick withdrew its membership, as did several other companies at that time. Barrick nevertheless continued to adopt global CSR practices that had been developed in keeping with the norm of sustainable development, so that its practices are aligned with the norm, even though it does not embrace it as an overarching framework for its CSR.

Influence of global CSR/sustainable development norms

By the mid-2000s, Barrick's rapidly growing size and the large degree of industry buy-in to industry collaboration under the ICMM, made it difficult for the company to continue outside that organization. Evolving global CSR/sustainable development standards/norms have had a significant influence on Barrick's policies and practices

(Executive 1, May 6, 2003; Executive 3, May 5, 2011). In the mid-2000s, Barrick rapidly expanded its membership in a range of global voluntary programs. This activity coincided with the significant expansion of its CSR initiatives and organizational competency around the same time. These activities are consistent with the growing influence of global CSR and sustainable development norms, and management actively scanned for global best practices in informing its CSR policy development and practices (Executive 1, October 14, 2011; Executive 3, May 5, 2011). Although Barrick evinced a preference for the concept of CSR over sustainable development, it was not immune to stakeholder pressure to demonstrate its commitment to sustainable development.

In 2005, Barrick adopted the GRI reporting indicators as a means to measure and report on its economic, social, and environmental performance (Barrick 2011a: 19). In effect, Barrick was preparing the groundwork for rejoining the ICMM, as reporting against the GRI indicators is a condition of membership. In 2006, Barrick rejoined the ICMM, after having inherited its membership from Placer Dome. A further condition of membership is that companies adhere to the ICMM's Sustainable Development Framework, so Barrick had to take steps to ensure it was operating in conformity with the Framework. Later, in 2008, Barrick began to report against the Mining and Metals Sector Supplement to the GRI, in keeping with the ICMM's adoption of the MMSS. Membership in the ICMM is key to learning around CSR/sustainable development, as collaboration with leading industry organizations fosters knowledge creation and dissemination of best practices.

Other notable organizations/voluntary programs which Barrick joined with a bearing on sustainable development include the UN Global Compact (which it joined in 2005), the ICMC (2005), the Carbon Disclosure Project (2005), the Extractive Industries Transparency Initiative (2006), and the Voluntary Principles on Security and Human Rights (2010) (for a complete list, see Barrick 2011a: 18–19). The dates at which the company joined these various initiatives show that there was a major push in the mid-2000s to align Barrick's policies and practices with global industry standards and growing public expectations (Executive 3, May 5, 2011).

Although Barrick adheres to the conceptual framework of CSR to guide its policies, the many policy initiatives adopted in the mid-2000s make explicit reference to sustainable development. Barrick's CSR Charter (adopted 2004), for example, formally reiterates the World

Bank's definition of CSR, but also declares the company's commitment to foster "sustainable development in the communities and countries where we operate" (Barrick 2004b). Under the "Community" pillar of the four pillars of CSR (Ethics, Employees, Community, and EHS), Barrick commits to facilitating "long-term and beneficial resources development," while giving priority to "building partnerships in entrepreneurial endeavors that contribute to enhancing local capacity," an approach entirely consistent with sustainable development (Barrick 2004b). Under the EHS pillar, Barrick commits to planning that ensures that "the environment is protected for future generations, and that the sustainability of nearby communities is safeguarded" (Barrick 2004b).

As the title indicates, Barrick's Community Engagement and Sustainable Development Guidelines (adopted 2006) explicitly embrace sustainable development as a norm informing its approach to the Community pillar of the CSR Charter. In developing the guidelines, Barrick drew on the IFC Performance Standards, as well as on other international standards, industry guidelines, and best practice at Barrick and among industry peers. The Guidelines include a set of five Community Management Standards (CMS), including:

Permitting phase

- CMS1: Social Impact Assessment: conduct a ESIA and develop a *Social Management Plan*
- CMS2: Indigenous Peoples' Consultation Plan: to be developed where applicable
- CMS3: Resettlement Plan: in the event of involuntary resettlement, a *Resettlement Action Plan* is developed (in accordance with the IFC Performance Standards)

Construction, operations and closure phase

- CMS4: CE&SD Plan: to be developed at all sites, building on the *Social Management Plan* and updated annually
- CMS5: Closure Social Impact Assessment: to be completed three years prior to closure of any operation.

(Barrick 2006a)

Barrick's extensive relations with development-oriented NGOs is a key component of its sustainable development strategies, as it reflects the recognition that sustainable development is not something that mining companies can accomplish on their own. Developing partnerships to promote a range of developmental initiatives in local communities also reflects double loop learning, changing how things are done in order to produce more positive results. In a presentation to the World Mines Ministries Forum in 2008, Barrick's Senior Director, CSR, stressed that collaboration with partners (other companies, NGOs, community representatives, governments, donor agencies) is fundamental to the goal of promoting sustainable development arising from mining activities (Senior Director, CSR, 2008). Barrick has established a thick web of organizational linkages to promote sustainable development in the countries in which it operates. A sampling of these include the African Medical and Research Foundation (AMREF), AIDS Business Coalition (Tanzania), CARE International (Tanzania), Nature Conservancy (US), Porgera District Women's Association (PNG), USAID, and World Vision Canada (for full list, see Barrick 2011a: 20).

In addition to the explicit nod to sustainable development in the community relations side of CSR, commitment to sustainable development is also embedded in Barrick's Environmental Policy. The Environmental Policy cites the Brundtland Commission understanding of the term: "Barrick believes that we can contribute to the sustainable development of our host communities ... We are committed to meeting the needs of current members of that community without jeopardizing the ability of future generations to meet their needs" (Barrick 2003e). In ongoing efforts to improve its environmental performance, Barrick has looked to the global ISO 14001 Environmental Management System standard. As noted in the *Environmental Policy Statement* (embedded in the code), Barrick's Environmental Management System Standard (EMSS), developed in 2005, was designed to be consistent with ISO 14001. The EMSS is being implemented with a view to moving Barrick's operations to ISO 14001 registration. As of 2011, all of Barrick's South American and North American mines have achieved ISO 14001 registration, and other operations in Australia are pursuing registration (Barrick 2011a: 35).

Although sustainable development does not provide a conceptual frame for Barrick's CSR activities, the above discussion clearly demonstrates the influence of emerging global sustainable development norms on Barrick. The buy-in by major mining companies is important, as Barrick risked being on the outside of the momentum around sustainable development as a norm informing mining industry practices. The mining industry's acceptance of the GRI as key reporting indicators denoting commitment to sustainable development clearly influenced Barrick's decision to adopt them for its own reporting. Furthermore, management's efforts to bring Barrick's CSR practices in line with the IFC Performance Standards and the ISO 14001 EMS is clearly in keeping with the growing weight of sustainable development norms and standards.

Learning around sustainable development

Given the preference for CSR as an organizational concept informing its CHESS policies, Barrick has not employed sustainable development as a means to integrate the various components of CSR functions, in the way that Placer Dome did. The lessons learned about the importance of the social side of CSR, however, draw on a similar rationale, as understood by Noranda and Placer Dome (Executive 3, May 5, 2011). These companies had understood sustainable development as a means to address or comprehend the social side of their responsibilities. As the Senior Director, CSR, noted in his PowerPoint presentation to the World Mines Ministries Forum in February 2008, a core part of the CSR function is to manage relationships, mitigate risks, and deliver benefits; doing so produces (hopefully) mine/community harmony, which translates into business sustainability and a social license to operate (Senior Director, CSR, 2008).

To address negative community perceptions about the impact of mining, an independent review of Barrick's Tanzania operations was conducted, known as the Advisory Committee for Environmental and Social Sustainability (ACESS) (Senior Director, CSR, 2008). These undertakings represent an important milestone in terms of approaches to community engagement that involves not just consultation, but listening to, and learning from, the local communities to develop appropriate development strategies.

ABG's most recent development in Tanzania is the Buzwagi mine, which commenced operations in 2009. As a new development, the mine offered Barrick the opportunity to get things right from the start, and it had the benefit of not having to deal with legacy issues (Goldstuck and Hughes 2010: 69–74). Guided by global best practices, great care and attention was paid to the environmental and social impact assessment (ESIA) and the Relocation Action Plan (RAP). Extensive consultations took place with local communities, village leaders, and regulatory working groups, and Barrick committed that it would not proceed with Buzwagi until the RAP had been approved by all stakeholders and every affected family. Community projects were launched during the project development phase, including the establishment of the Mwendakulima Cooperative Farm, and the expansion and upgrading of the Mwendakulima High School. The full cost of the RAP was approximately US$13 million, of which $10 million went towards mine compensation payments (Goldstuck and Hughes 2010: 72).

The challenges are complex, and poverty is pervasive; although mining can make a significant contribution to social and economic development, "success is not guaranteed" (Senior Director, CSR 2008). In light of all the community initiatives undertaken by Barrick, one can readily understand the major disappointment over the recent setback at North Mara (York 2011c). Barrick's overall record around sustainable development, however, has been recognized by external stakeholders. Starting in 2008, Barrick was added to the Dow Jones Sustainability Index – World, and starting in 2007, was added to the Dow Jones Sustainability Index – North America. For the first time in 2010, Barrick was placed on the NASDAQ Global Sustainability Index of the top one hundred companies worldwide. These accomplishments are important to the company, as they are understood to counteract criticism from NGOs, ethical investors, and other external stakeholders.

Conclusion

In the mid-2000s, Barrick implemented substantial internal organizational change and policy innovation across the full range of CSR. Although this chapter has focused mostly on the social side of Barrick's initiatives, there was a major push in the mid-2000s to strengthen the full range of Barrick's CSR, covering Community, Health, Environment, Safety, and Security. Barrick has also sought to change the culture of the organization, through, for example, the Courageous Leadership awards promoting safety, Environmental Excellence awards for continuous improvement, and, starting in 2010, new CSR Champion awards that recognize employees across the company for their commitment to CSR.

The timing of these transformative changes can be attributed to the important role of leadership. Although Barrick has faced intense external pressures from a variety of sources, ultimately it is up to senior management, with direction from the Board, to decide whether and how to respond to external pressures. After doing reasonably well with the environmental aspects of CSR in the 1990s in North America, Barrick experienced a CSR leadership lacuna that did not come to be adequately addressed until the mid-2000s. At the same time, the strengthening of global CSR norms and standards has played a formative role in influencing both the timing and the need to align with global standards, touching on reporting, management systems, and performance. Throughout this process, Barrick's efforts confirm that CSR adoption requires a variety of learning styles. Effective CSR demands that companies reach out to external stakeholders and partner with other organizations at the local, national, regional, and global levels, in order to be in a position to anticipate and respond to evolving societal expectations and stakeholder constellations. Such learning processes entail risks in their own right, once again pointing to the essential role of support at the very top of the organization.

It takes a long time to foster a culture of commitment to CSR. Although there was a major push to improve CSR policies and practices in the mid-2000s, it appears always to be catching up, as societal expectations and global norms continue to evolve. Barrick has gotten better at anticipating changing societal expectations, but continues to face challenges at some of its more socially complex sites, including legacy sites inherited through acquisitions. Barrick recognizes that to improve its reputation, it must do more than claim to adhere to global CSR standards. It has to be able to demonstrate a culture of commitment to the environmental, social, and economic components of CSR/ sustainable development. For this reason, Barrick has come to recognize the benefits of joining the ICMM, and participating in industry collaboration to promote standards such as the Assurance Process, that will gain credibility with external stakeholders. Engagement with industry associations and external stakeholders serve the important purpose of legitimizing and reinforcing the efforts of those within the company who are trying to promote change. The process requires a champion at the top (Executive 3, May 5, 2011), as Barrick, and Noranda and Placer Dome before it, have demonstrated.[1]

---

[1] The CEO of Barrick was fired on June 6, 2012. It remains to be seen whether or not Barrick's CSR will continue to have a champion at the top.

7 | Global collaboration towards sustainable development

Introduction

Having examined the internal, firm-level dynamics that influenced the evolution of the cases studies' unilateral CSR policies and practices, this chapter turns back to global developments. Specifically, this chapter traces the global collaborative efforts of major mining companies based in the advanced industrialized economies to promote industry self-regulation. The role and motivation of the early movers that assumed a leadership role in promoting private global norms for the mining sector is examined, through case-study analysis of Noranda and Placer Dome. Barrick was influenced by these global normative developments and the efforts of the mining industry to develop a specific set of standards consistent with the norm of sustainable development. Barrick's role will be contrasted in order to identify the global sub-set of specific voluntary standards applicable to mining that became institutionalized by the mid-2000s, and which influenced Barrick's choice of CSR initiatives.

It is argued that leading mining companies were prepared to absorb the collective action costs of free riding and shirking for several reasons. First, they hoped to realize early mover advantages, which would see them at the front of the pack and in a position to shape global standards for the industry as a whole. Second, as highly visible major mining companies, they recognized that it was necessary to take action in order to address the bad reputation of the industry as a whole. Third, persistent and strong external pressures have driven the industry to progressively strengthen its CSR practices over time. This pressure contributed to a shift in attitudes discernible within the mining industry as a whole regarding acceptance of environmental and social responsibilities, together with evidence of responsiveness to the global norm of sustainable development. These dynamics are consistent with the overall argument that a combination of instrumental and normative motives are at play.

Overview of relevant theory

The preceding case-study chapters employed the three-level institutional analysis outlined in Chapter 2 in order to set out the external national and global institutional context, and the response of the case-study companies to the pressures emanating from their external environment. The three institutional approaches help explain the timing of adoption of unilateral CSR policies, and in turn, are drawn upon here to explain the timing and motivation of early movers in collaborative efforts to promote industry self-regulation at the global level. The Canadian institutional context helps explain why Canadian companies such as Noranda and Placer Dome took on a leadership role at the global level.

Drawing on constructivist approaches in international relations theory, it is argued that firms are responsive to, and influenced by, global normative shifts, even as they act strategically to respond to them. As early movers, Noranda and Placer Dome played the role of norms entrepreneurs in promoting industry acceptance of practices associated with sustainable development, confirming the importance of internal leadership. Barrick rejected the norm of sustainable development as an overall frame for its CSR initiatives, but has adopted global standards designed to be consistent with sustainable development. The decision to rejoin the ICMM in late 2005, after having pulled out in 2002, meant that Barrick had to adopt the ICMM's sustainable development principles, as a condition of membership. By the mid-2000s, practices associated with sustainable development had achieved sufficient acceptance within the industry that it was difficult for a major company such as Barrick to stay on the outside.

The literature on learning, which was demonstrated to be relevant to how firms interpret, understand, and act on their CSR responsibilities, is equally relevant to how firms engage in industry collaboration. The key lessons for mining companies concern why collaboration was necessary to promote the industry's interests, and how the industry should collaborate to address the pressing need to improve its reputation. The literature on the impact of professional orientation is relevant to the industry as a whole, because one of the key challenges was for executives trained in mining and other engineering disciplines to comprehend how sustainable development might be understood and acted upon in the mining sector.

When competitive firms move beyond unilateral CSR initiatives and seek to collaborate in promoting CSR for the industry as a whole, new dynamics come into play. Firms encounter different challenges when undertaking unilateral CSR initiatives than when undertaking collaborative ones. In explicating the role of institutional approaches in the three-level analysis, a distinction is made between unilateral (individual firm) efforts to promote CSR and collaborative efforts to promote CSR across the global mining sector. The explanatory weight assigned to specific institutional approaches in the three-level analysis varies depending on whether the explanation focuses on unilateral or collaborative CSR initiatives. The focus in this chapter is on collaborative initiatives.

Industry self-regulation faces collective action problems (King and Lenox 2000; Olson 1965; Ostrom 1990; Prakash and Potoski 2007b; Rees 1997; Sethi 2005). Industry associations need to be able to avoid adverse selection or free riding, where companies join to hide their poor performance and bask in the glow of more responsible members, and shirking or symbolic adoption, where companies claim to be adhering to standards advocated by the association, but are not in fact doing so (King and Lenox 2000: 670; Prakash and Potoski 2007b: 778). Rational choice theory assumes that as competitive actors, firms are rational egoists, and will not participate in collaborative self-regulation unless the pay-off is at least as high as it would be without participation (Alberini and Segerson 2002; Prakash and Potoski 2007b). New institutional approaches emphasize normative dynamics and cognitive processes, which, through collaboration, can alter how managers perceive their roles and interests (Fligstein 1990; Galaskiewicz 1991; King and Lenox 2000; Ostrom 2000).

A major justification for self-regulatory institutions is that they can provide benefits that no firm acting unilaterally could realize. Voluntary industry associations are able to institutionalize rules and procedures that make it difficult for firms to change their minds about the externalities they are prepared to absorb, thereby conferring the benefit of legitimacy to the efforts of firms (Prakash and Potoski 2007b). Sethi argues that a necessary pre-condition for viable collaborative industry initiatives is that in the early stages, a small group of forward-looking companies take the lead in promoting standards for the industry (2005: 82). Doing so can minimize the free-rider problem, because all companies have agreed in advance to certain standards of conduct, and it eliminates the problem of adverse selection because membership is by invitation only, so that the worst performers are selected out at the outset.

Early movers enjoy certain advantages, including the ability to design standards that are appropriate to their industry and are cost effective, and to establish rules that other more skeptical companies will feel pressured to follow (Sethi 2005). By setting the process in motion, early movers can essentially set the rules for the industry, and increase the burden on non-participating companies to fall in line. Early movers also enjoy the initial advantage of being able to differentiate themselves from poor performers, although this advantage diminishes as more companies improve their CSR practices.

Collective action problems may be overcome when industry leaders are prepared to tolerate the private costs posed by free riders, in the belief that efforts to improve the performance of the industry as a whole will safeguard their own reputations (King and Lenox 2000; Meyer and Rowan 1997). In short, where the private benefits of collective improvement exceed the private costs of free riding, individual companies may be prepared to absorb the costs (and risks of drawing attention to themselves). As Prakash and Potoski (2007b) argue, an industry's reputation is "held in common"; the bad actions of one company spill over to taint the entire industry. According to Olson's "privileged" group model, members of small groups are more likely to bear the burden of collective goods provision (Olson 1965: 49–50).

Another consideration is the visibility of individual companies. The possibility that major mining companies' reputations are disproportionately hurt by the negative externalities caused by others in the industry explains the willingness of some to take on a leadership role in forming an industry club (Prakash and Potoski 2007b). King and Lenox found a strong correlation in their research on the chemical industry between visibility of firms and their inclination to participate in self-regulatory initiatives (2000), which is borne out in the mining sector. Ostrom reminds us that Olson did not rule out the potential for collective action to promote public goods where the actions of group members are highly noticeable (Ostrom 1990: 6). Major mining companies are "noticeable" to each other, in that one serious tailings spill on the part of a major mining company with sloppy environmental practices affects the reputation of the industry as a whole in a negative way.

Institutional context, collective action, and early efforts at global industry collaboration

Overview of global collaborative initiatives

In 1991, major mining companies around the world established the International Council on Metals and the Environment (ICME), in order to address a range of challenges confronting their industry. In the face of a growing and ever louder crescendo of opposition to mining, a number of CEOs of major mining companies launched, in 1999, the Global Mining Initiative (GMI). The GMI's first major initiative was to conduct a two-year study on the contribution of mining to sustainable development; the Mining, Minerals and Sustainable Development (MMSD) project (MMSD 2002). The other key initiative was to create, in 2001, the International Council on Mining and Metals (ICMM), which replaced the ICME. Through the ICMM, sustainable development has been actively promoted as a means for mining companies to frame their CSR policies, and as the framework guiding initiatives to improve their performance.

Efforts to improve the industry's reputation through voluntary mechanisms can be seen to be a strategic response to external pressures and constraints. The unevenness in regulatory environments in many parts of the developing world where mining companies now operate pointed to the need for more effective efforts at industry-wide collaboration at the global level. Rational choice institutionalism advances the explanation of why it was mining companies from the advanced industrialized economies which began to adopt unilateral CSR policies and promote collaborative initiatives in the 1990s. The damage to mining's reputation due to negative publicity over major disasters and controversies and the external pressures experienced by mining companies from the advanced industrialized economies form the key elements of the critical juncture faced by the mining industry in the mid-to-late 1990s. By the mid-1990s, mining companies found their access to land, markets, and finance increasingly restricted. Institutional approaches in organization theory shed light on the thinking informing managerial actions and the role of managerial discretion.

The critical juncture faced by the industry set the stage for new initiatives to address the industry's reputational problems. Still, it was not a foregone conclusion that mining companies would take action; the willingness of some major mining companies to assume a leadership role explains the major push from the late 1990s. What was critical was the perception on the part of some company CEOs that the industry had reached a crisis, which induced leading companies to step outside the ICME process by launching the GMI. The growing global presence of major mining companies put the spotlight on social and environmental performance in developing countries with weak regulatory frameworks (Nash, past-President, ICME, May 26, 2006). The industry recognized the need to address and minimize externalities associated with its operations in responding to NGO pressure and public concerns.

Strategies employed by the industry include consensus-building through multistakeholder engagement, international networking with other countries' industry associations and governments, international organizations, and global environmental NGOs, and the promotion of voluntary agreements at the national and global levels. These strategies are similar to what individual mining companies were undertaking unilaterally and through national mining associations, especially the Mining Association of Canada (MAC) and the Australian Minerals Council (AMC) (Fonseca 2010; Sanchez 1998: 524–8). The ICME was primarily focused on influencing policy development affecting mining, through engagement with multilateral organizations such as the Organisation for Economic Co-operation and Development (OECD) and the United Nations Environment Program (UNEP). The ICMM has focused less on policy and more on developing self-regulatory initiatives with a view to improving the industry's reputation (ICME, Executive 1, December 2, 2011).

The International Council on Metals and the Environment

The creation of the ICME in 1991 represented the mining industry's first effort to coordinate its activities at the global level. The ICME was established in part to coordinate the efforts of various national mining associations, as well as to address the industry's bad reputation. Although the ICME was not set up to promote industry self-regulation, major mining companies hoped to find mechanisms to distinguish between good and bad performers at the global level (Nash, May 26, 2006). The ICME provided an institutional setting at the global level through which the mining industry's interests could be represented and strategic alliances with other resource-producing countries fostered. The primary agenda of the ICME was to provide an industry relationship with multilateral organizations that were involved in the global development of standards and regulations affecting mining (Placer Dome, Executive 2, July 30, 2002). As a major player in the global mining industry, Canadian mining companies had a strong interest in global collaboration to influence global public policy.

The initial impetus behind the decision to launch a global industry association for mining came from Canada. Gary Nash, then a senior official in the Mining Association of Canada, developed the initial concept of a global industry association and was able to get Canadian mining companies onside. Due to Noranda's prominence and contacts within the global mining industry, Nash worked to persuade then President Keith Hendrick to promote the idea (Nash, November 29, 2011). Noranda then presented the idea in 1990 at a meeting of the London Metal Exchange (Nash, May 26, 2006). An eleven-member organizing committee was established, chaired by Nash, to look into how such an international industry association would be constituted. In late 1990, the decision was made to found the ICME, and Nash was appointed CEO.

The newly formed ICME was headquartered in Ottawa, Canada, a reflection of the fact that the initiative came from MAC and was spear-headed by a Canadian mining company. As the first national mining association to produce an *Environmental Policy Statement* in 1989, MAC (also based in Ottawa) influenced the development of ICME's first Environmental Charter (Nash, May 26, 2006). Much of the ICME's senior staff was Canadian, all experienced technical persons with both industry and government experience (Nash, November 29, 2011). They were able to substantively discuss technical issues with member company representatives.

Throughout the mid-1990s, the ICME gave high priority to market access issues, as reflected in ICME budget allocations. A key focus of activity was directed at the Basel Convention on the Control of Transboundary Movements of Hazardous Wastes and their Disposal, which was negotiated to address concerns about the growing traffic and dumping of hazardous wastes into developing countries. In 1994, the ICME Board decided that the ICME should become an active industry participant on the Basel Convention issue, through Basel's Technical Working Group (TWG).

In 1995, Basel Convention negotiators decided to ban the export of hazardous wastes (including those intended for recycling) from developed to developing countries (Decision 111/1). Given the inclusion of many metals in the Convention list of hazardous waste, the mining industry was greatly concerned about the effects on the metals recycling trade (ICME 1998a: 3). The ICME lobbied governments not to ratify the recyclables ban amendment until the TWG had completed its work on the listing of recyclables which should be excluded from the scope of the Convention (ICME 1995a).

The ICME took a science-based approach, by addressing definitional problems around waste definition (i.e., removing recyclables from the waste definition), dealing with toxicity issues, distinguishing between metals versus liquids, and other technical issues (Nash, November 29, 2011). According to Alex Balogh, then deputy chair of Noranda, and at the time, Chair of the ICME, "this thing [Basel] is so broad and pervasive that it's ridiculous . . . we have no problem with its objectives, it's the way it's being implemented" (McKenna 1995). In light of these concerns, ICME's goal was to prevent the creation of environmental trade barriers under the Convention which would ban the export of recyclables, including metal scraps and residues, from OECD to non-OECD countries.

In the view of one participant, the ICME was able to influence global public policy in a constructive and responsible manner (Placer Dome, Executive 2, November 13, 2011). Initiatives to promote improved performance took the form of a broad statement of principles, and efforts at industry self-regulation were not part of its agenda. The ICME's Environmental Charter, for example, was approved by the Board in 1993 (ICME 1994: 4–5), and consisted of Environmental Stewardship Principles and Product Stewardship Principles. Its significance lies in the fact that it represented the first attempt to apply environmental principles for the mining industry on a worldwide basis, by providing a common framework of principles for all companies.

The ICME sought to promote best practices by educating its members about how to improve their environmental performance, as well as about evolving global environmental management standards. For example, in October 1995, the Safe Use of Metals Committee of the ICME held a workshop on environmental risk assessment to disseminate information about best practices surrounding the principles and methodologies of risk assessment and the management of chemicals (ICME 1995b). As a heavy user of chemicals, their safe management is an area of upmost importance to the mining industry. The ICME tracked developments in the International Organization for Standardization (ISO), including the development of the 14000 environmental management series.

Although the ICME performed effectively within its mandate, it became apparent by the late 1990s that it was unable to counter the reputational crisis the industry was facing. The ICME was set up to address issues of a scientific/technical nature and was not well-equipped to address reputational issues. The communications function was to promote broad principles, rather than concrete standards for the industry. The *Environmental Charter*, for example, which was revised in 1998, remained a statement of broad aspirational principles, although the list had expanded from the earlier version (ICME 1998). Such a strategy could not compete with the string of major environmental disasters, the resultant further deterioration in the industry's reputation, and shifting societal values with respect to the environment.

Indeed, from the perspective of NGOs, the major priorities of the ICME reflect an organization keen to forestall changes adverse to the industry, but with little reciprocal collaborative effort to promote standards for the industry. For example, after the tailings dam failure in Guyana (Cambior/Golden Star Resources) in 1995, the UNEP became concerned and wanted to work with the ICME on this issue. Noranda supported this idea, but the ICME board was opposed. According to the Minutes of the October 1995 Environmental Stewardship Committee (ESC) meeting, "a strong view was expressed that ICME should not be jointly involved with UNEP in tailings dam issues" (ICME 1995a). In light of subsequent tailings dam failures (Marcopper, Placer Dome, 1996; Spain, Bolidan, 1998), this decision on the part of ICME appears to have been an unfortunate one (Foot 1998). Indeed, after subsequent tailings dam failures, the ICME and UNEP moved in 1998 to identify tailings issues as a key challenge and priority for the industry (*Northern Miner* 1998: 4). The industry's reaction after the fact gave the impression it was engaging in damage control.

Learning and norms dissemination: evolution of the sustainable development norm

Shifts in thinking about sustainable development

By the mid-to-late 1990s, the global mining industry had taken note of the continued and growing momentum behind sustainable development. While mining company executives were aware of the implications for the legitimacy of the mining industry, the adoption of sustainable development as a means to frame their CSR policies was by no means an inevitable or pre-determined outcome. Although there has been convergence around the norm of sustainable development as it relates to mining, institutional factors and norms dissemination dynamics are a necessary part of the explanation for the isomorphic processes that have taken place.

Many major mining companies in the mid-1990s were uncomfortable with the concept, as well as the implications, of sustainable development for the mining industry (Cooney 2008). Aside from the fact that mining involves the extraction of a depletable resource, sustainable development at the time was a concept more closely associated with the industry's adversaries: environmental and social advocacy groups, public officials, academics, and left-leaning politicians (Cooney 2008).

When preparation of a sustainable development charter was being considered by the ICME in the late 1990s, for example, a member of ICME's Communications and Public Policy Committee (CPPC) prepared a discussion paper entitled: "Sustainable Development – The Socialism of the 1990s" (Company A, Executive 1 1998). As the title implies, sustainable development is seen as an attack on free-market capitalism by the "intellectual class," who, with the demise of socialism after the end of the Cold War, are seen to employ the "environmentalist critique of capitalism" as the new "legitimating doctrine." In recommending against the ICME's adoption of sustainable development, the author suggests that it would be equivalent to ICME "wearing clothes designed for others and handed down many times . . . it would be an embarrassing display of ill-fitting apparel" (Company A, Executive 1 1998).

The views expressed above are broadly representative of the mining industry in the 1990s and into the early 2000s (Placer Dome, Executive 2, August 11, 2011). Although the value and importance of avoiding environmental degradation and promoting economic development were appreciated, the concern was about buying into an integrated paradigm or set of interrelationships that were not fully understood. There was a widespread sense that sustainable development was the creation of European social democrats, and that by adopting sustainable development, the industry would be caving in to adversaries (Placer Dome, Executive 2, August 11, 2011).

This view was not the preserve of those in the mining industry. In an address to the Prospectors and Developers Association of Canada, Patrick Moore, a founding member of Greenpeace, opined that, with the fall of the Berlin Wall, "the international peace movement had a lot less to do," and many pro-Soviet groups in the West moved into the environmental movement (Moore 1997). That having been said, Moore suggested that the best way for mining companies to counter "environmental extremism" was to get their own house in order, and adopt "the philosophy of sustainability as their central goal for strategic planning" (Moore 1997).

The belief that business was caving in to unreasonable demands from environmentalists is reflected in the following view point: "some business groups seem willing to cede the moral and intellectual high ground in return for the right to collaborate on the design of the resulting [international environmental] regulations ... business may even be granted 'consultative' status – as long as they refrain from questioning the basic principles of modern environmental orthodoxy" (Competitive Enterprise Institute 1995).

These perhaps extreme views aside, discussions began behind closed doors within the ICME around 1996 about the significance of sustainable development to mining (Nash, May 26, 2006). These discussions were led by Nash, and Canadian mining companies such as Noranda and Placer Dome played an important role in gaining support for sustainable development. Given that the ICME staff was largely Canadian, and that key companies such as Noranda and Placer Dome had become convinced about the normative validity of sustainable development, strong country-of-origin effects influenced the direction the ICME was heading.

There is evidence that, by the late 1990s, industry was beginning to see a connection between sustainable development and the social impacts of their operations. For example, when the ICME revised the *Environmental Charter* (1998), a section on "community responsibility principles" was added, in addition to the statement of product stewardship principles and environmental stewardship principles. The community responsibility principles included a commitment to "respect the cultures, customs and values" of local communities affected by mining, the recognition of local communities as stakeholders, and to "contribute to and participate in the social, economic and institutional development of communities where operations are located and mitigate adverse effects in these communities to the greatest practical extent" (ICME 1998b).

It was in relation to the social issues arising from mining that sustainable development came to have some meaning for the industry. The impact of mining on communities, and the need for better understanding of the different cultural contexts where mining takes place, drove the connection between the social issues the industry was facing, and sustainable development (Nash, May 26, 2006). Evidence that the ICME was gathering information about what sustainable development might mean for the mining sector is reflected in a 1998 issue of the ICME *Newsletter*. In an article by a World Bank official, the key elements of a sustainable development strategy for the mineral sector are discussed (Ackermann 1998). A key point made in the article is that sustainable development is not just about environmental sustainability, but social sustainability as well. The author pushes for social assessments, in addition to the by-then-accepted environmental assessments, as an acknowledgment of the legitimacy of all stakeholder perspectives (ibid.: 2). The point was driven home that the World Bank Group had developed environmental and social guidelines that it was implementing when considering funding projects (ibid.: 6) (a key concern for mining companies seeking financing for projects in developing countries).

At the same time (1998) that the *Environmental Charter* was being revised, there was an internal push within the ICME to rename the Charter a "Sustainable Development" Charter. Led by Placer Dome, the thinking was to convert the existing environmental charter with a "minimum of change" (Placer Dome, email exchange, 1998b). The email exchange included a strategy for out-maneuvering a member of ICME's Communications and Public Policy Committee, who was expected to resist the changes, by bringing the draft revised document to the ICME board, where it was expected the individual would be more easily outvoted (Placer Dome, email exchange, 1998b).

The resistance to sustainable development was not simply a reflection of a refusal to recognize the need to improve the industry's record; the industry found the concept genuinely challenging. In seeking to address the environmental challenges confronting the industry, there was a strong emphasis on science-based technological improvements (McAllister 2007). The ICME's *Environmental Charter*, for example, reflected a very strong preference for science-based approaches to addressing the industry's environmental problems: "ICME emphasizes the importance of *sound science* and technical and economic analyses to support its position and to improve environmental and health standards internationally" (ICME 1993–4: 4–5). Similar wording appeared in the revised 1998 *Environmental Charter*: "ICME ... emphasizes the importance of sound science and technical and socio-economic analyses to support its position," as well as in the 2000 *Sustainable Development Charter* (ICME 2000).

Efforts to address the environmental aspects of sustainable development fit the engineering mindset reasonably well because sustainable development seeks to deliver measurable outcomes, which are more readily obtained in measures of environmental performance (Placer Dome, Executive 2, November 13, 2011). Social dimensions of sustainable development are less amenable to measurement, and it is harder to conceptualize what the optimal outcome should be. As the saying goes, "if it can't be measured, it can't be managed," which made the moving target of social issues difficult for the mining mindset to deal with.

Efforts to address the political and social challenges confronting the industry were therefore more challenging, as these are often not conducive to technological solutions. As McAllister notes, the mining industry had traditionally been "educated in such fields as geology, engineering and finance . . . and none of these disciplines adequately equip the personnel with the tools required to operate" in the complex external environment that had emerged in the 1990s (McAllister 2007: 200). One key aspect of the "mining/engineering mindset" is a preference for results-oriented problem-solving, where the outcome is clear and predictable (Dashwood 2007a; Placer Dome, Executive 2, November 13, 2011). Engineers and miners are trained to deal with well-defined problems, where causality is clear and solutions clear-cut. Sustainable development is quite ambiguous, and therefore, was seen as problematic.

A key aspect of the problem on the social side is with respect to interaction with local communities. In pushing the need for public consultation at the community level, it was noted that "the biggest failing in this area is that the first people into a new prospect are usually geologists with little or no training in working with local communities, particularly those of another culture" (Moore 1997). The answer was not to hire public relations specialists, as some mining companies were doing, but rather, to hire professionals with knowledge of local community dynamics (Moore 1997). Rio Tinto, for example, was one of the first mining companies to hire a social anthropologist, to better understand the local communities where it was operating.

The lack of attention to the social side of sustainable development was reflected in industry as a whole in the 1990s. For example, the World Business Council for Sustainable Development (WBCSD) tended to focus on the "eco-efficiency" side of sustainable development, to the general neglect of the social side (Focus Report 1997). By the late 1990s, the WBCSD had become more proactive in stressing the social side of sustainable development as well. As the then President, Bjorn Stigson noted, for companies to be able to secure a "social licence to operate," they must learn to strike the right balance between economic growth, environmental protection, and social progress (Stigson 1998: 1). That balance, he argued, influences a company's growth potential, earnings and investor confidence, affecting the risk and value considerations of prospective investors (Stigson 1998: 2).

Evolving thinking within the WBCSD influenced mining companies, as they saw that other industries were beginning to accept sustainable development (Nash, May 26, 2006). WMC, Rio Tinto, and Noranda were members of the executive of the WBCSD, and even if not all these companies were convinced about sustainable development, broader trends within industry reinforced the importance of the norm. The WBCSD's evolution towards appreciating the social side of sustainable development influenced Noranda in gaining internal acceptance of the norm (Noranda, Executive 2, October 23, 2011).

In a similar vein, John Elkington's famous notion of the "triple bottom line," popularized in the late 1990s, represented a call for industry to wake up to the social side of sustainable development (Elkington 1998). Among his key insights of relevance for mining was the need for business to recognize the shift in values, from growth at any cost to sustainability, the movement away from sole dependence on facts and science to emotions and perceptions, and the movement away from one-way, passive communication to multi-way, active dialogue (Elkington 1998). Reacting to what at the time was the new notion of the "triple bottom line," an editorialist for the business section of Canada's leading newspaper declared that "Canada's business sector has set itself up for a takeover by an ideology that is completely at odds with its own best interests" (Corcoran 1998).

Initially, mining companies in the ICME saw sustainable development as a communications challenge, reflecting the belief that the economic, social, and environmental performance of the mining industry was better than the public perception (Cooney 2008). It was thereby felt that the appropriate strategy should be to close the "perception gap" by persuading the public that mining is consistent with sustainable development (Cooney 2008). The weakness of this communications strategy was that it was one-way, ignoring the need for dialogue with mining's external stakeholders.

In 2000, after further discussions and informal consultation with NGOs, the ICME's Sustainable Development Charter was released. Although the broad features of the Sustainable Development Charter resemble the updated Environmental Charter produced in 1998, it included a considerably expanded list of environmental and community responsibility principles. In the preamble, for example, it is stated that "ICME members recognize the benefits of integrating environmental, social and economic aspects into their decision-making processes" (ICME 2000). The preamble further notes that "ICME members acknowledge that sustainable development is a corporate priority." A key addition to the community responsibility principles was a commitment to "assess the social, cultural, environmental and economic impacts of proposed activities and engage with local communities and other affected organizations in the design of community development strategies." In a nod to the life cycle approach, a further commitment was to "reduce to acceptable levels the adverse environmental and social impacts on communities of activities related to exploration, extraction and closure of mining and processing facilities" (ICME 2000).

The release of the Sustainable Development Charter reveals that there was growing consensus among major mining companies about the appropriateness of adopting sustainable development to frame CSR initiatives. The work of the ICME was carried out largely by ICME staff and senior management, however, and CEOs feared they were losing control of the process (Placer Dome, Executive 2, November 13, 2011). By the time the Sustainable Development Charter was released, CEOs of major mining companies had already launched the Global Mining Initiative, and momentum was building to replace the ICME with the ICMM.

The Global Mining Initiative and the Mining, Minerals and Sustainable Development project

The path towards consensus around sustainable development that was reached by the mid-2000s was neither smooth nor linear. In December 1998, CEOs from nine major mining companies came to the view that a bold new initiative was needed to turn things around, leading to the launch of the GMI. Mining CEOs recognized that the industry was in danger of being "legislated out of business," and that it was necessary to reposition the mining industry (Noranda, Executive 2, October 28, 2003). At the same time, the CEOs felt that the

ICME was moving too fast, and wanted to take control of the process (Nash, November 30, 2011; Placer Dome, Executive 2, August 11, 2011; ICME, Executive 1, December 2, 2011). In effect, CEOs decided to "step outside the industry position that was emerging in the ICME Charter and outside the established network of relationships centered on the ICME" (Cooney 2008).

The ultimate industry-wide acceptance of sustainable development was not inevitable and it took concerted leadership from the top to move mining companies along. Some more forward-thinking CEOs recognized that the industry had little credibility in the eyes of governments, NGOs, and international agencies, and were cognizant of the fact that the industry's critics maintained control of the communications agenda (Cooney 2008). As noted by the CEO of BHP, although initiatives to address sustainable development were already under way, "these actions appear to lack the critical mass required to achieve the shift in performance that is clearly required" (McNeilly 2000). He further noted in the same address that the purpose of the GMI is to "listen, learn and engage." The key concern, then, was reputational, and a desire to move the industry away from the "dumb, dirty and dangerous" image it had in some circles.

Under the leadership of Sir Robert Wilson, at that time CEO of Rio Tinto, the original group of companies included Noranda, Placer Dome, Anglo American, Western Mining Company (WMC), Codelco, BHP, (BHP subsequently merged with Billiton in 2001), Phelps Dodge (which pulled out in October 2002), and Newmont. Some of these companies were members of the Mining and Minerals Working Group of the WBCSD (for details, see ICMM 2005). The WBCSD was the organization of choice to spearhead the GMI. As Sir Robert Wilson noted, "I would say that the WBCSD has a voice and authority which is remarkably free of the taint of being a lobby group and is listened to seriously by governments, inter-governmental agencies and NGOs, as well as by industry" (WBCSD 2004). As noted already, the shift in thinking about sustainable development within the WBCSD was an important influence on Noranda (Executive 2, October 23, 2011). The CEOs of these leading companies sought to "project a strong image of being open-minded and willing to listen with fresh attention" (Cooney 2008).

The WBCSD also provided CEOs with the means to step outside the organizational base of the ICME (ICME, Executive 1, December 2, 2011). By stepping outside the larger ICME, and forming a smaller grouping, it was easier to assert control and manage the GMI process.

Some executives hoped to buy time in the face of concerns that their companies' own practices needed a chance to catch up (Placer Dome, Executive 2, August 11, 2011).

As fiercely competitive mining companies, not all the members of the GMI were driven by the same motivations, but many were driven by early mover considerations. Interviews with Noranda and Placer Dome confirm that they were motivated by conviction about the appropriateness of sustainable development. These companies also, however, sought to project a different image from their competition, in the expectation that better performers would be distinguished from weak performers (Placer Dome, Executive 2, January 25, 2006).

Placer Dome came to an understanding about the business case for sustainable development, based on the belief that adherence would strengthen society's support for mining, reduce exposure to environmental and social risks, provide a competitive advantage in accessing business opportunities, and facilitate the permitting and development of projects (Cooney 1998). This thinking was echoed by R. J. McNeilly, Executive Director and President of what was then BHP Minerals: "While on the one hand the mood of disquiet presents many challenges, it also provides those of us who are willing to get out on the front foot in addressing the issues, and engaging in the dialogue, with a very significant opportunity to create a major competitive advantage" (McNeilly 2000).

From the initial meeting of the GMI in December 1998, the 2002 World Summit on Sustainable Development was at the top of everyone's mind, and the industry needed to prepare a position piece (Noranda, Executive 2, October 28, 2003). The mining industry felt that at the Rio Conference on Environment and Development in 1992, mining had been mentioned only as a problem, because government representation had been by Environment Ministries (ICME, Executive 1, May 25, 2006). Of further concern to mining companies was that NGOs were increasingly involved not just in setting the environmental agenda, but in participating in decision-making in global fora, as became clear at Rio. CEOs hoped to influence the agenda at the World Summit, and anticipated the need to have an industry position on sustainable development. In May 1999, to move forward on this task, members of the GMI launched the Mining, Minerals and Sustainable Development (MMSD) project.

The MMSD was a major program of participatory analysis and research, whose key objective was to advance understanding about how the mining and mineral sector's contribution to sustainable development at the global, national, regional, and local levels could be maximized (Dashwood 2005; Sethi 2005). Drawing on Kingdon's framework (1995), it could be argued that the looming 2002 World Summit provided a "policy window" which presented an opportunity for change agents to push the industry forward on sustainable development. Collaborative efforts serve as a vehicle through which mining companies seek to frame and influence CSR norms as they relate to the mining sector. The creation of the ICME and later, the ICMM, allowed the mining industry to have direct representation in the various international bodies dealing with an array of issues that were, or had the potential to, affect mining. As noted by Noranda, the "ICMM recognized the need for a global voice, or risk being deemed irrelevant" (Executive 2, October 28, 2003). Another objective was "to avoid reactionary market closures based on incomplete information and maintain land access for mining" (Noranda 2000: 21).

The MMSD project was an exercise in collective education, as members of the GMI recognized that the mining industry itself had to learn about the role of mining in sustainable development, in light of all the skepticism. It further reflected recognition that if industry was to make a convincing case that it was not undermining sustainable development, it would have to come to an understanding of what sustainable development would entail in the context of mining. As much as the MMSD project hoped to convince the public that the industry is committed to sustainable development, it was also about transforming the concept into something understandable to the mining community (ICME, Executive 1, December 2, 2011).

The MMSD project reflected an emerging consensus that in order for the mining industry to address the crisis it was facing, the GMI could not just be a mining initiative, but would have to include other stakeholders as well. In this respect, inspiration was drawn from the Whitehorse Mining Initiative (WMI) launched in Canada in the early 1990s. Supporters of the GMI and MMSD process recognized that sustainable development is not something that mining companies can achieve on their own; it requires collaboration with stakeholders and other relevant institutions (Cooney 2008). A key lesson of the MMSD was that everybody (industry, government, NGOs) has a role to play in promoting sustainable development (Noranda, Executive 2, December 2, 2011).

The format of the MMSD was modeled on the WMI, but was globally based, and grew to include almost forty mining companies, at a cost of over US$9 million, not including the Toronto Conference (Noranda,

Executive 2, December 2, 2011). In addition to mining companies, NGOs, and industry associations, academics and other stakeholders were invited to participate. The process culminated in May 2002 with the publication of the MMSD's final report, *Breaking New Ground* (MMSD 2002) and with a major GMI conference hosted by Noranda in Toronto, Canada, which brought together all of the major players within the global mining sector. At this international conference, the Toronto Declaration was issued, which set out a list of commitments for implementation, drawing on the report (www.icmm.com/library).

Although there were detractors, such as some critical NGOs and global indigenous organizations, at the time the project was the largest such multistakeholder process in any industrial sector (McPhail 2008; Sethi 2005; Young 2005). *Breaking New Ground* was not intended as a consensus document between all the various participants, as this would have been difficult to achieve. Such high-profile NGOs as Earthworks and Mining Watch Canada refused to participate in the MMSD process. Some NGOs, such as Project Underground (now defunct) and indigenous organizations, such as the Indigenous Peoples' International Centre for Policy Research and Education, were suspicious of the MMSD project, and did not endorse the final report (Tauli-Corpuz and Kennedy 2001). A key challenge for the ICMM would thereby be to counter criticisms that the MMSD was not merely a public relations exercise, and demonstrate through action that it was prepared to follow up on the recommendations flowing from the MMSD process.

In late 2001, it was decided that the ICME be transformed into the ICMM, so as to provide a more effective organizational architecture that would strengthen industry representation, promote a more ambitious mandate than had been pursued by the ICME, and support the industry transition to sustainable development (McPhail 2008). (Politics were also a factor, as the ICME was headquartered in Ottawa, and the new ICMM is headquartered in London, headquarters of the spearheading company, Rio Tinto.) Significantly, the ICMM was granted a larger mandate to promote change than had been the case with the ICME (Noranda, Executive 2, October 23, 2011). Furthermore, the creation of the ICMM was meant to ensure that policy recommendations flowing from the MMSD actually be acted upon, a lesson learned from the Canadian Whitehorse Mining Initiative, which dropped the ball because there was no individual or organization mandated to carry the findings forward (Noranda, Executive 2, October 23, 2011; Weitzner 2010).

One positive outcome that made this more likely was the creation through the ICMM of a mechanism for ongoing consultation between the mining industry and leading international NGOs, such as the International Union for the Conservation of Nature (IUCN). The ICMM also created an Association Committee, to which all commodity and mining associations were invited to join, in order to encourage communications and collaboration between the various associations (Noranda, Executive 2, October 23, 2011). They attend their own meeting, semi-annually, along with the ICMM's meetings, and participate in the various working groups.

Founding members of the GMI that subsequently joined the ICMM include Noranda (whose CEO served as Chair of the Executive Committee), Newmont, Placer Dome, WMC, Anglo American, BHP-Billiton, and Rio Tinto. Not all of the original members of the ICMM had launched the GMI, but they did all subsequently participate in the MMSD. These included Alcoa, AngloGold, Freeport-McMoRan, Sumitomo, Mitsubishi, Nippon, Pasminco, and Umicore. At the inaugural meeting of the ICMM in September 2002, four members – Phelps Dodge, Codelco, Inco, and Barrick – withdrew voluntarily. Phelps Dodge pulled out because of a change of leadership, which came as a total surprise to the retiring CEO (Noranda, Executive 2, December 2, 2011). Codelco pulled out because executives were uncomfortable with what they saw as intrusion in their independence (as a state-owned company). Inco and Barrick had previously stated that there was a lack of budget control, and formally announced their resignations at the meeting (Noranda, Executive 2, October 23, 2011). The smaller size of the ICMM relative to the ICME ensured a more cohesive group of members who, even if still uncertain about sustainable development, were prepared to commit to sustainable development as a norm informing future initiatives of the ICMM. Barring the impact of mergers and acquisitions, the ICMM's membership remained stable for the next few years, and started to attract new members, including from emerging economies, after it had established itself from the mid-2000s.

In addition to the need to represent industry at the World Summit, the second immediate task of the ICMM was to provide representation for the mining industry at the World Bank's Extractive Industry Review (EIR) process (www.eir.com). The EIR was the direct result of pressure from some NGOs and governments, which felt that the GMI/MMSD had been too industry-centric and that too much had been conceded to mining at the World Summit (Placer Dome, Executive 2, January 25, 2006). The mining industry was very concerned about the EIR process, fearing it was losing the agenda to NGOs (Executive 1, ICME, May 25, 2006). As a multistakeholder process, it was considered risky to treat governments as merely stakeholders, which were perceived by the mining industry to be largely absent in the decision-making process.

The EIR was of particular concern, as some NGOs with representation (such as Greenpeace) were of the view that the Bank should not be lending to the extractive industry at all if prior and informed consent of the local communities affected by the operations had not been attained (Placer Dome, Executive 2, January 25, 2006). There was also a concern on the part of industry that, through the EIR process, expectations would be raised too high (Nash, May 26, 2006). The fear that NGOs could indirectly influence regulations through their advocacy of tougher international standards for mining (Walde 2005) served as another incentive to form the ICMM.

The EIR was directed by Emil Salim, the former Environment Minister of Indonesia, and ended in 2004 with a call for the Bank to withdraw all investment in oil and gas projects for a period of five years (Anonymous 2004). Although the Bank's Board did not adopt this recommendation, the EIR process ultimately resulted in the development of the International Finance Corporation's (IFC) Policy and Performance Standards on Social and Environmental Sustainability (IFC 2006). The IFC Performance Standards are very influential, because private financial institutions, through the Equator Principles, also adhere to these standards.

ICMM sustainable development initiatives

Perhaps the most significant outcome of the MMSD was that it fostered learning at the global level about what are the most significant challenges facing the industry, and it was a major learning mechanism for mining companies in terms of what sustainable development should mean for the industry. The MMSD process also produced a significant shift in attitudes on the part of mining companies, and helped break down resistance to change. One hundred NGOs were invited to attend the Toronto Conference, and their participation helped bring the temperature down, both on the part of industry and NGOs. Recognition of the importance of moving the industry to a higher level was reflected in the fact that twenty-three CEOs were brought together in the same room at the Toronto Conference, quite an accomplishment (Noranda, Executive 2, December 2, 2011).

Although the title of the MMSD project makes it seem as though embracing sustainable development was a fait accompli, the key task before the industry was to define sustainable development in the context of mining. The self-assessment of past industry performance that came out of the MMSD report was quite frank, with words such as "bad" and "abysmal" used to refer to environmental performance, including the implementation of environmental management systems (MMSD 2002).

The need to incorporate social impact assessment into the environmental impact assessment process was one key insight of the MMSD, and one that had been acknowledged in the past, but was now clearly recognized as needing to be acted upon (MMSD 2002: xxi). The proposal for Community Sustainable Development Plans marked an important advancement for the industry, providing companies with a framework and set of tools for moving forward in this critical area (MMSD 2002: xxviii).

The motivations for industry collaboration found their way into the stated strategy of the ICMM, namely to: 1. repair the mining industry's bad reputation through dissemination of best practices; 2. earn a seat at the table of international organizations such as the World Bank, where standards affecting mining were being set; and 3. enhance the legitimacy of mining through engagement with external stakeholders (ICMM 2003b). In treating sustainable development as a fundamental principle guiding operations, it is hoped that "continued access to land under clear and equitable rules; continued market access and recognition of minerals and metals as materials of choice" (ICMM 2003b) will be attained.

The most important initiative launched by the ICMM is the Sustainable Development Framework (ICMM 2003a). Adherence to the Sustainable Development Framework is a condition of membership, and was seen as a way to differentiate good performers from bad ones as well as a means to avoid the problem of free riders (Noranda, Executive 2, October 23, 2011). The ICMM defines sustainable development as "investments [that are] financially profitable, technically appropriate, environmentally sound and socially responsible" (ICMM 2003a).

The second major initiative of the ICMM is to establish reporting mechanisms for the mining sector, against which mining companies can report on their environmental, social, and economic performance (ICMM 2003a). Although criticized for a variety of reasons, the GRI emerged as one of the foremost global standards for reporting on environmental and social performance (Fonseca 2010). In 2000, the GRI was revised to incorporate "sustainability" indicators ("G2") and in 2005, the third revised version was published ("G3") (GRI 2006). There was some pushback from industry against the GRI, as many companies did not want to take on the burden of reporting, "just for the sake of reporting" (Executive 1, past Vice-President, MAC, May 26, 2006).

In light of this, the ICMM worked with the GRI to prepare a separate mining and metals supplement, and to develop reporting indicators relevant to the mining industry (GRI 2007). The Mining and Metals Sector Supplement (MMSS) of the GRI was adopted by the ICMM in 2005, so as to provide a set of common indicators that could be uniformly applied across the industry.

The third element of the Sustainable Development Framework is the commitment to independent third party assurance. Third party assurance is a condition of membership in the ICMM, but the problem has been finding a credible, independent assurance process recognized as legitimate by external stakeholders (a problem widely noted in the literature as applicable to all industries) (Dando and Swift 2003; Fonseca 2010; MacLean and Revernak 2007). To address this problem, the ICMM developed a pilot assurance procedure, based on AccountAbility's AA1000 standard (www.accountability21.net) and the global accounting industry's International Standard for Assurance Engagement (ISAE) ISAE3000 standard.

The AA1000AS standard was chosen for external verification of reports because it incorporates principles that are considered more inclusive and responsive to stakeholders' concerns (AccountAbility 2008; Fonseca 2010). Starting with reports published in 2010 for the 2009 reporting year, member companies are required to provide external assurance on both their commitment to the Sustainable Development Framework principles, as well as reporting in accordance with GRI guidelines (McPhail 2008). The mining industry is at the forefront of industry in reducing the information asymmetries inherent in industry reports to external stakeholders (Fonseca 2010). In a context where repairing reputation is a key motivating factor for ICMM members, the ICMM has been compelled to introduce increasingly stringent conditions of membership, culminating with the verifiable external independent assurance initiative.

At the global level, there are now a set of global voluntary standards that represent accepted practice for adherence to sustainable development in the industry. In addition to the Sustainable Development Framework and GRI Mining and Metals Sector Supplement developed under the auspices of the ICMM, a number of other initiatives developed outside the ICMM have acquired wide acceptance. Virtually all members of the ICMM have started to have their sites certified under ISO 14001, an indication of the status of that environmental management standard as an accepted norm of business practice for major mining companies.

Other initiatives developed outside the ICMM have seen some uptake amongst members of the ICMM. The IFC Performance Standards (2006, revised 2011), for example, were the result of multi-stakeholder consultations with government, industry, and NGOs in the aftermath of the World Bank's Extractive Industry Review. Although not "voluntary" in the strict sense, some companies are adopting the Performance Standards as corporate policy, regardless of whether or not they have a particular project being financed by the Bank. Private financial institutions, through the Equator Principles, also uphold the Performance Standards. The Extractive Industries Transparency Initiative (EITI) is another example of a tri-partite initiative involving government, NGOs, and extractive companies. Once again, although "voluntary," once a government decides to join the EITI, mining companies must report the royalties paid to government. The Voluntary Principles on Security and Human Rights incorporates a tri-partite governance structure, and they have become an important indicator of a company's ability to manage its human rights challenges, and respect human rights at its operations.

Involvement of individual companies

Noranda and Placer Dome

Why were some mining companies early movers, and why did some take on a leadership role in promoting industry-wide collaboration? In addressing these questions, there are two different challenges that firms in the mining sector face. First, there is the challenge they face individually in considering how to respond to the pressure for sustainable development norms. Second, there is the challenge of how to coordinate CSR initiatives across firms so as to fend off NGO pressure and possible regulation, but also to protect against the bad actions of single firms tarnishing the industry as a whole. The internal attributes that influenced early movers with their unilateral CSR initiatives also inform why some of these companies chose to play a leadership role. The firm-level decisions of the case-study companies shed light on the motives behind, and challenges inherent in, industry collaboration.

The experiences of Noranda and Placer Dome in stakeholder consultation and engagement through the WMI influenced their approach to global collaborative efforts. The WMI taught some Canadian mining companies the value of engaging with their critics (Placer Dome, Executive 2, November 13, 2011). They also had early exposure to the concept of sustainable development, and what it might mean for mining. Early movers such as Noranda and Placer Dome were cognizant of the growing global importance of sustainable development by the early 1990s. The shifting global normative context was identified by the company executives interviewed for this study as an important influence on their decision to adopt sustainable development.

Noranda and Placer Dome had extensive external relations with a wide range of stakeholders, including governments, NGOs, international organizations, and national and global industry associations. Senior management recognized the need to manage external relations effectively, and to be able to keep abreast of evolving thinking on CSR, and to respond to issues as they emerged (Noranda, Executive 2, October 28, 2003; Placer Dome, Executive 2, January 25, 2006). Both companies saw the advantage of being proactive, rather than reactive, to shifting societal norms. Placer Dome sought to construct alliances with other institutions that have credibility around the world, such as international financial institutions, bilateral aid agencies, NGOs focused on economic development and social and environmental issues, and with local communities (Executive 2, January 25, 2006). Such a strategy would not only improve the company's reputation through association with legitimate agencies, but allow it to continually acquire information and learn about emerging issues and shifting societal expectations.

Noranda also had extensive external relations. It participated, for example, in the ISO initiative to develop the ISO 14000 guidelines and several senior managers were members of Canada's management team on ISO 14000. Noranda sat on the Board of the World Industry Council on the Environment (WICE), and when WICE merged with the Business Council on Sustainable Development in 1995, Noranda's Chair and

CEO, David Kerr, sat on the newly formed World Business Council for Sustainable Development and in 1997, he served as Vice-Chair.

Senior management at Placer Dome recognized that the company was part of a larger whole, and that it needed to look at the bigger picture beyond its own corporation (Executive 2, January 25, 2006). Since the nature of mining companies' operations mean that "they are in for the long term," they "need to demonstrate good performance" in order to obtain permits and a license to operate (Noranda, Executive 2, October 28, 2003). Such thinking demonstrates that early movers were already pre-disposed to play a leadership role in promoting global collaborative engagement. Companies that found the ICMM appealing were those that saw themselves as leaders, and on the leading edge of voluntary initiatives (Executive 1, then Vice-President, MAC, May 26, 2006).

The thinking in Noranda and Placer Dome was echoed by other early movers as well. Although WMC cannot be said to have been sold on sustainable development, Hugh Morgan, then CEO of WMC, observed that "at WMC, sustainable development is emerging as part of our business strategy and as a potential source of competitive advantage ... viewing investment and operational decisions through this 'frame' provides insight that may not otherwise be available" (Morgan 1998: 2).

As reflected in the interviews with executives at Noranda and Placer Dome, a variety of factors influenced thinking on the desirability of global collaboration. Global coordination was seen as necessary to deal with "big ticket" issues affecting the industry, allowing companies to confront and address common problems facing them all (Noranda, Executive 2, October 28, 2003). By the late 1990s, it became apparent to leaders in the industry that a concerted collaborative effort was necessary to combat reputational issues. The visibility of the major mining companies, and the targeting of them by NGOs, while lesser-known mid-tier and junior companies slipped under the radar, provided another incentive for major mining companies to assume a leadership role.

In keeping with an understanding of the institutional forces at work within industry associations, it was anticipated that a global industry association would provide a forum to discuss contentious issues, thereby "lowering the temperature of dialogue" within individual companies, and minimizing push-back against change (Noranda, Executive 2, October 28, 2003). With more and more companies and their national mining associations taking on CSR initiatives, there was growing concern over the fact that various companies and national associations were doing different things. The ICMM was seen as a means to coordinate various initiatives at the national level, to ensure companies and national associations were going down the same road (Noranda, Executive 2, October 28, 2003).

Barrick Gold Corporation

The response of Barrick to the emerging norm of sustainable development, as well as its approach to global collaboration, can be contrasted with that of Placer Dome and Noranda. As noted above, the mining industry as a whole had significant reservations about the ambiguity surrounding how sustainable development should be defined. Placer Dome, and especially Noranda, shared these reservations about sustainable development, yet these companies responded in very different ways. Management at Placer Dome and Noranda became convinced that sustainable development was an appropriate normative frame in which to promote industry self-regulation at the global level, and opted for a proactive stance in promoting industry-wide global efforts to give meaning to sustainable development relevant to mining. These companies' status as major mining companies, and the global scope of their operations, provided a strong incentive for them to address reputational issues through global collaboration. There was a strategic calculus about the benefits of being early movers in shaping mining industry norms, but also a degree of conviction about the intrinsic value of aligning the mining industry with the norm of sustainable development.

In Barrick's case, the lack of a global profile and what at the time was still a modest position within the industry in terms of production, meant the incentives to participate in a global collaborative industry-wide effort were not as strong. Barrick assumed a leadership role in developing the International Cyanide Management Code (ICMC), an initiative specific to its business of gold mining, but stepped back from industry-wide collaboration after the ICME was replaced by the ICMM. Barrick joined the ICMM during the initial transition process, and then pulled out shortly thereafter (as did Inco, Codelco, and Phelps Dodge) (Executive 1, October 14, 2011).

Barrick continues to evince a preference for CSR as a concept framing its various CSR initiatives. Whereas Noranda changed the title of its EHS reports to "sustainable development" reports, and Placer Dome moved to name its first report a "sustainable development" report,

Barrick continues to use the concept of CSR to frame its initiatives, preferring to call its reports "Responsibility Reports." Nevertheless, sustainable development informs Barrick's community engagement guidelines and the company undertakes many voluntary initiatives that are consistent with sustainable development. What explains the differences in Barrick's response to common external pressures relative to Noranda and Placer Dome? Although structural dynamics are clearly relevant, one must look to managerial discretion in order to provide a complete explanation.

Interviews with Barrick officials reveal that part of the concern with the ICMM was that management felt the initiatives were too broad in scope, involving all global mining companies (Executive 2, May 28, 2003). Management also felt that the costs of trying to promote global collaborative efforts through the ICMM were disproportionate with expected results, and that Barrick's money would be better spent on the ground (Executive 1, May 6, 2003). Management expressed concern that the initiatives being proposed by the ICMM were so broad in scope that they would be too watered down to be meaningful, and could lead to rising expectations that might not get fulfilled (Executive 2, May 28, 2003). As one executive noted, "the fear is not making commitments, but making commitments that are perceived to have failed" (Executive 2, May 28, 2003).

At the time (2001), there was general concern that the GMI/MMSD process was being co-opted by then Chair of the GMI, Robert Wilson of Rio Tinto (Executive 2, May 28, 2003). This concern was not altogether unfounded, given Rio Tinto's motivations for leading the GMI, and the decision to move the ICMM to London. (Wilson also apparently did not think the global collaboration process should be "driven from the colonies," in a context where Canadian and Australian mining companies had spear-headed change within the ICME.) (Placer Dome, Executive 2, August 11, 2011). The ICMM had a difficult start, as it experienced significant cost over-runs, and management felt it was in danger of over-reaching itself. Barrick was concerned about being involved in a venture where the ICMM's priorities were not deemed directly relevant to the company, and where there was likely to be little traction for the resources to be expended (Executive 1, May 6, 2003). Barrick was undergoing internal transition at the time, having just merged with Homestake, and did not want its limited resources to be spread too thin (Executive 1, October 14, 2011).

Barrick management was more comfortable with more focused initiatives, such as the International Cyanide Management Code. In response to a cyanide spill from a Romanian gold mine in 2000 that polluted the Danube River, a multistakeholder steering committee was formed by the ICME, together with UNEP. Barrick assumed an industry leadership role on the committee that developed the code, which is voluntary, but involves a third-party audit to certify compliance with code requirements (Barrick 2011b). Barrick's Cowal mine became the first facility in the world to achieve code certification in 2006, at the pre-operational stage (Barrick 2006b). As at August 1, 2011, nineteen sites are certified, excluding joint ventures, and twenty-one are certified, including joint ventures (some sites do not use cyanide at all) (ICMC).

Having stepped away from the ICMM, what influenced Barrick's decision to rejoin the organization? Although the immediate impetus behind Barrick's rejoining the ICMM was the membership inherited from Placer Dome, there are a variety of factors that influenced the decision. A major factor was the change in staffing and management at Barrick as it enhanced its organizational competency around CSR (Manager 2, November 3, 2011). The appointment of Greg Wilkins as CEO in 2003 served as a catalyst for formalizing existing CSR activities, implementing organizational change, and adopting new CSR intiatives. Those within Barrick who might have resisted joining came to recognize the case for rejoining the ICMM.

A driving factor in this change of heart can be attributed to Barrick's larger visibility within the global mining sector. Even prior to the Placer Dome acquisition, Barrick had become a major gold-mining company, with growing operations around the world. Management came to recognize the opportunity for learning that the ICMM provides, and wanted to work with industry peers on issues of mutual concern (Manager 2, November 3, 2011). Membership in the ICMM provided the potential for cross-fertilization of best practices, where Barrick could learn from its peers, rather than reinventing the wheel when entering new jurisdictions (Executive 1, October 14, 2011). At the same time, Barrick wanted to contribute to the ongoing development of standards (Manager 1, November 3, 2011) and add its expertise based on the experience acquired from its own operations (Executive 1, October 14, 2011).

Earlier concerns about the ICMM overstepping itself were alleviated by management's impression that the ICMM was producing results, such as the Metal and Mining Sector Supplement to the GRI. Management was impressed with the clear criteria for membership, through the Sustainable Development Framework (Executive 1, October 14, 2011). Barrick is now actively engaged with the ICMM, with senior management involved at the executive committee level and on the many Working Groups covering health and safety, environment, and society. On the social side, for example, Barrick participates in the Community and Social Development Task Force, the Artisanal Mining Working Group, the Resource Endowment Initiative Working Group, the Indigenous People's Working Group, and the Business and Human Rights Working Group (Barrick 2011b: 55). The Working Groups have provided an excellent forum for promoting learning around best practices, and Barrick has been able to contribute in a significant way, including in the Indigenous People's Working Group, which developed the "Good Practices Guide: Indigenous Peoples and Mining" in 2010 and features best-practice case studies from companies including Barrick (Manager 2, November 3, 2011).

Management viewed the membership of the ICMM to be strong, consisting of the world's top mining companies (Executive 1, October 14, 2011). Barrick wanted to be included among the global group of major mining companies, and, by working with its industry peers, maximize the benefits of membership (Executive 1, October 14, 2011). These benefits include association with top industry peers, the potential for collaboration, and acceptance of the more focused sustainable development agenda adopted by the ICMM (Executive 1, October 14, 2011). A key priority identified by Barrick is the continued need for the industry to better communicate the benefits of mining, a challenge which can best be addressed through collaboration (Executive 1, October 14, 2011). Barrick participated in the ICMM's Resource Endowment initiative towards this end, which included a case study of mining in Tanzania, where Barrick has significant investments through its subsidiary company, African Barrick Gold.

The fact that Barrick by the mid-2000s was adopting sustainable development as a means to inform its CSR initiatives points to the importance of global normative shifts that have influenced Barrick's adoption of practices consistent with sustainable development. In contrast to earlier years, Barrick now recognized the benefits of collaborating in industrywide initiatives supportive of responsibility and sustainability. Having become a major global player, and after eclipsing Newmont as the world's largest gold producer after the acquisition of Placer Dome, Barrick now considered membership in the ICMM to be beneficial to its interests.

As a relative newcomer in terms of engaging in industry collaboration through the ICMM, Barrick was more of a "taker" of voluntary standards developed by the industry (with the exception of the International Cyanide Management Code). It commenced reporting according to the GRI indicators in 2005, and moved towards having its sites certified under the ISO 14001 EMS (all of Barrick's South American sites and North American operations are certified under ISO 14001). A further benefit of membership is therefore the ability to participate in developing industry standards, rather than adopting standards other companies have developed. For example, Barrick participated in the development of the ICMM's Assurance Process. Since 2009, Barrick has undergone third-party assurance of its annual Responsibility Reports, which confirms both its adherence to the GRI's MMSS, but also the ICMM's sustainable development principles.

In 2006, Barrick adopted Community Management Standards as part of its Community Engagement and Sustainable Development Guidelines, which were developed in keeping with the IFC Performance Standards. Barrick applies the IFC Performance Standards to all sites that receive financing from IFC and Equator Principle financial institutions.

The Extractive Industries Transparency Initiative is another important tri-partite voluntary initiative in which Barrick participates (starting in 2006). Since 2005, Barrick has participated in the United Nations Global Compact, which is applicable to all industry sectors and is popular amongst mining companies, but has little credibility in the view of many NGOs.

The only standard adhered to by other companies, but not by Barrick, is the Occupational Health and Safety Assurance Standard (OHSAS). However, the Barrick Health and Safety System is aligned with OHSAS 18001, which was confirmed through a gap assessment in 2009. Barrick did not feel it necessary to seek OHSAS certification because the certification process is primarily a paper-based audit. The audit process performed by Barrick is a more comprehensive audit based on field level risk assessments along with worker and management interactions (Manager 2, November 3, 2011).

Table 7.1 identifies which companies are reporting against the standards most commonly reported against by members of the ICMM. As Table 7.1 reveals, Barrick now leads other major mining companies in terms of the number of voluntary and tri-partite standards it adheres to. This development reflects both the growing influence of sustainable

Table 7.1 ICMM members' adherence to global voluntary standards (2010)

Company	ISO 14001	GRI	ICMC	IFC performance standards	Global compact	OHSAS 18001	EITI	VP's
ARM	✓	✓	X	X	X	✓	✓	X
Anglo American	✓	✓	X	X	✓	✓	✓	✓
AngloGold Ashanti	✓	✓	✓	✓	✓	X	✓	✓
Barrick-Gold	✓	✓	✓	✓	✓	X	✓	✓
BHP-Billiton	✓	✓	X	✓	✓	X	✓	✓
Freeport-McMoRan	✓	✓	X	X	X	✓	✓	✓
Gold Fields	✓	✓	✓	X	✓	✓	✓	X
Lihir Gold Limited	✓	✓	✓	✓	✓	✓	✓	X
Lonmin	✓	✓	X	X	✓	✓	✓	✓
Mitsubishi Materials	✓	✓	X	X	X	X	X	X
Newmont	✓	✓	✓	✓	✓	✓	✓	✓
Nippon Mining & Metals	✓	✓	X	X	✓	✓	✓	X
OZ Minerals	X	✓	X	X	X	X	X	X
Rio Tinto	✓ North America	✓	X	✓	✓	✓	✓	✓
Sumitomo	✓	✓	X	X	X	X	✓	X
Teck	✓	✓	X	X	✓	X	✓	✓
Vale	✓	✓	✓	✓	✓	X	X	✓
Xstrata	✓	✓	X	✓	✓	✓	✓	✓

Source: 2010 Corporate sustainable development/sustainability reports (www.icmm.com).

development norms, but also the strong desire by management to align Barrick's policies with leading global CSR standards applicable to mining.

Sustainable development and the institutionalization of CSR initiatives

A long-term strategic goal of the ICMM includes increased sector-wide action in support of the ICMM's sustainable development objectives (ICMM 2003b). This means promoting sustainable development both among members of the ICMM (with adherence to principles a condition of membership), and within the industry as a whole. The ICMM has performed the mimetic function of enhancing the legitimacy of voluntary reporting mechanisms within the mining industry (important for buy-in) and disseminating information on best practices, not just among members of the ICMM, but across the industry as a whole. As reputation is a benefit that is "held in common" (Prakash and Potoski 2007b), the ICMM's efforts have to be directed at all mining companies, not just members. In responding to public concerns over the negative environmental and social externalities of mining, the challenge for the industry was to take steps that would mitigate these impacts, and justify the continued existence of mining companies (Hamann 2003).

The approach of the ICMM has been to make information on best practices in the industry widely available, so that non-members might improve their performance as well. Drawing from learnings from the MMSD, the ICMM recognized that "if civil society groups put pressure only on a large few companies and fail to recognize progress, the rest will ride free" (MMSD 2002: xxiii). Concerns about the free-rider problem of non-members, especially among smaller mining and exploration companies, drove the ICMM to encourage all mining companies, regardless of membership, to improve their practices. While membership in the ICMM is affordable only to the largest mining companies, mid-tier and junior companies can point to best practices promoted by the ICMM, even where certification is too costly (Dashwood and Puplampu 2010). The significant increase in stand-alone sustainable development reports from the early 2000s (KPMG 2006) suggests that the ICMM has played a role in facilitating the dissemination of sustainable development as a norm informing legitimate business practice in the mining sector. The framing of CSR reports in terms of sustainable development provides a conceptual framework through which mining companies can integrate the social side of their initiatives with their environmental initiatives, a point emphasized in the MMSD report (MMSD 2002). At the same time, variation in the uptake of global CSR standards reveals the role of managerial discretion in determining which standards to adopt, beyond those required by the ICMM.

Conclusion

As a participant in the South American team of the MMSD noted, "they [GMI, MMSD, EIR initiatives] have generated accumulative learning processes in which all of us involved stakeholders have developed an increased capacity for dialogue and have also enriched our knowledge of the complexities involved in mining development" (Echavarria 2004: 3, 5). Acting on the perception of leading mining executives that the mining industry had reached a critical juncture, and fixated on the policy window provided by the need to position mining as sustainable at the 2002 World Summit, the MMSD process marked a significant departure for the industry, as it sought to show it was prepared to listen to, engage with, and learn from other stakeholders.

The account in this chapter of industry collaboration through the ICME and later, the ICMM, supports the literature on the importance of industry associations in fostering learning by increasing the sensitivity of mining companies to the interests of external stakeholders. The processes of dialogue and engagement moved the industry away from the view that the industry merely needed to communicate to the public its good intentions and address perception gaps, to a recognition that the industry would have to work with external stakeholders to develop standards that would lead to improvement in performance and greater accountability (Cooney 2008; Noranda, Executive 2, October 28, 2003).

This chapter confirms that professional orientation and culture can influence how an industry addresses its CSR challenges. Faced with the need to come to grips with the norm of sustainable development, the "engineering mindset" of many in the industry made this undertaking a particularly daunting challenge. In addressing the social side of its operations, the mining industry had to "unlearn" traditional approaches to problem solving and re-think how to approach its social responsibilities. The ICMM has effectively applied the learnings of the MMSD to give meaning to sustainable development in the context of mining. At the same time, initiatives such as the EIR and the IFC Performance Standards, as well as ongoing intense scrutiny from NGOs, has kept the "screws" on the industry to continuously improve its performance and demonstrate greater accountability to external stakeholders through independent certification of its performance.

The variation in firm responses to common external pressures confirms the salience of managerial discretion and leadership, and the need to look at dynamics internal to the firm. Using the examples of Noranda, Placer Dome, and Barrick, this chapter explains how managers interpret pressures in their external environment in order to understand the differences in response and strategy. Ultimately, isomorphic pressures brought Barrick in line with other major mining companies, as evidenced by management's decision to rejoin the ICMM and, by extension, accept the ICMM's Sustainable Development Framework. Social structural determinants are therefore important, but are not a sufficient part of the explanation for Barrick's actions.

The very bad reputation garnered by the mining industry drove leading mining companies to push for global industry self-regulation to address the strong need for legitimacy, and to justify the continued existence of mining. The actions of the mining industry supports other research findings, which suggest that a major reason for accepting the institutional constraints and loss of autonomy associated with collaboration is to manage a company's image (Howard et al. 1999). In considering the calculus of the leaders in the mining industry, early mover advantages were a factor. The willingness of leading companies to tolerate the private costs posed by free riders bears out research which demonstrates that managers may be prepared to, unilaterally or collectively with a few other firms, work to improve the performance of an industry as a whole, and thereby safeguard their own reputations (King and Lenox 2000; Meyer and Rowan 1977).

At the outset, leading mining companies were prepared to absorb the costs of free riding and shirking, because of the benefits that are believed to accrue to early movers, and because it was recognized that some major companies needed to play a leading role to address the industry's reputational problems. The relatively small group of nine leading mining companies that launched the GMI and established the ICMM had a global presence and high visibility, consistent with Olson's "privileged group" model (Olson 1965). Barrick's decision not to participate in industry-wide collaboration through the ICMM supports this theory, as concern about escalating costs was a major factor in Barrick's decision to pull out in 2002.

The genesis and initial conception of the ICMM met the pre-conditions identified by Sethi (2005) as necessary for avoiding some collective-action problems. The requirement that members adhere to the ICMM's Sustainable Development Framework reveals a commitment to avoid problems of shirking or strategic adoption. New members are vetted by an Independent Review Panel, which adjudicates all applicants to assure that they can meet the requirements of membership.

Continued pressure from mining's external stakeholders has been important in motivating the ICMM and its members to strengthen their reporting mechanisms. The ICMM has thus progressively moved from a weak sword to a medium sword club, with the introduction of third-party certification through the AA1000 standard, and public disclosure (Prakash and Potoski 2007b), confirming the necessity of these elements to demonstrate the credibility of self-regulatory initiatives (Sethi 2005). Verifiable, independent assurance that is publicly disclosed is a necessary condition for winning credibility in the eyes of external stakeholders.

Isomorphic processes are also evident in the major uptake of sustainable development as a norm informing mining companies' CSR policies and practices. The framing of CSR reports in terms of sustainable development is evidence of mimetic processes at work in the mining industry. The near-universal consensus around the norm of sustainable development suggests that companies are strongly motivated to enhance the legitimacy of their operations, a strategic calculus, but one that does not translate into immediate gains (Howard et al. 1999). Although Barrick has explicitly chosen not to frame its overall CSR policies in terms of sustainable development, it moved with the crowd in framing its community relations initiatives explicitly in terms of that norm. These findings confirm research that has found that where reputation is at stake, companies are more likely to mimic successful peers (isomorphism) (Campbell 2007; Howard et al. 1999: 285).

8 | Conclusion

Introduction

This book asks how and why emerging global CSR norms influenced the strategies and practices of mining multinationals. Three major empirical findings informed the methodological and theoretical approach adopted to address this central question. First, the vast majority of major mining companies had come by the mid-2000s to frame their CSR policies and practices in relation to the global norm of sustainable development. Second, some mining companies took on a leadership role in promoting global CSR norms through industry collaboration, and some were early movers in adopting CSR standards in their policies and practices. Third, the operational challenges of mining in home and host countries (developed and developing) informed CSR adoption.

The first finding leads to the theoretically relevant observation that firms are responsive to global norms. The literature on norms dissemination in international relations theory (Keck and Sikkink 1998; Risse et al. 1999), which seeks to explain how global norms such as human rights change state behavior, showed potential in explaining the receptiveness of mining companies to emerging global CSR norms. Although broadly applicable, the literature assumes that NGOs are the only credible actors in promoting norm-consistent behavior on the part of states, and that profit-maximizing firms neither promote norms nor are motivated by them. In the face of clear evidence that mining companies had adopted sustainable development as the normative referent for their CSR policies and practices, this book analyzed the process by which the global norm of sustainable development influenced firms and their CSR policies and practices.

Not only are mining companies responsive to global normative developments, they actively seek to disseminate global CSR norms within the global mining industry. In other words, they are both receptors of

253

global norms, as well as norms entrepreneurs. The global governance literature, with its early focus on NGOs, has been slow to analyze and explain the fact of firms as normative actors in global governance. Recent contributions to the global governance literature expands upon the role of firms as political actors shaping global public policy (Flohr et al. 2010; Fuchs 2007; Sell and Prakash 2004), a key insight informing this book. Major mining companies participated in multilateral organizations to represent their interests in global decision making, and in the process, were influenced by evolving global norms.

The global governance and norms-dissemination literature was found wanting in explaining the variation between mining companies in terms of the timing of CSR adoption and the leadership role played by some companies. In order to explain this variation, this study argues that emerging global CSR norms, on their own, are insufficient to explain CSR adoption. To understand why firms adopt CSR, factors internal to the firm and institutional context must be brought into the analysis. The role of leadership on the part of senior management was found to be decisive in determining when, how, and why mining companies moved forward with CSR. A necessary part of the explanation for firms' CSR responses is the interaction between external, intra-organizational, and internal leadership factors.

The emphatic emphasis of senior management on the critical importance of the role that the experience of mining in their countries of operation played in shaping CSR policies and practices pointed to the need to incorporate institutional approaches into the analysis. This book adopts a three-level institutional framework, drawing on rational choice institutionalism, institutionalism in organization theory, and historical institutionalism, in order to advance understanding of both convergence around sustainable development as a normative frame, and variation in terms of the timing of CSR adoption and commitment to CSR. The research design consists of a comparison of three major Canadian mining companies, Noranda, Placer Dome, and Barrick Gold. The choice of Canadian mining companies controls for country-of-origin effects, and these companies vary in terms of early mover status, leadership role, and the nature of the influence of sustainable development. Table 8.1 outlines the indicators found to be important in determining early mover status, the role of leadership (internal and global), and the manner and extent to which the case-study companies were socialized to the norm of sustainable development (norms-socialization process). Structural,

Table 8.1 *Key explanatory indicators*

Structural	• Expansion beyond North America • Prominence in industry (size, production, earnings)
Internal/organizational	• Role of leadership/norms entrepreneurs • Release of stand-alone CSR reports • Creation of EHS/CSR positions • Introduction of EHS management systems • Adoption of voluntary CSR standards • Sustainable development norm socialization • Role of learning, professional background, culture
External engagement (Local/national/global)	• Leadership in industry collaboration • Degree of external engagement (with stakeholders, critics, industry associations, IGOs)

internal/organizational, and external engagement indicators were found to be relevant in explaining the variation between the three companies.

Noranda and Placer Dome were early movers in terms of expansion into the developing world, CSR adoption, external reporting, organizational change, external engagement, and leadership in industry-wide collaboration. All three companies questioned the applicability of sustainable development to mining, but Noranda and Placer Dome were early movers in framing their CSR policies in terms of sustainable development. Of the two, Placer Dome moved furthest in accepting the normative validity of sustainable development at the discursive level and in adopting practices consistent with sustainable development. These companies had attained "prescriptive status" (Risse et al. 1999) by the late 1990s because they referred to sustainable development as the norm informing their policies and practices, and they worked to continually improve their practices with a view to aligning their CSR performance with the goal of sustainable development (which was a work in progress).

Barrick was an early mover in terms of the development of environmental policies and the creation of a VP, Environment position in the mid-1990s. Until the late 1990s, however, Barrick's operations were confined to North America and its community engagement initiatives were understood as largely discretionary, philanthropic undertakings. Organizational change to address the full range of Barrick's CSR responsibilities and improve competency commenced in the early-to-mid 2000s. The first stand-alone CSR report was released in 2003 for the 2002 reporting year. Compared with Noranda and Placer Dome, Barrick was a late mover, although Barrick was in line with industry practice as a whole in most respects. Barrick was a member of the ICME and provided leadership in global industry collaboration in its specific business area (gold mining – International Cyanide Management Code), but in 2002 withdrew from industry-wide collaboration through the ICMM. Most interestingly, although Barrick has adopted most of the major global standards developed in keeping with sustainable development, management prefers to identify its policies in terms of CSR and has not adopted sustainable development as an over-arching frame for its CSR. In this respect, Barrick differs from most of the mining industry, which has widely adopted sustainable development (or sustainability) as a normative frame informing its CSR initiatives. The following section outlines the explanation advanced in this book for the variation between Noranda, Placer Dome, and Barrick across these indicators.

Analysis of findings

This book employs a multivariate and multi-level analysis of the influences on CSR adoption. Such an approach accounts for the complex, dynamic, and fluid nature of the influences shaping the CSR policies and practices of major mining companies. The immediate downside of such an approach is that there is no one variable that can be isolated out as crucial, because the variables at the external (global, national, local), internal, and intra-organizational levels together influence firms' CSR responses. There is a trade-off between theoretical parsimony and the explanatory comprehensiveness that the case-study analysis of Noranda, Placer Dome, and Barrick afford. Crucial to the explanation of CSR adoption is the temporal ordering of developments at the global, national, and local levels, and process tracing of change over time. Timing is highly salient to theories on early mover status, critical juncture, and the life cycle of norms dissemination. Processes of change are critical to understanding what drove the evolution of managerial attitudes towards CSR, norms socialization, and the degree of firm commitment to CSR. The connection between temporal ordering and process tracing of change is at the heart of the explanation for unilateral and collaborative CSR adoption.

Structure, path dependence, and critical juncture

Structural changes within the industry and individual mining companies are an appropriate starting point for explaining firms' responses to CSR. In the 1990s, major mining companies became truly global in their operations, with the opening up of investment opportunities in developing countries. Critics of globalization have argued that it produced a "race to the bottom," where it is presumed that companies seek destinations with cheap labor and weak or non-existent environmental laws. The lack or ineffectiveness of regulatory oversight in developing countries might arguably have led mining companies to neglect their CSR responsibilities. Instead, as this book has demonstrated, the CSR practices of mining companies steadily expanded and improved, even in the absence of regulatory oversight (see also Borzel and Risse 2010). Globalization created incentives for mining companies to engage with CSR.

Mining companies were attracted to developing countries because of the introduction of mining laws friendly to foreign investment, but unlike other industries such as textile and clothing, mining companies lack mobility because they must locate where the ore is. Rather than avoiding regulatory oversight, major mining companies were motivated to develop global self-regulation to compensate for regulatory deficiencies in developing countries. Anti-mining activism on the part of NGOs and growing public concern about the negative environmental effects of mining meant that well-publicized accidents negatively affected the industry's reputation as a whole. Reputational concerns provided the impetus behind global industry self-regulation, which in turn was partly a response to structural changes in the industry as mining companies expanded into the developing world.

Noranda and Placer Dome significantly expanded their global operations during the 1990s, yet both companies already had operations outside of North America. Structural change, namely industry-wide expansion into the developing world, cannot be said to have been the primary impetus for CSR adoption for these companies, although they drew on their experiences operating in remote communities in Canada, as well as in developing countries, to develop their CSR policies. Barrick, on the other hand, did not expand beyond North America until the late 1990s, and there is a stronger correlation between the changes in its CSR policies and practices and this global expansion. Significant organizational and CSR policy development commenced in the early-to-mid 2000s, as Barrick sought to address the challenges of operating in developing countries. Furthermore, management in the early 2000s did not see the company as a prominent player within the industry, which diminished the incentive to participate in industry-wide collaborative arrangements. Even for Barrick, however, an explanation for CSR adoption that depends on structural changes in the industry and Barrick's business only goes so far, as managerial discretion played a significant role in explaining the nature and timing of CSR adoption.

Structural factors have a bearing on why Noranda was an early mover and industry leader. Mining and metals is a broad category, and both Placer Dome and Barrick are almost exclusively gold-mining companies. In addition to mining, Noranda's mining business included smelting, recycling, and the production of sulfuric acid at its zinc plant in Quebec (CEZinc). Noranda management was sensitized to the long-term vulnerabilities of this side of its business by the 1979 Mississauga train derailment just outside of Toronto, requiring a mass evacuation, followed a few years later by the Bhopal tragedy. These events influenced Noranda's early mover status as the company recognized that the nature of its business exposed it to increased regulatory scrutiny and potential public outrage. Yet, recognition of these risks does not automatically lead to a proactive approach to CSR; management might well have chosen to deny or take a minimalist approach. Reliance on structural arguments overlooks management's interpretation of the external environment and how that influenced Noranda's response to its CSR challenges.

As rational choice institutionalism expects, major mining companies from the advanced industrialized economies began to adopt CSR policies and practices because they all faced broadly similar external constraints and incentive structures. The regulatory context influenced the CSR considerations of Noranda, Placer Dome, and Barrick, as it did for all companies with headquarters in the advanced industrialized economies. Mining companies adapted by creating positions, such as VP, Environment, and improving their competency in the area of environmental monitoring and auditing in response to tightening environmental regulation. Companies also came to appreciate the value of communicating their CSR efforts to external stakeholders through stand-alone CSR reports, and by the mid-2000s, the majority of major mining companies were doing so.

Institutional context is significant in explaining the operational challenges confronting Noranda and Placer Dome, as well as the mode of adoption of CSR policies (but has less predictive power in explaining the timing). The experience of mining in North America and developing countries led senior management to recognize the need to improve CSR competency and policies and influenced the specific practices adopted. At Placer Dome, CSR adoption was lateral, in that organizational challenges at specific operations prompted the adoption of initiatives that were then incorporated into company-wide policies. Placer Dome's first CSR report was released in 1997 for the Asia Pacific region one year in advance of company-wide reporting, a reflection of the challenges the company had been addressing at its operations in the region (Philippines and PNG in particular). Noranda had a highly decentralized organizational structure, and separate business units and the specific mine sites undertook initiatives that head office then sought to coordinate in a more formalized manner. Noranda's CEZinc operation in Valleyfield, Quebec, for example began communicating to external stakeholders in 1987, three years ahead of the company-wide commencement of reporting.

Institutional context was also an important influence on Barrrick, where the VP, Environment was based in the United States, the location of its flagship Goldstrike property. When the company expanded into the developing world, it sought to apply its existing CSR practices (the Goldstrike Model), a clear example of country-of-origin effects. Management learned that the developing-country context required a different approach to CSR, which led Barrick to move away from the earlier philanthropic approach to a more expansive understanding of the need to contribute to socio-economic development. Institutional context, together with the need for local community support, influenced the type of CSR initiatives Barrick adopted.

The critical-juncture concept in historical institutionalism provides a convincing explanation of the impetus behind unilateral CSR adoption and global collaborative efforts on the part of the mining industry. Mining companies based in the advanced industrialized economies faced a number of constraints in their external environment. A series of serious environmental accidents in the 1990s intensified NGO and media scrutiny, compromising the industry's reputation and very legitimacy. Experiences such as opposition to Noranda's New World mining project near Yellowstone National Park in the US, and the denial of a permit for the Windy Craggy project in British Columbia were significant markers of the increasing difficulty mining companies in the advanced industrialized economies were encountering gaining access to land. Although new opportunities opened up in developing countries, the mining industry faced new "green" conditionalities as private and public lending institutions sought to reduce their exposure to environmental liability and respond to growing NGO pressure. New environmental treaties, such as the Basel Convention, threatened to limit access to markets for their metal products. The coming together of these developments, declining access to land, markets, and finance, combined to create a critical juncture for the mining industry in the mid-to-late 1990s. The critical juncture provided the "push" that led the industry to improve upon and communicate their unilateral CSR practices, and helped propel leading mining companies towards revitalized efforts at global industry collaboration.

Convergence, isomorphism, and sustainable development

This book argues that a major influence on unilateral CSR adoption and global industry collaboration was the global normative weight of sustainable development. National governments, including many in the developing world, had adopted sustainable development in their national environmental policies. Initiatives in international governmental organizations towards protecting the environment were informed by sustainable development. NGOs had adopted the discourse of sustainable development informing their efforts to advocate on behalf of environmental causes. The global mining industry found itself out of step with these global developments and some leading mining companies recognized the need to come to terms with the normative consensus around sustainable development.

By the mid-2000s, the majority of major mining companies from the advanced industrialized countries had converged around the norm of sustainable development. The evidence for this lies in the framing of unilateral CSR policies and practices in terms of sustainable development and the adoption of sustainable development by the ICMM as the normative frame for the development of specific voluntary standards. The industry's efforts to develop CSR policies and practices led to a degree of isomorphism, as mining companies implemented organizational changes to increase competency around CSR. Evidence for this can be found in the creation of VP, Sustainability/Sustainable Development positions, the creation of CSR groups to support senior management, the development of internal monitoring and auditing systems covering OHS and the environment, and the creation of middle-management positions such as Community Relations Managers at the mine sites.

New institutionalist approaches would look to these developments as evidence of the paramount importance of structural determinants leading to convergence around sustainable development. Once a critical number of major mining companies had adopted sustainable development, other mining companies came onside with their industry peers. Upon accepting sustainable development at the discursive level, companies then had to institute organizational changes in order to be able to act on their stated commitment to sustainable development through CSR policies and practices. When one actually examines the responses of the case-study companies, however, an explanation that relies solely on structural forces is found to be inadequate.

Of the three case-study companies, Barrick comes closest to meeting the expectations of convergence theories. Senior management acknowledged the importance of global normative developments in guiding the development of its CSR policies and practices in the mid-2000s. By this time, a number of specific voluntary standards had been institutionalized within the industry, which influenced Barrick's choice of CSR initiatives. In addition to the ICMM's Sustainable Development Framework and the GRI's Mining and Metals Sector Supplement, the ISO environmental management systems had gained widespread acceptance within the industry, as had the International Cyanide Management Code. By the mid-2000s, sustainable development had been institutionalized by the mining industry at the global level, and as such, sustainable development norms were more influential in CSR adoption. Beyond these structural determinants, however, there are some awkward anomalies that give pause to assigning too much causal weight to convergence around common structural incentives.

Although Barrick frames its community-engagement protocols in terms of sustainable development, management continues to evince a preference for CSR, as opposed to sustainable development, as an overall frame for its initiatives, as reflected in its stand-alone reports, comments within those reports, and as confirmed by interviews. Structural determinism ignores the process by which mining companies came to accept a concept that they found deeply troubling because of its lack of definitional clarity, and because it incorporated social dimensions which were somewhat alien to what many within the industry had been trained to deal with. Structural determinism also ignores the fact that leading companies such as Noranda and Placer Dome themselves acted as agents in the promotion of global CSR norms and were influenced by the experience of mining in the countries in which they had operations. The findings of this study tilt decisively in favour of explanations that can account for variation and agency.

Agency, leadership, and organizational attributes

Country-of-origin effects are often an important factor in explaining variation in multinational firms' responses to their external environment. At a broad level, the largely similar institutional context in the advanced industrialized economies explains why it was companies headquartered in those countries that moved forward with unilateral and collaborative CSR initiatives. Accounting for variation between firms headquartered in different countries was well beyond the scope of this study, which opted instead to control for country-of-origin effects by analyzing the CSR responses of Canadian mining companies. In this study, it was found that both the country of origin and country of operation influenced CSR strategies. There is nevertheless variation between the Canadian case-study companies, even after controlling for country-of-origin effects.

All three companies were clearly influenced by developments in their external environment, and as noted above, structural industry factors are also relevant. These factors, while important, leave some questions unanswered. Why were Noranda and Placer Dome early movers in adopting CSR and sustainable development, and why did Barrick, after practicing good CSR in the 1990s, witness some early missteps in its CSR initiatives in the early 2000s? How can the shift in managerial attitudes about the nature of their responsibilities be accounted for? Why did Noranda and Placer Dome adopt sustainable development as a normative frame for their CSR, while Barrick has not? This book demonstrates that internal dynamics, including the role of leadership, organizational attributes, and learning are essential to answering the above questions.

Leadership was decisive in all companies in terms of their CSR response to external pressures. Management at Noranda took a proactive stance to the CSR challenges it was facing, and took long-term value into account in strategic planning. Management rejected a defensive stance, opting instead to reach out to external stakeholders, including critics, through outreach initiatives such as the New Directions Group and the Friday Group. Leadership at Placer Dome, especially after the appointment of the new CEO in 1992, also played a decisive role in moving the company forward on its CSR policies and reporting. The disastrous Marcopper tailings spill might well have led senior management to backpedal on CSR, because of the liability issues associated with the accident. Instead, management opted to improve its CSR performance, and communicate its intentions to external stakeholders. Furthermore, senior management had already been discussing the adoption of sustainable development prior to Marcopper, so the commencement of external reporting was not merely a reaction to enhance image.

By all accounts, Barrick had strong CSR leadership in the 1990s, with a well-regarded senior executive, Robert Smith, spearheading the company's CSR initiatives in North America. His passing in 1998 left a CSR-leadership lacuna that happened just as Barrick commenced operations in developing countries. The appointment of a new CEO in 2003 served as a catalyst for substantial policy and organizational changes in order to improve Barrick's CSR competency and performance. Under the leadership of the current CEO, appointed in 2009, a cultural shift is beginning to occur alongside the transformation in CSR policies and practices. The evidence for this is in the greater responsiveness to external critics, the willingness to acknowledge mistakes in recent serious human rights incidents at its North Mara and Porgera operations, and openness about corrective steps to be taken to rectify those mistakes.

The role of leadership is directly correlated with the complex learning processes that firms must undertake in tackling CSR (Cooksey 2003). Without supportive leadership at the top, any learning about how to improve upon or transform CSR practices will be unlikely to permeate throughout the entire organization. The internal challenges of CSR adoption were similar in all companies; simply improving on current ways of doing things (single loop learning) proved inadequate. All three companies had to adopt new practices, employ new strategies (double loop learning), and engage with external stakeholders on an ongoing basis (deutero learning) in order to adapt to changing societal expectations. Learning is ultimately reflected in shifting corporate attitudes towards their environmental responsibilities, and the rich case-study analysis employed in this study allowed this process to be traced in detail. The extent to which companies change their CSR policies and practices as a result of lessons learned provides a means to differentiate between companies according to their degree of commitment to CSR. A shift in attitudes came very early at Noranda, while the shift in thinking at Placer Dome occurred in the 1990s (still early by overall industry standards). At Barrick, the shift away from a compliance-based and discretionary approach to CSR gave way by the mid-2000s to transformative change in attitudes and practices.

In thinking about learning, one must be mindful of who the teachers are. In the case of Noranda and Placer Dome, learning was derived from the experience of mining in Canada and around the world. Both had experience in developing countries, which was incorporated in the 1990s in their corporate-wide CSR policies and practices. Barrick learned the wrong lessons from its North American operations and had to make adjustments in order to meet the needs of communities in developing countries affected by its operations. By the mid-2000s, an important "teacher" was the existence of well-established global CSR standards that Barrick could align its practices with.

Learning from membership in industry associations exerted an important influence on Noranda and Placer Dome. Due to the nature of its business, Noranda was a member of the Canadian Chemical Producers' Association, which responded to the Bhopal disaster by developing the Responsible Care® program. Participation in the CCPA taught Noranda the benefits of public outreach, and exposed it to management systems for EHS. The rise of management systems through the ISO served as another important teacher, and Noranda's CEZinc was the first zinc plant in the world to achieve certification under ISO 9000. Placer Dome had extensive external relations with a wide variety of actors and was a key player in the ICME. The WBCSD played a very important role in influencing the movement of all industry towards alignment with sustainable development. A small number of major mining companies, including Noranda and Placer Dome, were members of the WBCSD, which served as an important reinforcement in support of the move towards sustainable development within mining. All of the mining companies who were members of the WBCSD were among the group of nine companies which launched the GMI in 1999. Barrick's membership in the World Gold Council promoted learning on responsible gold mining and Barrick was a member of the ICME when leading companies pushed for acceptance of the Sustainable Development Charter. Leadership and learning is also correlated with the extent to which there is a culture of commitment to CSR, another source of differentiation between firms. Many of the organizational indicators of commitment were present in all three companies from the perspective of the 1990s (although Noranda was a pioneer in this regard). All three had created VP, Environment positions by 1995 and were working to improve their environmental management systems. A culture of commitment can be discerned by the extent to which firms scan for information about improving their CSR performance (a necessary element of learning), and the incentive structure for employees around achieving CSR goals. Noranda and Placer Dome possessed these attributes in the 1990s, as did Barrick on the environmental side, but transformational change did not commence at Barrick on the social side until after the creation of the Director, CSR position in 2005. Noranda and Placer Dome proved to be reasonably responsive and willing to engage with external stakeholders (even those critical of their operations) whereas Barrick has only evinced such willingness in the past few years.

Different organizational cultures can explain variance in approaches to CSR pressures, and as the literature expects (Howard-Grenville 2006), CSR norms entrepreneurs in mining companies must appeal to the dominant role that risk avoidance/mitigation plays in corporate strategy. The need to present a business case for improved CSR was paramount in all three companies, but the arguments for the business case differed. Noranda sought to promote a "win–win" approach, while Placer Dome was acutely aware that aligning its policies with sustainable development might help it secure permits for new projects and expedite the permitting process. For Barrick, costly disruptions to its operations is a key risk to be avoided, driving its efforts at community engagement.

Although professional background was found to be relevant in explaining industry-wide discomfort with sustainable development, the "mining mindset" was not found to be a determining factor in any of the case-study companies. For industry as a whole, resistance in the

1990s to sustainable development stemmed in part from the fact that those with backgrounds in mining and geology are used to working with clearly defined, measurable objectives. Professional background was also a barrier to responding effectively to the social side of sustainable development in terms of responding to communities affected by mining. By the 2000s, the industry had started to address these concerns by identifying measurable indicators of sustainable development, and hiring people with backgrounds in anthropology and sociology to handle the "human," non-technical side of their operations.

Senior management at Noranda had doubts about sustainable development because of the lack of definitional clarity around the concept. To make the concept meaningful to those at the operational level who would have to implement it, the company set about to develop some measurable indicators consistent with sustainable development, the first mining company to do so. To the extent that sustainable development can be measured, it becomes a better fit with the engineering mindset. On the operational side, the challenge in implementing sustainable development arose from the very decentralized structure of Noranda, as much as from the professional training of mine managers.

At Placer Dome, the senior manager responsible for external engagement had a background in philosophy, and developed an early understanding of the relevance of sustainable development to mining. He played a central role as a norms entrepreneur, but other senior managers had mining backgrounds (including the CEO) but were nevertheless able to grasp the significance of sustainable development. The leadership team at Placer Dome is central to understanding why the company was an early mover in the adoption of sustainable development to frame its CSR initiatives and reporting.

Barrick's issues with sustainable development are definitional, in the sense that management perceives CSR to be a better conceptual frame for its policies. When Barrick came to grapple with how sustainable development would apply to its community-engagement practices in developing countries in the mid-2000s, measurable indicators had already been developed at the global level which the company drew upon to develop its community-engagement guidelines. Furthermore, Barrick hired outside the mining discipline when it created the Director, CSR position in 2005.

The possession of various organizational attributes, supportive and committed leadership from the top, scanning for new information, the perception of CSR improvement as an opportunity, the degree of responsiveness to external stakeholders' concerns, and the extent of collaborative interactions with stakeholders, as well as incentives for employees to implement CSR, are all highly relevant to explaining why Noranda and Placer Dome took on a leadership role at the global level. Management perceived their companies to be CSR/sustainable development leaders, and therefore to be in a position to take on a leadership role. Management in the early 2000s at Barrick was preoccupied with the 2001 merger with Homestake, and the company did not have the same prominent position within the industry it now has.

Interests, norms, and norm dissemination

The possession of organizational attributes conducive to developing CSR, together with strong leadership from the top and a proclivity to listen to, and engage with, external stakeholders, meant Noranda and Placer Dome were well placed to take on a leadership role globally. Equally important was the fact that these companies had accepted the validity of the sustainable development norm at the discursive level, and were taking steps to align their CSR policies with sustainable development. The companies had become convinced about the normative validity of sustainable development in the context of mining. Without such conviction on the part of even a small number of the world's leading mining companies, the mining industry would not have moved forward with sustainable development at the global level. The adoption of sustainable development by mining companies as a normative framework for their CSR policies was not inevitable. The role of agency was important, as norms entrepreneurs played an essential role, through global collaboration, to bring about change.

Mining companies were motivated by interest-based considerations while also responding to evolving global CSR norms. For all mining companies, including the three analyzed in this study, strategic considerations drove unilateral CSR adoption and collaborative efforts. Framing justifications for CSR in terms of the business case and risk avoidance/mitigation was essential for internal buy-in for all three companies. Early mover advantages are evident in the considerations of Noranda and Placer Dome's unilateral and collaborative CSR initiatives. As the first early mover, Noranda hoped to garner positive relations with government and NGOs, and shape the content of any future regulation.

Placer Dome hoped to differentiate itself from other mining companies by being among the first to frame its CSR policies in terms of sustainable development, and to release a sustainable development report. Yet Placer Dome was also motivated by the desire not to be the only company to have adopted sustainable development, motivating it to collaborate globally for sustainable development adoption. At the global collaborative level, both companies saw the advantage of being in a position to set the agenda and launch specific practices which other major mining companies would then feel pressured to follow. The privileged group status (Olson 1965) and visibility of these companies as major mining companies gave them the incentive to assume the private costs of global collective action. As the literature predicts, reputational concerns were a major part of the calculus (King and Lenox 2000).

Even at the level of interests, however, there were interesting differences. Management at Noranda treated the need for environmental expenditure as an opportunity to promote win–win gains, through the development of energy-saving technology. Noranda grew its recycling business both to take advantage of consumer demand for recycled products, but also to be in sync with the value society had come to attach to recycling. Noranda also based its strategic planning on the enhancement of long-term value, another intangible consideration. Placer Dome advanced the business case, but it was understood in less tangible terms, such as gaining advantages in securing permits, as much as it was about the more measurable benefits of risk avoidance. Furthermore, Placer Dome sought to integrate sustainable development into a core value system for the company, after a CEO-led, corporate-wide exercise to identify the values the company would adhere to and seek to promote.

Barrick's interests in the 2000s have been driven primarily by the need for community acceptance of its operations, a different interpretation of interests than was the case for the other two companies. This is partly to do with timing, because of Barrick's rapid expansion in the 2000s, but also because by the mid-2000s there were established global practices for engaging with local communities. The IFC Performance Standards, for example, came into effect in 2006, meaning practices with respect to community engagement had become institutionalized. Global norms institutionalization has altered how Barrick defines its interests; there are consequences for production, and hence profitability, if community conflict and/or opposition is severe. Furthermore, external pressure on the mining industry continues to intensify, with the entry of new players such as socially responsible investors, so the institutional context in which Barrick operates is characterized by a high level of scrutiny.

Global collaboration commenced in the early 1990s under the ICME primarily because of concerns about market access. After the 1992 Rio Summit, all the major international organizations and many governments in the developed and developing worlds adopted sustainable development as the normative framework for their environmental initiatives. NGOs had captured the global agenda, and international business was not in an all-powerful position (Fuchs 2007). Leading mining companies understood the need to align their practices with sustainable development in order to improve their reputation, a strategic consideration, but one that is not easily measured in narrow cost-benefit terms. Leading mining companies also recognized the need to be able to speak the language of sustainable development, a strategic consideration (Wheeler et al. 2003), but one which recognized the normative value of participating in dialogue about appropriate standards of behavior for the mining sector.

As documented in the previous chapter, strategic considerations aside, the process by which mining companies came to adopt sustainable development as a normative frame was neither linear nor inevitable. Due in part to professional background (engineering) and uncertainty about what an open-ended concept such as sustainable development should/would mean for the industry, there was considerable industry-wide resistance to embracing this normative frame. The impetus for change came from the recognition by CEOs of major mining companies that the industry had reached a critical juncture. Leadership through the GMI was critical in moving the industry towards consensus on sustainable development at the discursive level (much work still had to be done to determine what specific practices would constitute sustainable development in the context of mining). There was some urgency, because the industry needed to develop a position in advance of the 2002 World Summit that would align it with sustainable development in public discourse. In this respect, the World Summit opened a "policy window" (Kingdon 1995) which presented policy entrepreneurs (mining CEOs) with the opportunity to break down resistance and address the reputational crisis the industry was grappling with.

Norms socialization is a type of learning where mining companies became sensitized to, and then acted upon, shifting societal norms with respect to the environment and human rights. The MMSD process was important for promoting learning about the meaning of sustainable development for mining, fostering engagement with external stakeholders and bringing about a change in attitudes on the part of mining executives. Since major mining companies had adopted CSR to varying degrees, part of the norms-socialization process involved defining how already existing practices aligned with sustainable development. Sustainable development also taught mining companies about the need to think more systematically about the social impact of their operations. Through the ICMM, specific "voluntary" practices informed by sustainable development have been developed to promote rule-consistent behavior on the part of member companies.

Drawing on the norms dissemination literature, Noranda and Placer Dome had achieved prescriptive status through their acceptance of the normative validity of sustainable development, as evidenced by the references to sustainable development, and as evidenced by efforts to improve CSR practices in line with sustainable development. They did not reach this path in an identical manner, however, and Barrick, which has also achieved prescriptive status, differs in its approach to sustainable development. Barrick has not adopted sustainable development as an over-arching frame, but rather, prefers the concept of CSR, calling its reports "Responsibility Reports." Barrick has adopted the language of sustainable development in its policies on community engagement, and its voluntary initiatives are consistent with sustainable development as defined by the mining industry. The significance of this is that individual companies differ in how they interpret and act upon sustainable development norms. There was a norms cascade/convergence around sustainable development in the mid-2000s (see Figure 2.1), but an explanation for this drawing solely on structural factors would not catch these nuances.

Theoretical implications

This study has shown how norms and interests work together, and how they are conditioned by specific institutional contexts in the emergence of CSR programs in the mining sector. Norms work their influence on profit-maximizing firms in a variety of ways. The findings in this research clearly demonstrated that firms are responsive to the shifting global normative context. Firms, just like NGOs (Sell and Prakash 2004), act strategically to achieve their goals, and will adopt CSR policies as a form of instrumental, strategic adaptation. The act of adopting sustainable development at the discursive level entails acceptance of its normative validity. In deciding on how to implement CSR, firms make fundamentally normative choices that cannot be readily equated to cost-benefit analysis. In their engagement with local communities, complex social dynamics can mean that there is rarely a clear-cut course of action that will ensure smooth operations. Decisions around what role the company can/should play in contributing to socio-economic development in the local communities where they operate in developing countries is an inherently normative exercise.

The interplay between the logic of consequences and the logic of appropriateness resonates with stakeholder theory. Stakeholder approaches that seek to separate out norms and interest-based engagement create a false dichotomy between the two bases of action. The literature distinguishes between approaches that look at the impact of external stakeholders on the firm (instrumental) and the impact of the firm on external stakeholders (normative). It is better to see the dynamic interaction between the two approaches, and recognize the normative dimension of being responsive to societal concerns and values (Donaldson and Preston 1995).

The fact that the mining industry must locate where the ore is makes mining companies vulnerable to local community opposition. During the Cold War, it might have been possible for mining companies to collaborate with authoritarian regimes to override community opposition, but political liberalization in developing countries after the Cold War and NGO scrutiny have necessitated strategies for stakeholder engagement at the local level. As the mining industry discovered, if too large a gap emerges between corporate behavior and societal values, the very legitimacy of the industry can be undermined, dictating the need to earn and maintain a social license. To effectively earn a social license to operate (Gunningham et al. 2003), mining companies have recognized effective community engagement is both a strategic necessity, as well as the right thing to do.

The stakeholder literature interprets CSR as a stakeholder risk-management strategy, an overly firm-centric understanding of how companies manage their external relations (Sagebien and Lindsay 2011). As such, it provides too narrow an understanding of the stakeholder dynamics mining companies grapple with. One of the key learnings for mining companies about sustainable development is that they are but one of many players involved in the process of fostering socio-economic development. Legitimacy theory holds promise in its understanding of the normative nature of the business–society relationship, which varies according to different institutional contexts (Idemudia 2007).

In arguing that emerging global CSR norms are an important influence on CSR adoption, an approach that can explain how and why norms work their influence on firms, is a central part of the explanation. In explaining how and why global CSR norms became influential, constructivist approaches, when adapted as in this study to include firms, allows for analysis of the role mining companies played in developing standards for the mining industry consistent with the norm of sustainable development. Recent global governance literature that recognizes the role of firms as contributing to global governance as actors in their own right (Avant et al. 2010; Flohr et al. 2010; Meckling 2011) captures collaborative efforts at industry self-regulation through the ICMM.

The business literature tends to emphasize the learning and socialization processes that occur through engagement in industry associations (Campbell 2006). While important, this literature overlooks the important learning that took place in multilateral organizations. Noranda and Placer Dome, for example, were extensively involved in organizations such as UNEP, the OECD, and the World Bank. Their objective was to ensure their companies' interests were represented in global public policy decision-making affecting mining. In the process of participating in these organizations, however, they interacted with other players, including NGOs, which influenced their thinking on sustainable development. The business literature needs to pay more attention to norms-socialization processes through external engagement outside of professional associations. By joining constructivist and global governance literatures, as this study did, a more comprehensive understanding is afforded of the impact of firm participation in institutions of global public governance.

Constructivist explanations of the norms-socialization process (when adapted to apply to firms, as in this study) shed light both on how mining companies accepted sustainable development, as well as on variation in their degree of commitment to the norm. Noranda and Placer Dome, as norms entrepreneurs, played an important leadership role in bringing the industry around to sustainable development. Through their words and actions, they had achieved prescriptive status. As expected in the norms dissemination literature, Barrick in the mid-2000s was influenced by global CSR norms to a greater degree and adopted practices consistent with sustainable development (prescriptive status). What is interesting, though, is that Barrick interpreted and acted upon sustainable development differently than have most mining companies. Norms socialization, therefore, does not necessarily lead to common outcomes except at the broadest level, which means that research needs to delve into individual cases.

These findings suggest that caution must be employed in relying on an overly structuralist explanation of norms dissemination and convergence. Norms dissemination is not simply a top-down process, so that analysis of the bottom-up, institutionally conditioned sources of norms that become influential at the global level is essential (Katzenstein 1996). This study found that the institutionally derived, bottom-up nature of norms dissemination was crucial at the early stages. Noranda and Placer Dome were effective norms entrepreneurs because they had shown leadership in their own CSR policies, which in turn, were influenced by their experience of mining in Canada and around the world. The lessons learned from mining in specific institutional contexts were then applied at the global level. The efforts of leading mining companies, the MMSD process, and the ICMM produced a norms cascade in the mid-2000s.

As the literature expects, once sustainable development was institutionalized within the mining industry through the identification of specific practices consistent with the norm, then it can be said that norms began to filter from the top (global level) on down to influence the CSR practices of specific mining companies (as was the case with Barrick). Developments in the mining industry support the argument that structure and agency are mutually constitutive (Finnemore 1996), with agency on the part of early movers having played a crucial role in establishing institutionalized practices at the global level that then provided the structural context that exerts influence on late movers (or newcomers to the mining big leagues).

Structural factors clearly did work their influence on the mining industry, but in explaining unilateral CSR adoption and collaborative initiatives, the role of leadership is a crucial part of the explanation. In comparing Noranda and Placer Dome with Barrick, it is the one factor that can decisively be said to have influenced the differences in approach between these companies. Not only are managerial attitudes towards CSR crucial, but leadership influences the organizational attributes that signal a commitment to CSR, namely learning, organizational change and the adoption of institutionalized practices, and ultimately, a culture of commitment to CSR. Leadership from the top can also help overcome obstacles, such as the influence of professional background on the industry's perception of sustainable development, as well as subcultures within an organization that may be resistant to change (Gunningham and Sinclair 2009; Howard-Grenville 2006).

CSR research agenda

This book has contributed to the analysis of the conditions under which CSR is likely to be adopted by embedding the explanation solidly in the institutionalist and global governance literatures. It expands on those literatures by drawing on organization theory to show how internal factors interact with global ones to produce specific CSR outcomes. This study has sought to build bridges between different theoretical approaches and disciplines, a necessary step towards moving the CSR research agenda forward.

There are a number of important questions/issues that arise from this research. To be truly considered global norms, the CSR standards established by the ICMM have to be adopted by all the major players in the mining industry. Increasingly, the major players are coming from countries such as China, India, and Brazil. How do these countries interpret and act upon global CSR norms? As the research in this study reveals, one cannot assume uniformity in these matters.

To move the global norms dissemination literature forward, it is important to consider what happens to CSR practices when companies from China, for example, invest in countries such as Canada. China is not known to have a great track record on OHS, but what happens when it invests in advanced industrialized countries where OHS standards are much higher? Will the experience of mining in advanced industrialized countries influence the practices of Chinese companies back home, or in other countries of operation? Understanding how institutional context influences the CSR practices of mining companies from emerging economies is important to moving the CSR research agenda beyond companies headquartered in the advanced industrialized economies. The three-level institutional analysis provides a basis for addressing these questions.

This research drew attention to the vulnerability of mining companies to community opposition, and the importance of earning a social license at the local level as an important driver of CSR adoption. What has been especially challenging for mining companies operating in developing countries is that although there are broad similarities between countries (poverty, weak state capacity, etc.), the specific dynamics in individual countries (and even between different communities in the same country) can make the establishment of uniform standards challenging. There are two implications of this reality. First, classifying countries simplistically as "fragile" states or "areas of limited statehood" masks what is considerable diversity between, say, a South Africa and a Mali, with implications for CSR adoption. Second, the absence of "one-size-fits-all standards" means that individual mining companies must develop their own customized practices for their areas of operation. These realities help explain why there is considerable variation between mining companies in terms of the uptake of global voluntary standards applicable to mining.

More research is needed on the organizational antecedants for successful CSR in developing countries (Puplampu and Dashwood 2011), as well as the factors that produce variation between major mining companies in adopting specific CSR standards observed in the previous chapter. To what extent does leadership in one set of CSR issues get transferred to another set of CSR issues? What influences which CSR initiatives firms undertake, and the timing of CSR adoption in specific contexts? To what extent do firms learn from their prior experiences, and how does this inform their future CSR initiatives? These questions are especially important in the developing country context, where regulations may be weak or weakly enforced. As the case of Barrick reveals, there is no necessary linear progression in the adoption of CSR.

Although there is much evidence to suggest that professional background (which has traditionally centered on mining engineering) disadvantaged the mining sector in addressing the dynamic social effects of their operations, this was not found to be a key factor explaining variation between the three companies examined in this study. One reason for this is that this study focused largely on corporate-level CSR initiatives and attitudes. There is an important literature that looks at the influences on CSR implementation at the mine site, with professional orientation and the existence of sub-cultures resistant to change being important explanatory variables (Gunningham and Sinclair 2009). It is quite possible to have highly committed leadership at the corporate level, but with significant variation between mine sites within the same company and in the same country in terms of CSR performance. More research is needed on what influences variation in CSR implementation between sites owned by one company, in the same country and across countries. Such research would build on the CSR research agenda by both controlling for country-of-origin effects (different sites in the same country) and analyzing the impact of institutional context (same company operations in different countries). It would also shed light on why strong corporate commitment to CSR does not always translate into successful implementation at the mine site, a problem that Barrick is grappling with at some of its more challenging operations.

References

AccountAbility 2008, *AA1000 Assurance Standard 2008*, London.

Ackermann, R. (World Bank) 1998, "Is Mining Compatible with Sustainable Development: A World Bank Perspective," *ICME Newsletter* 6, 2: 1–6.

Aguilera, R. V. and Jackson, G. 2003, "The Cross-National Diversity of Corporate Governance: Dimensions and Determinants," *Academy of Management Review* 28, 3: 447–65.

Alberini, A. and Segerson, K. 2002, "Assessing Voluntary Programs to Improve Environmental Quality," *Environment and Resource Economics* 22, 1/2: 157–84.

Alexandre, B., Lorne, J., and Thomas, S. 2004, *A Case Study of Conservation in the Abitibi Region (Quebec–Ontario Border)*, prepared for the National Round Table on the Environment and the Economy, as part of its Conserving Canada's Natural Capital: The Boreal Forest Program, Ottawa: AborVitae Environmental Services, Boldon Group.

Amnesty International 2010, "Undermining Rights: Forced Evictions and Police Brutality around the Porgera Gold Mine, Papua New Guinea," www.amnesty.org/en/library/asset/ASA34/001/2010/en/2a498f9d-39f7-47df-b5eb-5eaf586fc472/asa340012010eng.pdf (accessed June 20, 2011).

Anderson, M. H., Gold, R., and Bravin, J. August 27, 2008, "Supreme Court Rules Exxon Valdez Payout," *Globe and Mail: Report on Business*, Toronto: B10.

Anonymous 2004, "The Challenges of Transition," in Echavarria, C. (ed.), *Mining and Sustainable Development Series: Global Processes* Ottawa: International Development Research Centre (IDRC) and Mining Policy Research Initiative (MPRI), pp. 7, 10.

Antal, A. B. and Sobczak, A. 2004, "Beyond CSR: Organisational Learning for Global Responsibility," *Journal of General Management* 30, 2: 77–98.

Aragon-Correa, J. A. 1998, "Strategic Proactivity and Firm Approach to the Natural Environment," *Academy of Management Journal* 41: 556–67.

Argyris, C. 1990, *Overcoming Organizational Defenses: Facilitating Organizational Learning*, Boston, MA: Allyn and Bacon.

  1999, *On Organizational Learning*, Boston, MA: Blackwell Business.

Argyris, C. and Schon, D. 1978, *Organizational Learning: A Theory of Action Perspective*, Reading, MA: Addison Wesley.

1996, *Organisational Learning II: Theory, Method and Practice*, Reading, MA: Addison Wesley.

Avant, D., Finnemore, M., and Sell, S. 2010, *Who Governs the Globe?*, Cambridge University Press.

Aziz, M. L., Ferguson, K. D., and Ferris, G. 1998, "Perspectives of Environmental Risk at the Equity Silver Mine," unpublished manuscript.

Balkau, F. and Parsons, A. 1999, "Emerging Environmental Issues for Mining in the PECC Region," paper presented at the First Pacific Economic Cooperation Committee Minerals Forum, Lima, Peru, April 22, www.natural-resources.org/minerals

Bansal, P. and Penner, W. J. 2002, "Interpretations of Institutions: The Case of Recycled Newsprint" in A. Hoffman and M. Ventresca (eds.), *Organizations, Policy and the Natural Environment: Institutional and Strategic Perspectives*, Stanford University Press, pp. 311–26.

Barrick Gold 2000, *1999 Annual Report*, Toronto.

2002a, "Community Focus," www.barrick.com/5_Corporate_Responsibility/5_02_Global_Community_Focus.asp (accessed April 29, 2003).

2002b, "Independent Report at Bulyanhulu," www.barrick.com/CorporateResponsibility/KeyTopics/IndependentReport/default.aspx (accessed July 6, 2011).

2003a, *2002 Responsibility Report*, Toronto.

2003b, *2002 Annual Report*, Toronto.

2003c, *Code of Business Ethics*, www.barrick.com/Company/Corporate Governance/CodeofEthics/default.aspx (accessed June 30, 2011).

2003d, *Safety and Health Policy*, www.barrick.com/Company/Corporate Governance/CodeofEthics/default.aspx (accessed June 30, 2011).

2003e, *Environmental Policy Statement*, www.barrick.com/CorporateResponsibility/Environment/default.aspx (accessed June 29, 2011).

2004a, *2003 Responsibility Report*, Toronto.

2004b, "Corporate Social Responsibility Charter," www.barrick.com/Theme/Barrick/files/docs_ehss/CSR_Charter.pdf (accessed June 20, 2011).

2005, *2004 Responsibility Report*, Toronto.

2006a, *Community Engagement and Sustainable Development Guidelines*, www.barrick.com/Theme/Barrick/files/docs_csr/CESD-Guidelines.pdf (accessed June 20, 2011).

2006b, *2005 Responsibility Report*, Toronto.

2006c, "Pascua Lama," www.barrick.com/CorporateResponsibility/KeyTopics/PascuaLama/default.aspx (accessed July 6, 2011).

2007, "The Facts and CorpWatch," www.barrick.com/Corporate Responsibility/KeyTopics/TheFacts&Corpwatch (accessed June 23, 2011).

2008, *2007 Responsibility Report*, Toronto.

2009, "Special Focus on Indigenous Peoples," *Beyond Borders*, Toronto.

2010, *2009 Responsibility Report*, Toronto.

2011a, *2010 Responsibility Report*, Toronto.

2011b, *2011 First Quarter Report*, www.barrick.com/Theme/Barrick/files/docs_annualquarterly/2011/2011-Q1-Report_v001_u52cd8.pdf (accessed August 19, 2011).

2011c, *Beyond Borders*, (March) Toronto.

2011d, "Statement from Barrick Gold Corporation Concerning the North Mara Mine, Tanzania," (May 31) www.barrick.com/News/PressReleases (accessed June 10, 2011).

Bastida, E., Wälde, T., and Warden-Fernández, J. (eds.), 2005 *International and Comparative Mineral Law and Policy: Trends and Prospects*, The Hague/Frederick, MD: Kluwer Law International.

Baumgartner, F. and Jones, B. D. 1993, *Agendas and Instability in American Politics*, University of Chicago Press.

Benedetto, K. 1999, *Testimony to the Subcommittee on Forests and Public Land Management, Committee on Energy and Natural Resources* (US Senate, May 1999), www.nwi.org/Testimony/testmay99.html.

Berger, S. 1996, "Introduction," in Berger and Dore (eds.), pp. 1–25.

Berger, S. and Dore, R. (eds.) 1996, *National Diversity and Global Capitalism*, Ithaca, NY: Cornell University Press.

Bernstein, S. 2006, "Legitimacy in Global Environmental Governance," *Journal of International Law and International Relations* 1: 139–66.

Bernstein, S. and Cashore, B. 2007, "Can Non-State Global Governance be Legitimate? An Analytical Framework," *Regulation and Governance* 1: 347–71.

Bernstein, S. and Coleman, W. D. (eds.) 2009, *Unsettled Legitimacy: Political Community, Power and Authority in a Global Era*, Vancouver: UBC Press.

Bernstein, S. and Pauly, L. 2007, *Global Liberalism and Political Order: Toward a New Grand Compromise?*, New York: State University of New York Press.

Billette, R. and Robertson, J. D. 1994, "The Integration of Environmental Factors in All Phases of a Mine," paper presented in Caracas, September 30.

Bird, F. 2004, "Ethical Reflections on the Challenges Facing International Businesses in Developing Areas" in F. Bird and S. Herman (eds.), *International Businesses and the Challenges of Poverty in the Developing World*, Hampshire/New York: Palgrave Macmillan, pp. 14–33.

Boardman, R. 1992, "The Multilateral Dimension: Canada in the International System" in R. Boardman (ed.), *Canadian Environmental*

Policy: Ecosystems, Politics and Process, Toronto: Oxford University Press, pp. 224–45.

Borzel, T. and Risse, T. 2010, "Governance Without a State: Can it Work?," *Regulation & Governance* 4: 113–34.

Brehaut, H. 1991, "Environmental Management from a Corporate Perspective," paper presented to a session on the management of environmental issues, Canadian Institute of Mining, Metallurgy and Petroleum (CIM), location unknown.

1996, "Responsible Mining: A Key to Sustainable Development," paper presented to the Third Annual Conference on the Latin American Market, November.

Brenton, T. 1994, *The Greening of Machiavelli*, London: Royal Institute of International Affairs.

Buhner, R., Rasheed, A., Rosenstein, J., and Yoshikawa, T. 1998, "Research on Corporate Governance: A Comparison of Germany, Japan and the United States," *Advances in International Comparative Management* 12: 121–55.

Burton, B. 2005, "Canadian Firm Admits to Killings at PNG Gold Mine," www.ipsnews.net/news.asp?idnews=31074 (accessed June 26, 2011).

Business Wire 2002, "Barrick's New Growth Plan," www.barrick.com/News/PressReleases/PressReleaseDetails/2002/BarrickSetsOutNew GrowthPlan172002207261/default.aspx (accessed June 25, 2011).

Buthe, T. 2010, "Private Regulation in the Global Economy: A (P)Review," *Business and Society* 12, 3: 1–38.

Campbell, J. L. 2006, "Institutional Analysis and the Paradox of Corporate Social Responsibility," *American Behavioural Scientist* 49, 7: 925–38.

2007, "Why Would Corporations Behave in Socially Responsible Ways? An Institutional Theory of Corporate Social Responsibility," *Academy of Management Review* 32, 3: 946–67.

Carroll, A. and Buchholtz, A. 2006, *Business and Society: Ethics and Stakeholder Management*, Mason, OH: Thomson South-Western.

Carroll, A. B. 1999, "Corporate Social Responsibility: Evolution of a Definitional Construct," *Business and Society* 38, 3: 268–95.

Cashore, B. 2002, "Legitimacy and the Privatization of Environmental Governance: How Non-State Market-Driven (NSMD) Governance Systems Gain Rule-Making Authority," *Governance* 15: 502–29.

Cashore, B., Auld, G., and Newsom, D. 2004, *Governing Through Markets: Forest Certification and the Emergence of Non-State Authority*, New Haven: Yale University Press.

Chemers, M. M. and Ayman, R. (eds.) 1993, *Leadership Theory and Research: Perspectives and Directions*, San Diego, CA: Academy Press.

Chwieroth, J. 2007, "Testing and Measuring the Role of Ideas: The Case of Neoliberalism in the International Monetary Fund," *International Studies Quarterly* 51: 5–30.

Cioffi-Revilla, C. 1998, "The Political Uncertainty of Interstate Rivalries: A Punctuated Equilibrium Model," in P. F. Diehl (ed.), *The Dynamics of Enduring Rivalries*, Chicago: University of Illinois Press, pp. 64–97.

Clapp, J. 1998, "The Privatization of Global Environmental Governance," *Global Governance* 4: 295–316.

Clark, A. L. 1997, "Emerging Challenges and Opportunities for the Minerals Industry in the 21st Century," paper presented at the Fifth Annual Asia-Pacific Mining Congress, Jakarta, Indonesia.

Clark, A. L. and Clark, J. C. 1999, "The New Reality of Mineral Development: Social and Cultural Issues in Asia and Pacific Nations," *Resources Policy* 25: 189–96.

Coglianese, C. and Lazar, D. 2003, "Management-Based Regulation: Prescribing Private Management to Achieve Public Goals," *Law and Society Review* 37: 691–730.

Coglianese, C. and Nash, J. (eds.) 2006, *Leveraging the Private Sector: Management-Based Strategies for Improving Environmental Performance*. Washington, DC: Resources for the Future.

Cohen, M. 1996, "A New Menu for the Hard-Rock Café: International Mining Ventures and Environmental Cooperation in Developing Countries," *Stanford Environmental Law Journal* 15: 130–86.

Cohen, S. D. 2007, *Multinational Corporations and Foreign Direct Investment: Avoiding Simplicity, Embracing Complexity*, Oxford University Press.

Company A, Executive 1, 1998, "Sustainable Development – the Socialism of the 1990s," notes for the ICME's Communications and Public Policy Committee on the words "Sustainable Development," May 6.

Competitive Enterprise Institute 1995, "The Despairing Optimist," *Newsletter*, August 31.

Compliance Advisor Ombudsman (World Bank) 2002, "Tanzania/Bulyanhulu Project-01-Kankola," www.cao-ombudsman.org/cases/case_detail.aspx?id=113 (accessed June 24, 2011).

2006, *Final Assessment Report: Complaint Regarding the Antamina Mining Project in Huarmey, Peru*, CAO, May 11.

Cooksey, R. W. 2003, "'Learnership' in Complex Organisational Textures," *Leadership and Organization Development Journal* 24, 4: 204–14.

Cooney, J. 1995, "Global Mining: Three Priorities in a Politically Challenging World," paper presented at the Annual International Convention of the Northwest Mining Association, Spokane, Washington, December 4–8.

1998, "Corporate Social Responsibility in the Era of Globalization," paper presented at the Centre for Asia Pacific Initiatives Student Forum, University of Victoria, Victoria, BC, March 18.

2008, "Sustainable Mining and the Oil Sands," paper presented at the Alberta Environment Conference, Calgary.

Cooney, J. and Willson, J. 1997, "Globalization Offers Social Environmental Opportunities," speech given to the Canadian Club, reproduced in *North American Mining* (November): 14–16.

Corcoran, T. 1998, "Corporate Green Turns Red," *Globe and Mail*, March 21.

Corporate Governance, 2008, "Business in Society and the Emerging Global Governance Paradigm," special issue, guest editors, G. Lenssen, D. Arenas, P. Lacy and S. Pickard.

CorpWatch 2007, *Barrick's Dirty Secrets: Communities Worldwide Respond to Goldmining's Impacts*, www.foei.org/en/resources/publications/pdfs/2000–2007/Barrick_final_sml.pdf/view

Council of Canadians 2001, "Canadians Accused of Burying Africans Alive," (September 27) Ottawa: Council of Canadians, www.canadians.org.

Cragg, W. (ed.) 2005, *Ethics Codes, Corporations and the Challenge of Globalization*, London: Edward Elgar Publishing.

Cragg, W. and Greenbaum, A. 2002, "Reasoning about Responsibilities: Mining Company Managers on What Stakeholders are Owed," *Journal of Business Ethics* 39, 3: 319–35.

Crossan, M., Lane, H., and White, R. 1999, "An Organizational Learning Framework: From Intuition to Institution," *Academy of Management Review* 24, 3: 522–37.

Culpeper, R. and Whiteman, G. 1998, "The Corporate Stake in Social Responsibility," in M. Hibler and R. Beamish (eds.), *Canadian Development Report, 1998: Canadian Corporations and Social Responsibility*, Ottawa: The North–South Institute, pp. 14–33.

Cutler, A. C. 2003, *Private Power and Global Authority: Transnational Merchant Law in the Global Political Economy*, Cambridge University Press.

2006, "Transnational Business Civilization, Corporations, and the Privatization of Global Governance" in May (ed.), pp. 199–227.

Cutler, A. C., Haufler, V., and Porter, T. (eds.) 1999, *Private Authority and International Affairs*, Albany: State University of New York Press.

Dalupan, M. C. 2005, "Mining and Sustainable Development: Insights from International Law" in Bastida, Walde, and Warden-Fernandez (eds.), pp. 149–69.

Dando, N. and Swift, T. 2003, "Transparency and Assurance: Minding the Credibility Gap," *Journal of Business Ethics* 44: 195–200.

Danielson, L. J. 2005, "Evolution of Global Standards in the Extractive Sector: The Growing Role of the World Bank Group," in Bastida, Walde and Warden-Fernandez (eds.), pp. 197–216.

Dashwood, H. S. 2005, "Canadian Mining Companies and the Shaping of Global Norms of Corporate Social Responsibility," *International Journal* 60, 4: 977–98.

2007a, "Canadian Mining Companies and Corporate Social Responsibility: Weighing the Impact of Global Norms," *Canadian Journal of Political Science* 40, 1: 129–56.

2007b, "Towards Sustainable Mining: The Corporate Role in the Construction of Global Standards," *Multinational Business Review* 15, 1: 47–65.

2011, "Sustainable Development Norms and Self-Regulation in the Mining Sector," in Sagebien and Lindsay (eds.), pp. 31–46.

2012, "CSR Norms and Organizational Learning in the Mining Sector," *Corporate Governance*, vol. 12, issue 1: 118–38.

Dashwood, H. S. and Puplampu, B. B. 2010, "Corporate Social Responsibility and Canadian Mining Companies in the Developing World: The Role of Organizational Leadership and Learning," *Canadian Journal of Development Studies* 30: 175–96.

Diamond, J. 2005, *Collapse: How Societies Choose to Fail or Succeed*, New York: Viking Press.

Dias, A. K. and Begg, M. 1994, "Environmental Policy for Sustainable Development of Natural Resources: Mechanisms for Implementation and Enforcement," *Natural Resources Forum* 18, 4: 276–86.

DiMaggio, P. and Powell, W. 1991, "The Iron Cage Revisited: Institutional Isomorphism and Collective Rationality," in Powell and DiMaggio (eds.), pp. 63–82.

Dodge, J. 1997, "Reassessing Culture and Strategy: Environmental Improvement, Structure, Leadership and Control," in Welford (ed.), pp. 104–126.

Doering, R. and Runnalls, D. 1993, "Sustainability: The Key to Competitiveness in the 21st Century," *Prosperity and Sustainable Development for Canada: Advice to the Prime Minister*, Ottawa: National Roundtable on the Economy and Environment (NRTEE), March.

Doern, G. B. and Conway, T. 1994, *The Greening of Canada: Federal Institutions and Decisions*, University of Toronto Press.

Doh, J. P. and Guay, T. R. 2006, "Corporate Social Responsibility, Public Policy, and NGO Activism in Europe and the United States: An Institutional-Stakeholder Perspective," *Journal of Management Studies* 43: 47–73.

Donaldson, T. and Preston, L. E. 1995, "The Stakeholder Theory of the Corporations: Concepts, Evidence and Implications," *Academy of Management Review* 20, 1: 65–91.

Dore, R. 2000, *Stock Market Capitalism, Welfare Capitalism: Japan and Germany versus the Anglo-Saxons*, New York: Oxford University Press.

Doremus, P., Keller, W., Pauly, L., and Reich, S. 1999, *The Myth of the Global Corporation*, Princeton University Press.

Downs, A. 1957, *Inside Bureaucracy*, Boston: Little, Brown.

Earthworks/Oxfam America 2004, *Dirty Metals: Mining, Communities and the Environment* (Earthworks/Oxfam America), www.nodirtygold.org/pubs/DirtyMetals.pdf (accessed May 5, 2006).

Echavarria, C. 2004, "Complex Trade-Offs Between the Potential and the Viable" in Echavarria, C. (ed.), *Mining and Sustainable Development Series: Global Processes* Ottawa: International Development Research Centre (IDRC) and Mining Policy Research Initiative (MPRI), pp. 3, 5.

Economist (The), 2008, "Just Good Business: A Special Report on Corporate Social Responsibility," London, January 19, 1–24.

Ecos Corporation, 1998, "The Business Case for Sustainable Development at Placer: A Summary of the Arguments," Ecos Corporation, January.

Eggert, R. G. (ed.) 1994, *Mining and the Environment: International Perspectives on Public Policy*, Washington, DC: Resources for the Future.

Egri, C. P. and Herman, S. 2000, "Leadership in the North American Environmental Sector: Values, Leadership Styles, and Contexts of Environmental Leaders and their Organizations," *Academy of Management Journal* 43: 571–604.

Elkington, 1998, "The Triple Bottom Line: Seven Business Revolutions for the 21st Century," paper presented at the Globe 98 Conference, Vancouver, March 18, www.sustainability.co.uk.

Environmental Mining Council of BC, 1998, *Code of Environmental Conduct for Mining Operators*, September.

Environmental Protection Agency (EPA) 1995, Sector Notebook Project, *Profile of the Metal Mining Industry*, Washington, DC.

Ethical Funds Company (The) 2009, *Proxy Alert* (April 7), Calgary.

Executive 6 (Placer Dome) 1994, (PDI Environmental Group) "Proposed Strategy for Addressing Environmental/Social Issues for Exploration in Developing Countries," internal memo, Placer Dome, September 28.

1995, "The Impact from Omai and a Possible Strategy for Insurance for PDI from Future Similar Events," paper presented to the Public Affairs Round-Up, Vancouver, December.

1998, "Summary of 1998 Sustainable Development Report Development," Vancouver, May.

Eyton, T. 1997, "Sustainable Development: The Concept Theoretically and Practically for Canadian Natural Resources Businesses, with Particular Reference to the Noranda Experience," keynote address delivered to the Corporate Symposium on Sustainable Development, Toronto, June 5.

Falkner, R. 2003, "Private Environmental Governance and International Relations: Exploring the Links," *Global Environmental Politics* 3, 2: 72–87.

Feltmate, B. 2008, "Dr. Frank Frantisak: Reflections on Corporate Sustainable Development," *Corporate Knights* 6, 4: 30–1.

Finnemore, M. 1996, *National Interests in International Society*, Ithaca, NY: Cornell University Press.

Finnemore, M. and Sikkink, K. 1999, "International Norm Dynamics and Political Change," in P. Katzenstein, R. Keohane and S. Krasner (eds.), *Exploration and Contestation in the Study of World Politics*, Cambridge, MA: MIT Press, pp. 247–77.

Fitzpatrick, P., Fonseca, A., and McAllister, M. L. 2011, "From the Whitehorse Mining Initiative Towards Sustainable Mining: Lessons Learned," *Journal of Cleaner Production* 19, 4: 376–84.

Five Winds International 2000, *The Role of Eco-Efficiency: Global Challenges and Opportunities in the 21st Century, Part 2: Industry Case Studies*, Ottawa, May.

Fligstein, N. 1990, *The Transformation of Corporate Control*, Cambridge, MA and London: Harvard University Press.

Fligstein, N. and Freeland, R. 1995, "Theoretical and Comparative Perspectives on Corporate Organization," *Annual Review of Sociology* 21: 21–43.

Flohr, A., Rieth, L., Schwindenhammer, S., and Wolf, K. D. 2010, *The Role of Business in Global Governance: Corporations as Norm-Entrepreneurs*, New York: Palgrave Macmillan.

Florini, A. (ed.) 2000, *The Third Force: The Rise of International Civil Society*, Washington, DC: Japan Center for International Exchange and Carnegie Endowment for International Peace.

Focus Report 1997, "Sustainable Development: Is it Industry's Business?" *Business and the Environment*, February, 2–5.

Fonseca, A. 2010, "How Credible Are Mining Corporations' Sustainability Reports? A Critical Analysis of External Assurance under the Requirements of the International Council on Mining and Metals," *Corporate Social Responsibility and Environmental Management* 17: 355–70.

Foot, R. 1998, "Mining Firm Faces Lawsuits Threat: The Disaster in Spain is Only One of a Series Involving Canadian Mines Around the Globe," *Vancouver Sun*, April 28.

Forbes, L. C. and Jermier, J. M. 2002, "The Institutionalization of Voluntary Organizational Greening and the Ideals of Environmentalism: Lessons about Official Culture from Symbolic Organization Theory," in A. Hoffman and M. Ventresca (eds.), *Organizations, Policy and the Natural Environment: Institutional and Strategic Perspectives*, Stanford University Press, pp. 194–213.

Frantisak, F. 1990, "Environmental Management for 1990s and Beyond," paper presented to the Senior Management Committee, Ontario Hydro, Toronto, March 13.

1998, "Quo Vadis? Where Do We Go From Here?" paper presented to the Canadian Pulp and Paper Association Conference, Montreal, Quebec, January.

Fraser, D. 1997, Address to a group of shareholders on sustainable development, Toronto.

Freeman, R. E. 1984, *Strategic Management: A Stakeholder Approach*, Boston, MA: Pitman.

Friedman, M. 1970, "The Social Responsibility of Business is to Increase its Profits," *New York Times Magazine*, September 13, pp. 32–3.

Frynas, G., Beck, M., and Mellahi, K. 2000, "Maintaining Corporate Dominance after Decolonization: The 'First Move Advantage' of Shell-BP in Nigeria," *Review of African Political Economy* 27, 85: 407–25.

Fuchs, D. 2007, *Business Power in Global Governance*, Boulder, CO: Lynne Rienner Publishers.

Galaskiewicz, J. 1991, "Making Corporate Actors Accountable: Institution-Building in Minneapolis-St. Paul," in Powell and DiMaggio (eds.), pp. 293–310.

Gale Group 2007, *Encyclopedia of Global Industries*, 4th edn, Detroit: Thomson Gale.

Garvin, D. A. 1993, "Building a Learning Organization," *Harvard Business Review* (July–August), 79–91.

George, A. and Bennett, A. 2004, *Case Studies and Theory Development*, Cambridge, MA: MIT Press.

Gersick, C. 1991, "Revolutionary Change Theories: A Multilevel Explanation of the Punctuated Equilibrium Paradigm," *Academy of Management Review* 16, 1: 10–36.

Givel, M. 2006, "Punctuated Equilibrium in Limbo: The Tobacco Lobby and US State Policymaking from 1990 to 2003," *Policy Studies Journal* 34, 3: 405–18.

Goldstuck, A. and Hughes, T. 2010, "Securing a Social Licence to Operate? From Stone Age to New Age Mining in Tanzania," *Governance of Africa's Resources Programme* 7: 69–74.

Global Reporting Initiative (GRI) 2006, *Sustainability Reporting Guidelines, Version 3.0*. Amsterdam: GRI.

2007, *Mining and Metals Sector Supplement*, Amsterdam: Global Reporting Initiative. www.globalreporting.org (accessed June 10, 2010).

Government of Canada 1976-7, *James Bay and Northern Quebec Native Claims Settlement Act 32* (assented to July 14, 1977) http://laws-lois. justice.gc.ca/eng/acts/J-0.3/FullText.html

2005, *Government Response to the 14th Report of the Standing Committee on Foreign Affairs and International Trade*, www2.parl.gc. ca/HousePublications/Publication.aspx?DocId=2030362&Language=E &Mode=1&Parl=38&Ses=1 (accessed May 8, 2012).

2009, "Building the Canadian Advantage: A CSR Strategy for the Canadian International Extractive Sector," www.international.gc.ca/trade-agree ments-accords-commerciaux/ds/csr-strategy-rse-stategie.aspx?view=d (accessed August 21, 2011).

Government of Quebec 1975, *James Bay and Northern Quebec Agreement and Complementary Agreements* (1998 edn), http.//www3.publications duquebec.gouv.qc.ca/produits/conventions/lois/loiz.fr.html

Grande, E. and Pauly, L. 2005, *Complex Sovereignty: Reconstituting Political Authority in the Twenty-First Century*, University of Toronto Press.

Greenpeace 2003, *Noranda: From Canada to Patagonia, A Life of Crime*, Amsterdam, www.greenpeace.org/international/en/publications/reports/ noranda-from-canada-to-patago

Gunningham, N. 2008, "Occupational Health and Safety, Worker Participation and the Mining Industry in a Changing World of Work," *Economic and Industrial Democracy* 29: 336-61.

Gunningham, N., Kagan, R. A., and Thornton, D. 2003, *Shades of Green: Business, Regulation, and Environment*, Stanford University Press.

Gunningham, N. and Sinclair, D. 2009, "Organizational Trust and the Limits of Management-Based Regulation," *Law and Society Review* 43, 4: 865-99.

Guthrie, J. and Parker, L. D. 1990, "Corporate Social Disclosure Practice: A Comparative International Analysis," *Advances in Public Interest Accounting* 3: 159-75.

Haas, P. 1990, *Saving the Mediterranean*, New York: Columbia University Press.

1992, "Introduction: Epistemic Communities and International Policy Coordination," *International Organization* 46: 1-35.

Halifax Initiative Coalition 2003, *Seven Deadly Secrets: What the Export Development Canada Does Not Want You to Know* (NGO Working Group on the EDC), www.miningwatch.ca/en/seven-deadly-secrets-about-export.development-canada-does-not-want-you-know

Hall, P. 1997, "The Role of Interests, Institutions, and Ideas in the Comparative Political Economy of the Industrialized Nations," in I. L. Mark and S. Z. Alan (eds.), *Comparative Politics: Rationality, Culture and Structure*, Cambridge University Press, pp. 174–207.

Hall, P. and Taylor, R. 1996, "Political Science and the Three New Institutionalisms," *Political Studies*, 44: 936–57.

Hall, R. B. and Biersteker, T. J. (eds.) 2002, *The Emergence of Private Authority in Global Governance*, Cambridge University Press.

Halme, M. 2002, "Corporate Environmental Paradigms in Shift: Learning During the Course of Action at UPM-Kajaani," *Journal of Management Studies* 39, 8: 1087–109.

Hamann, R. 2003, "Mining Companies' Role in Sustainable Development: the 'Why' and 'How' of Corporate Social Responsibility from a Business Perspective," *Development Southern Africa* 20, 2: 237–54.

Hamann, R., Kapelus, P., and O'Keefe, E. 2011. "Mining Companies and Governance in Africa," in Sagebien and Lindsay (eds.), pp. 260–76.

Hansen, P. 1991, "BC Round Table on the Environment and the Economy: An Update on Sustainable Development and Reclamation," report prepared for the British Columbia Mine Reclamation Symposium, http://circle.ubc.ca/handle/2429/12560 (accessed July 2, 2011).

Hardy, C., Phillips, N., and Lawrence, T. B. 2003, "Resources, Knowledge, and Influence: The Organizational Effects of Interorganizational Collaboration," *Journal of Management Studies* 40, 2: 321–47.

Hart, S. L. and Ahuja, G. 1996, "Does it Pay to be Green? An Empirical Examination of the Relationship between Emission Reduction and Firm Performance," *Business Strategy and the Environment* 5, 1: 30–7.

Haufler, V. 1999, "Self-Regulation and Business Norms: Political Risk, Political Activism," in Cutler, Haufler, and Porter (eds.), pp. 199–221.

2001, *A Public Role for the Private Sector: Industry Self-Regulation in a Global Economy*, Washington, DC: Carnegie Endowment for International Peace.

2010, "Corporations in Zones of Conflict: Issues, Actors and Institutions," in Avant et al. (eds.), pp. 102–30.

Heaps, T. 2006, "The Acid Rain Formula," *Corporate Knights* 5, 1: 16–17.

Hedberg, B. 1981, "How Organizations Learn and Unlearn," in P. C. Nystrom and W. H. Starbuck (eds.), *Handbook of Organizational Design, Vol. 1: Adapting Organizations to their Environments*, New York and London: Oxford University Press, pp. 3–27.

Hemingway, C. and Maclagan, P. 2004, "Manager's Personal Values as Drivers of Corporate Social Responsibility," *Journal of Business Ethics* 50: 33–44.

Henao, L. D., 2010, "Argentine Lawmakers Pass Glacier Law to Curb Mining," www.protestbarrick.net/article.php?id=638 (accessed July 10, 2011).

Hoffman, A. 1997, *From Heresy to Dogma: An Institutional History of Corporate Environmentalism*, San Francisco, CA: New Lexington Press. Reprint 2001 (page references are to the original edition).

Howard, J., Nash, J., and Ehrenfeld, J. 1999, "Industry Codes as Agents of Change: Responsible Care Adoption by Chemical Companies," *Business Strategy and the Environment* 8, 5: 281–95.

Howard-Grenville, J. A. 2006, "Inside the 'Black Box': How Organizational Culture and Subcultures Inform Interpretations and Actions on Environmental Issues," *Organization and Environment* 19, 1: 46–73.

Howard-Grenville, J. A. and Hoffman, A. 2003, "The Importance of Cultural Framing to the Success of Social Initiatives in Business," *Academy of Management Executive* 17, 2: 70–84.

Huang, J., Newell, S., Galliers, R., and Pan, S. 2003, "Dangerous Liaisons? Component-Based Development and Organizational Subcultures," *IEEE Transactions on Engineering Management* 50: 89–99.

Human Rights Watch 2011, "Gold's Costly Dividend: Human Rights Impacts of Papua New Guinea's Porgera Gold Mine," www.hrw.org/node/95776 (accessed May 8, 2012).

ICMM, 2003a, International Council on Mining and Minerals, "About ICMM – Work Programme," www.icmm.com/our-work, last updated June 9, 2005.

2003b, International Council on Mining and Minerals, "ICMM Sustainable Development Framework: ICMM Principles," www.icmm.com/our-work/sustainable-development-framework, last updated June 9, 2005.

2005, "GMI," www.icmm.com/about-us/icmm-history (accessed July 22, 2005).

Idemudia, U. 2007, "Community Perceptions and Expectations: Reinventing the Wheels of Corporate Social Responsibility Practices in the Nigerian Oil Industry," *Business and Society Review* 112, 3: 369–405.

International Council on Metals and the Environment (ICME) 1993–4, *Environmental Charter*, reproduced in *ICME Newsletter* 1, 1: 4–5.

1994, *ICME Newsletter* 1, 1: 4–5.

1995a, Environmental Stewardship Committee, minutes of meeting, London, October 23.

1995b, "Forward," Workshop on Environmental Risk Assessment: Presentations and Recommended Actions, London, October 24.

1998a, *Environmental Charter*. Ottawa, ICME.

1998b, *ICME Newsletter* 6, 2.

2000, *Sustainable Development Charter*, Ottawa: ICME.

International Cyanide Management Code (ICMC), "Signatory Companies," www.cyanidecode.org/signatory_barrickgold.php (accessed August 21, 2011).

International Finance Corporation (IFC), 2006, *Performance Standards on Social and Environmental Sustainability* (IFC), www.ifc.org/wps/wcm/connect/topics_ext_content/ifc_external_corporate_site/ifc+sustainability/publications/publications_handbook_pps.

International Organization for Standardization (ISO), *Origins and ISO/TC 207*, www.iso.org/iso/iso_catalogue/management_and_leadership_standards/environmental_management/origins_and_iso_tc207.htm (accessed May 8, 2012).

Jacobs, D. and Getz, K. 1995, "Dialogue on the Stakeholder Theory of the Corporation: Concepts, Evidence, and Implications," *Academy of Management Review* 20, 4: 793–5.

Jenkins, H. 2004, "Corporate Social Responsibility and the Mining Industry: Conflicts and Constructs," *Corporate Social Responsibility and Environmental Management* 11, 1: 23–34.

Jenkins, H. and Yakovleva, N. 2006, "Corporate Social Responsibility in the Mining Industry: Exploring Trends in Social and Environmental Disclosure," *Journal of Cleaner Production* 14: 271–84.

Jermier, J., Slocum, J., Fry, L., and Gaines, J. 1991, "Organizational Subcultures in a Soft Bureaucracy: Resistance Behind the Myth and Façade of an Official Culture," *Organization Science* 2: 170–94.

Kairos (Canadian Ecumenical Justice Initiatives) 2002, *Principles for Global Corporate Responsibility: Bench Marks for Measuring Business Performance*, Toronto.

Katzenstein, P. J. (ed.) 1996, *The Culture of National Security: Norms and Identity in World Politics*, New York: Columbia University Press.

Keck, M. and Sikkink, K. 1998, *Activists Beyond Borders: Advocacy Networks in International Politics*, Ithaca, NY and London: Cornell University Press.

Kennedy, D. 1996, "Porgera: Arsenic and Gold," *Mining Monitor*, Sydney, May: 1–2.

Keohane, R. O. 2008, "Exploring the Governance Agenda of Corporate Responsibility: Complex Accountability and Power in Global Governance: Issues for Global Business," *Corporate Governance* 8, 4: 361–7.

King, A. and Lenox, M. 2000, "Industry Self-Regulation Without Sanction: The Chemical Industry's Responsible Care Program," *Academy of Management Journal* 43, 4: 698–716.

King, G., Keohane, R. O., and Verba, S. 1994, *Designing Social Inquiry*, Princeton University Press.

Kingdon, J. 1995, *Agendas, Alternatives and Public Policies*, 2nd edn, New York: HarperCollins.

Kirton, J. and Trebilcock, M. (eds.) 2004, *Hard Choices, Soft Law: Voluntary Standards in Global Trade, Environment and Social Governance*, Toronto: Ashgate.

Kollman, K. 2008, "The Regulatory Power of Business Norms: A Call for a New Research Agenda," *International Studies Review* (September) 10, 3: 397–419.

Kollman, K. and Prakash, A. 2001, "Green by Choice? Cross-National Variation in Firms' Responses to EMS-Based Environmental Regimes," *World Politics* 53: 399–430.

KPMG 2005, *International Survey of Corporate Responsibility Reporting*, www.kpmg.com/au/Portals/0/kpmg%20survey202005_3.pdf (accessed May 8, 2012).

2006, *Global Mining Reporting Survey 2006*, www.kpmg.ca/en/industries/enr/mining/documents/GMS2006.pdf (accessed March 26, 2010).

Levy, D. and Prakash, A. 2003, "Bargains Old and New: Multinational Corporations in Global Governance," *Business and Politics* 5, 1: 131–50.

Lieberman, M. and Montgomery, D. 1988, "First-Mover Advantages," *Strategic Management Journal* (Summer) 9: 41–58.

Lipschutz, R. 2000, *After Authority: War, Peace and Global Politics in the 21st Century*, Albany: State University of New York Press.

Lumsdaine, D. H. 1993, *Moral Vision in International Politics: The Foreign Aid Regime, 1949–1989*, Princeton University Press.

McAllister, M. L. 2007, "Shifting Foundations in a Mature Staples Industry: A Political Economic History of Canadian Mineral Policy," *Canadian Political Science Review* 1, 1: 73–90.

McAllister, M. L. and Alexander, C. J. 1997, *A Stake in the Future: Redefining the Canadian Mineral Industry*, Vancouver: UBC Press.

McGovern, S. 1998, "Goldberg says Public Confidence in Metal Industry has Weakened," *The Gazette*, May 5: F3.

McGuire, D. and Hutchings, K. 2006, "A Machiavellian Analysis of Organizational Change," *Journal of Organizational Change Management* 19, 2: 192–209.

McKenna, B. 1995, "Environmental Pacts Assailed," *Globe and Mail*, June 16.

MacLean, R. and Rebernak, K. 2007, "Closing the Credibility Gap: The Challenges of Corporate Responsibility Reporting," *Environmental Quality Management* 16, 4: 1–6.

McMillan LLP, 2009, *Mining: The Regulation of Exploration and Extraction in 32 Jurisdictions Worldwide*, Toronto: McMillan LLP.

McNeil, D. 1998, "Zambia Announces Deal to Sell Copper Mines," *New York Times*, December 21.

McNeilly, R. J. (BHP Minerals) 2000, "The Global Mining Initiative: Changing Expectations – Meeting Human Needs and Aspirations," address to the 2000 Minerals Industry Seminar, Minerals Council of Australia, June 7.

McPhail, K. 2008, "Contributing to Sustainable Development Through Multi-Stakeholder Processes: Practical Steps to Avoid the 'Resource Curse,'" *Corporate Governance* 8, 4: 471–81.

Maignan, I and Ralston, D. A. 2002, "Corporate Social Responsibility in Europe and the US: Insights from Businesses' Self-Presentations," *Journal of International Business Studies* 33: 497–514.

March, J. and Olsen, J. 1999, "The Institutional Dynamics of International Political Orders" in P. J. Katzenstein, R.O. Keohane, and S.D. Krasner (eds.), *Exploration and Contestation in the Study of World Politics*, Cambridge, MA: MIT Press.

Margolis, J. D. and Walsh, J. P. 2003, "Misery Loves Companies: Rethinking Social Initiatives by Business," *Academy of Management Review* 28: 268–305.

Maxwell, J. W., Lyon, T. P., and Hackett, S. C. 2000, "Self-Regulation and Social Welfare," *Journal of Law and Economics* 43, 2: 583–617.

May, C. (ed.) 2006, *Global Corporate Power: International Political Economy Yearbook*, Boulder and London: Lynne Rienner Publishers.

Meckling, J. 2011, *Carbon Coalitions: Business, Climate Politics, and the Rise of Emissions Trading*, Cambridge, MA: MIT Press.

Meyer, J. and Rowan, S. 1997, "Institutionalized Organizations: Formal Structure as Myth and Ceremony," *American Journal of Sociology* 83: 340–63.

Miller, C. G. 1997, "The Whitehorse Mining Initiative: A Case Study in Partnerships," in *Management of Commodity Resources in the Context of Sustainable Development: Social Impacts of Mining*, Geneva: UNCTAD

Mineral Policy Center 1999, *Mining Report Card: 14 Steps to Sustainability*, Placer Dome Inc., Washington, DC, July.

Minerals Council of Australia (MCA) 1996, *Code for Environmental Management*, www.minerals.org.au.

Mining Association of Canada (MAC) 1989, *Environmental Policy Statement*, Ottawa.

   2005, *Towards Sustainable Mining: Progress Report 2004*, Ottawa.

   2008, *Towards Sustainable Mining, Progress Report: 2007*, Ottawa.

Mining Journal 1996, "Latin America, Still Emerging," April 19.

Mining, Minerals and Sustainable Development (MMSD) 2002, *Breaking New Ground: Mining, Minerals and Sustainable Development*, London: International Institute for Environment and Development (updated December 6, 2002), www.iied.org/pdfs/9084IIED.pdf (accessed May 29, 2012).

Mining Watch Canada 2003, "Chilean Activist Builds Solidarity with Canadian Noranda Workers, Students, and Politicians," www.mining-watch.ca/chilean-achivist-builds-solidarity-with-canadian-noranda-workers-students-and-politicians (accessed May 8, 2012) June 3.

2006, Open Letter to Chilean President Ricardo Lagos Opposing Approval of Pascua Lama Project (February 7): http//www.miningwatch.ca/open-letter-chilean-president-ricardo-lagos-opposing-approval-pascua-lama-project

2011, "Request for Review: Porgera," March 1, www.miningwatch.ca/sites/miningwatch.ca/files/OECD_Request_for_Review_Porgera_March-1–2011.pdf (accessed July 8, 2011).

Miranda, M., Burris, P., Bingcang, J.F., Shearman, P., Briones, J.O., La Vina, A., and Menard, S. 2003, *Mining and Critical Ecosystems: Mapping the Risks*, Washington DC: World Resources Institute.

Moore, P. 1997, "Hard Choices for Environmentalists and the Mining Industry," paper presented at the Prospectors and Developers Association of Canada Annual Meeting, Toronto, March 10.

Morgan, H. 1998, "The Triple Bottom Line in Practice," *ICME Newsletter* 6, 3.

Natural Resources Canada 2004, *Canadian Minerals Yearbook, 2004*, Ottawa.

2006, *Overview of Trends in Canadian Mineral Exploration*, Ottawa.

Neu, P., Warsame, H., and Pendwell, K. 1998, "Managing Public Impressions: Environmental Disclosures in Annual Reports," *Accounting, Organizations and Society* 23, 3: 265–82.

New Directions Group, "History of the NDG": www.newdirectionsgroup.org/about/history/php (accessed July 29, 2008).

Noranda Inc./Falconbridge, Ltd. 2003, *2002 Sustainable Development Report*, Toronto.

2004, *2003 Sustainable Development Report*, Toronto.

Noranda (Minerals) Inc. 1991, *1990 Environmental Report*, Toronto.

1992, *1991 Environmental Report*, Toronto.

1993, *1992 Environmental Report*, Toronto.

1994, *1993 Environmental Report*, Toronto.

1995, *1994 Environment, Health and Safety Report*, Toronto.

1996a, *1995 Environment, Health and Safety Report*, Toronto.

1996b, *Environment 2000 Plus*, Toronto.

1997, *1996 Environment, Health and Safety Report*, Toronto.

1998, *1997 Environment, Health and Safety Report*, Toronto.

1999a, *1998 Environment, Safety and Health Report*, Toronto.

1999b, *Code of Ethics*, Toronto.

Noranda Inc. 2000, *1999 Sustainable Development Report*, Toronto.

2002, *2001 Sustainable Development Report*, Toronto.

Northhouse, P. G. 1997, *Leadership: Theory and Practice*, Thousand Oaks, CA: Sage.

North–South Institute, 1998, *Canadian Development Report: Canadian Corporations and Social Responsibility*, Ottawa.

Northwest Ethical Investments 2010, "Investing to Make a Difference. Corporate Engagement Report: Barrick Gold Corporation," (September 2010), www.neiinvestments.com/NEIFiles/PDFs/4.0%20Advisor% 20Tools_ESG_Corporate%20Engagement/Corporate%20Engagement %20Reports/Corporate%20Engagement%20Barrick_EN.pdf (accessed August 17, 2011).

2010b, "Turn SRI into $RI," www.neiinvestments.com/Pages/ethical-funds.aspx (accessed August 17, 2011).

O'Brien, R., Goetz, A. M., Scholte, J. A., and Williams, M. (eds.) 2000, *Contesting Global Governance: Multilateral Economic Institutions and Global Social Movements*, Cambridge University Press.

Ohmae, K, 1991, *The Borderless World*, New York: Harper.

Olson, M. 1965, *The Logic of Collective Action: Public Goods and the Theory of Groups*, Cambridge, MA: Harvard University Press.

Orlitzky, M., Schmidt, F. L., and Rynes, L. S. 2003, "Corporate Social and Financial Performance: A Meta-Analysis," *Organization Studies* 24: 403–41.

Ostrom, E. 1990, *Governing the Commons: Evolution of Institutions for Collective Action*, Cambridge University Press.

2000, "Collective Action and the Evolution of Social Norms," *Journal of Economic Perspectives* 108: 137–58.

Palan, R. 2000, *Global Political Economy: Contemporary Theories*, London: Routledge.

Pattberg, P. 2005, "The Institutionalization of Private Governance: How Business and Nonprofit Organizations Agree on Transnational Rules," *Governance* 18, 4: 589–610

Patterson, K. 2006, "Gold's Lustre Tarnished by Ecologically Hazardous Mining, Say Critics," (February 12) Toronto: CanWest News Service.

Pauly, L. W. and Reich, S. 1997, "National Structures and Multinational Corporate Behaviour: Enduring Differences in the Age of Globalization," *International Organization* 51, 1: 1–30.

People's Gold Summit 1999, "Statement of Unity," California: San Juan Ridge, California, June 2–8, rainforestinfo.org.au/gold/platform.htm (accessed May 8, 2012).

Peters, A., Keochlin, L., Forster, T., and Zinkernagel, G. 2009, *Non-State Actors as Standard Setters*, Cambridge University Press.

Pierson, P. 2004, *Politics in Time: History, Institutions, and Social Analysis*, Princeton and Oxford: Princeton University Press.

Pierson, P. and Skocpol, T. 2002, "Historical Institutionalism in Contemporary Political Science," in I. Katznelson and H. Milner (eds.), *Political Science: The State of the Discipline*, New York and Washington, DC: Norton, pp. 693–721.

Placer Dome Inc. 1990a, *Environmental Policy Statement*, Vancouver.

1990b, *Environmental Management*, Vancouver.

1994, *Environmental Policy Statement*, Vancouver.

1995, *Mission Statement*, Vancouver.

1997, *Summary Report of the 1997 Public Affairs Round-Up*, presentation summaries of Manager 3 and Manager 4, Vancouver (May 8).

1998a, *Sustainability Policy*, Vancouver.

1998b, email exchange, from Executive 6, Placer Dome to Executive 2, Placer Dome, and Gary Nash, President, ICME, February 14, 1998.

1999, *It's About Our Future: 1998 Sustainability Report*, Vancouver.

2000, *1999 Sustainability Report*, Vancouver.

2001, *2000 Sustainability Report*, Vancouver.

2002, *2001 Sustainability Report*, Vancouver.

2003, *2002 Sustainability Report*, Vancouver.

2004a, *2003 Sustainability Report*, Vancouver.

2004b, *Sustainability Charter*, Vancouver.

2005a, *2004 Annual Report*, Vancouver.

2005b, *2004 Sustainability Report*, Vancouver.

2005c, *Communication Brief on Our Safety Strategies*, Vancouver.

Placer Pacific Ltd. 1998a, *Proceedings of the "Sustainable Development Report and Indicators Workshop,"* Sydney, Australia (20 February).

1998b, *Taking on the Challenge: Towards Sustainability, 1997 Progress Report*.

Porter, M. 1991, "America's Green Strategy," *Scientific American* 264, 4: 168.

Porter, M. and van der Linde, C. 1995, "Toward a New Conception of the Environment-Competitiveness Relationship," *Journal of Economic Perspectives* 9, 4: 97–118.

Porter, T. 2005, "The Private Production of Public Goods: Private and Public Norms in Global Governance," in Grande and Pauly (eds.), pp. 217–37.

Potoski, M. and Prakash, A. 2005, "Covenants with Weak Swords: ISO 14001 and Facilities' Environmental Performance," *Journal of Policy Analysis and Management* 24, 4: 745–69.

Powell, W. and DiMaggio, P. (eds.) 1991, *The New Institutionalism in Organizational Analysis*, Chicago University Press.

Prakash, A. 2000, *Greening the Firm: The Politics of Corporate Environmentalism*, Cambridge University Press.

Prakash, A. and Potoski, M. 2007a, "Investing Up: FDI and the Cross-Country Diffusion of ISO 14001 Management Systems," *International Studies Quarterly* 51: 723–44.

2007b, "Collective Action Through Voluntary Environmental Programs: A Club Theory Perspective," *Policy Studies Journal* 35, 4: 773–92.

Price, R. 2003, "Transnational Civil Society and Advocacy in World Politics," *World Politics* 55: 579–606.

PricewaterhouseCoopers (PWC) 2004, *Mine: Review of Global Trends in the Mining Industry*, Johannesburg: PWC.

Prince, W. and Nelson, D. 1996, "Developing an Environmental Model: Piecing Together the Growing Diversity of International Environmental Standards and Agendas Affecting Mining Companies," *Colorado Journal of International Environmental Law and Policy* 7: 247–92.

Pring, G. W. 1999, "International Law and Mineral Resources," paper prepared for *Mining, Environment and Development*, a series of papers prepared for UNCTAD.

Protest Barrick 2010, "Huascoaltino Claim is admitted by the Inter-American Commission on Human Rights" (February), http://protestbarrick.net/ article.php?id=570 (accessed July 10, 2011).

Rees, J. 1997, "The Development of Communitarian Regulation in the Chemical Industry," *Law and Policy* 19, 4: 477–528.

Regent, A. 2011, "Barrick Gold and North Mara: The Search for Common Ground,' *Globe and Mail*, www.theglobeandmail.com/news/opinions/ opinion/barrick-gold/and-north-mara-the-search-for-common-ground/ article206932 (accessed June 22, 2011).

Resource Futures International 1997, *Placer Dome's Public Affairs Round Up: Sustainable Development Workshop – Results*, Ottawa, April 17.

Risse, T., Ropp, S. C., and Sikkink, K. (eds.) 1999, *The Power of Human Rights: International Norms and Domestic Change*, Cambridge University Press.

Roe, M. J. 2003, *Political Determinants of Corporate Governance: Political Context, Corporate Impact*, New York: Oxford University Press.

Ruggie, J. G. 1998, *Constructing the World Polity: Essays on International Institutionalization*, London and New York: Routledge.

2002, "The Theory and Practice of Learning Networks: Corporate Social Responsibility and the Global Compact," *Journal of Corporate Citizenship* 5: 27–36.

2004, "Reconstituting the Global Public Domain – Issues, Actors, and Practices," *European Journal of International Relations* 10, 4: 499–531.

2008, *Protect, Respect and Remedy: A Framework for Business and Human Rights. Report of the Special Representative of the Secretary-General (SRSG) On the Issue of Human Rights and Transnational Corporations and Other Business Enterprises*, UN Doc. A/HRC/8/5. www.unhcr.org/refworld/docid/484d2d5f2.html (accessed February 10, 2010).

Russo, M. V. and Fouts, P. A. 1997, "A Resource-Based Perspective on Corporate Environmental Performance and Profitability," *Academy of Management Journal* 40: 534–59.

Sagebien, J. and Lindsay, N. (eds.) 2011, *Corporate Social Responsibility and Governance Ecosystems: Emerging Patterns in the Stakeholder Relationships of Canadian Mining Companies Operating in Latin America*, New York: Palgrave-Macmillan.

Salop, S. C., and Scheffman, D. T. 1983, "Raising Rivals' Costs," *American Economic Review* 73, 2: 267–71.

Sanchez, L. E. 1998, "Industry Response to the Challenge of Sustainability: The Case of Canadian Nonferrous Mining Sector," *Environmental Management* 22, 4: 521–31.

Saunders S. 2009, "Norway Finds Canada's Largest Publicly-Traded Company, Barrick Gold, Unethical', CorpWatch, www.corpwatch.org/article.php?id=15286 (accessed June 23, 2011).

Schaferhoff, M., Campe, S., and Kaan, C. 2009, "Transnational Public–Private Partnerships in International Relations: Making Sense of Concepts, Research Frameworks and Results," *International Studies Review* 11, 3: 457–74.

Scharpf, F. 1997, *Games Real Actors Play: Actor-Centered Institutionalism in Policy Research*, Boulder, CO: Westview Press.

Schertow, J. A. 2009, "Western Shoshone Prevail at Ninth Circuit Court on Mining Sacred Land," December 6 http://intercontinentalcry.org/western-shoshone-prevail-at-ninth-circuit-court-on-mining-sacred-land/ (accessed July 7, 2011).

Schneiberg, M. 1999, "Political and Institutional Conditions for Governance by Association: Private Order and Price Controls in American Fire Insurance," *Politics and Society* 27, 1: 67–103.

Scholte, J. A. 2000, *Globalization: A Critical Introduction*, Houndmills, Basingstoke and New York: Palgrave-Macmillan.

Scott, P. 2000, "Reporting in the Mining Sector," *Mining Environmental Management* 8, 2: 10–12.

Scott, R. W. and Meyer, J. W. (eds.) 1994, *Institutional Environment and Organizations: Structural Complexity and Individualism*, Thousand Oaks, CA: Sage.

Sell, S. and Prakash, A. 2004, "Using Ideas Strategically: The Context Between Business and NGO Networks in Intellectual Property Rights," *International Studies Quarterly* 48: 143–75.

Senge, P. 1990, "The Leader's New Work: Building the Learning Organisation," *Sloan Management Review* 23: 1–17.

Senior Director, CSR 2008, "Barrick Gold Corporation: Achieving the Benefits of Mining," Toronto (February 29).

Sethi, S. P. 2005, "The Effectiveness of Industry-Based Codes in Serving Public Interest: the Case of the International Council on Mining and Metals," *Transnational Corporations* 14, 3: 55–99.

Sethi, S. P. and Elango, B. 1999, "The Influence of 'Country of Origin' on Multinational Corporation Global Strategy: A Conceptual Framework," *Journal of International Management* 5: 285–98.

Sharma, S. 2000, "Managerial Interpretations and Organizational Context as Predictors of Corporate Choice of Environmental Strategy," *Academy of Management Journal* 43, 4: 681–97.

Sharma, S. and Vredenburg, H. 1998, "Proactive Corporate Environmental Strategy and the Development of Competitively Valuable Organizational Capabilities," *Strategic Management Journal* 19: 729–53.

Slack, J. 2009, "Derailment Changed our History," November 10, www.mis sissauga.com/news/article/161133-train-derailment-changed-our-history (accessed October 3, 2011).

Sloan, P. 1999, *Placer Dome's Policy on Sustainability: Teaching Case*, National Management Education Project in Business and the Environment, Schulich School of Business, York University, Toronto, Canada.

Smith, S. 1995, "Ecologically Sustainable Development: Integrating Economics, Ecology, and Law," *Willamette Law Review* 31: 251–305.

Stacey, R. D. 2000, *Strategic Management and Organisational Dynamics: The Challenge of Complexity*, 3rd edn, Hemel Hempstead: Prentice-Hall.

Standing Committee on Foreign Affairs and International Trade (SCFAIT) 2005, *Report on Mining in Developing Countries and Corporate Social Responsibility*, www.parl.gc.ca/HousePublications/Publication.aspx? DocId=1901089&Language=E&Mode=1&Parl=38&Ses=1 (accessed May 8, 2012).

Stigson, B. (World Business Council for Sustainable Development) 1998, "Sustainable Business: Performing Against the Triple Bottom Line," *ICME Newsletter* 6, 3: 1.

Strange, S. 1996, *The Retreat of the State: The Diffusion of Power in the World Economy*, Cambridge University Press.

Stueck, W. 2009, "Chasing Prices, Losing Sleep," *Globe and Mail*, April 19: B18.

Suchman, M. C. 1995, "Managing Legitimacy: Strategic and Institutional Approaches," *Academy of Management Review* 20, 3: 571–610.

Supreme Court of Canada 1973, *Kanatewat v. James Bay Development Corp.*, 1.S.C.R. 48.

Szablowski, D. 2007, *Transnational Law and Local Struggles: Mining Communities and the World Bank*, Oxford University Press.

Taskforce on the Churches and Corporate Responsibility (TCCR) 1998, *Taskforce Memorandum: 10 March 1998 Meeting with Placer Dome Officials*, Toronto, March 10.

Tauli-Corpuz, V. and Kennedy, D. 2001, "An Activist Perspective on the Mining, Minerals and Sustainable Development Initiative," Project Underground, by permission of *Cultural Survival Quarterly*, 2001.

Taylor, D., Sulalaman, M., and Sheahan, M. 2001, "Auditing of Environmental Management Systems: A Legitimacy Theory Perspective," *Managerial Auditing Journal* 16, 7: 411–22.

Taylor, S. P. 2004, "Whose Rules? Forget the Feel-Good Homilies. There's No Win-Win-Win When Activists, Canada's Second-Largest Gold Company and an Indigenous People Battle to Define Social Responsibility," *National Post Business* (August): 24.

Thauer, C. 2009, "Corporate Social Responsibility in the Regulatory Void – Does the Promise Hold? Self-Regulation by Business in South Africa and China," unpublished PhD thesis, European University Institute, Florence.

Northern Miner 1998, "Editorial and opinion: Tailings Management Critical for Miners," *Northern Miner* (December 21–7) 84, 43: 4.

Thelen, K. 1999, "Historical Institutionalism in Comparative Politics," *American Review of Political Science* 2: 369–404.

Togolo, M. 1999, *Mining and Sustainability: Placer Niugini Ltd*, paper presented at the International Congress on Earth Science, Exploration and Mining around the Pacific Rim, Bali, Indonesia, October 10–13.

United Nations (UN) 2002, *Report of the World Summit on Sustainable Development*, Johannesburg, South Africa, August 26–September 4.

1996, *Expert Mission Assessment Report*, September.

2001, *The Role of Financial Institutions in Sustainable Mineral Development*, Paris: UNEP, Division of Technology, Industry and Economics.

United Nations Economic Commission for Europe (UNECE) 1979, *Geneva Convention on Long-Range Transboundary Air Pollution*, Geneva –

Aarhus Protocol on Heavy Metals, Aarhus, Denmark (1998). (Reference is to the 1998 protocol.)

United Nations Educational, Scientific and Cultural Organisation (UNESCO) 1972, *Convention Concerning the Protection of the World Cultural and Natural Heritage*, Paris.

United Nations Environment Program (UNEP) 1989, *Basel Convention on the Control of Transboundary Movements of Hazardous Wastes and their Disposal*, Basel, Switzerland.

1992, *Convention on Biological Diversity*, Nairobi.

US Census Bureau 2009, "Statistical Abstract: Natural Resources and Energy," Washington, DC.

Van Maanen J. and Barley, S. R. 1984, "Occupational Communities: Culture and Control in Organizations," *Research in Organizational Behaviour* 6: 287–365.

Vietor, R. H. K. 2002, *Noranda Inc.: Mining, Smelting and Sustainability?* Boston: Harvard Business School Publishing, Case No. N9–702–009.

Vogel, D. 2005, *The Market for Virtue: The Potential and Limits of Corporate Social Responsibility*, Washington, DC: Brookings Institution Press.

Voluntary Principles on Security and Human Rights, "Voluntary Principles Framework for Admission of New Companies," www.voluntaryprinciples.org/files/VPs_Company_Entry_Criteria_Final_127001_v1_FHE-DC.PDF (accessed August 21, 2011).

Waddock, S. A. and Boyle, M. 1995, "The Dynamics of Change in Corporate Community Relations," *California Management Review* 37, 4: 125–40.

Walde, T. 1992, "Environmental Policies Towards Mining in Developing Countries," *Journal of Energy and Natural Resources Law* 10, 4: 327–51.

2005, "International Standards: A Professional Challenge for Natural Resources and Energy Lawyers" in E. Bastida, T. Walde, and J. Warden-Fernandez (eds.), *International and Comparative Mineral Law and Policy: Trends and Prospects*, The Hague/Frederick, MD: Kluwer Law International, pp. 219–47.

Wapner, P. 1995, "Politics Beyond the State: Environmental Activism and World Civic Politics," *World Politics* 47: 311–40.

Warhurst, A. 1992, "Environmental Management in Mining and Mineral Processing in Developing Countries," *Natural Resources Forum* 16, 1: 39–48.

1994, "The Limitations of Environmental Regulation in Mining" in Eggert (ed.), pp. 133–72.

2001, "Corporate Citizenship and Corporate Social Investment: Drivers of Tri-Sector Partnerships" *Journal of Corporate Citizenship* 1: 57–73.

Warner, R. 2006, "The Canadian Environmental Foreign Policy Agenda: Competitiveness Versus Sustainability," in E. Laferriere and P. Stoett (eds.), *International Ecopolitical Theory: Critical Approaches*, Vancouver: UBC Press, pp. 17–33.

World Commission on Environment and Development (WCED) 1987, *Our Common Future*, New York: United Nations.

Weitzner, V. 2010, "Indigenous Participation in Multipartite Dialogues on Extractives: What Lessons Can Canada and Others Share?" *Canadian Journal of Development Studies* 30, 1–2: 87–109.

Welford, R. (ed.) 1997, *Corporate Environmental Management 2: Culture and Organizations*, London: Earthscan Publications.

Wendt, A. 1992, "Anarchy is What States Make of It: The Social Construction of Power Politics," *International Organization* 46, 2: 391–425.

1999, *Social Theory of International Politics*, Cambridge University Press.

Wheeler, D., Colbert, B., and Freeman, R. E. 2003, "Focusing on Value: Reconciling Corporate Social Responsibility, Sustainability and a Stakeholder Approach in a Network World," *Journal of General Management* 28, 3: 1–28.

Willson, J. 1997, *New Frontiers for Placer Dome and the Mining Industry*, paper presented to the 99th Annual General Meeting of the CIM, Vancouver, April 28.

World Bank 2002, *Peru: Country Assistance Evaluation*, Washington, DC: WB Operations Evaluation Department, September 25.

World Business Council for Sustainable Development (WBCSD) 2004, Interview with Sir Robert Wilson, Geneva, 2 September, www.wbcsd. org/plugins/DocSearch/detailsasp?type=DocDet&ObjectID=N2EwNg (accessed October 4, 2004).

World Commission on Environment and Development (WCED) 1987, *Our Common Future*, New York: United Nations.

Yakovleva, N. 2005, *Corporate Social Responsibility in the Mining Industries*, Aldershot, UK and Burlington, VT: Ashgate Publishing.

York, G. 2011a, "Allegations of Sexual Assault a Blow to Barrick and Add Urgency to Miner's Reforms in Lawless Lands," *Globe and Mail*, May 31: A1.

2011b, "In an African Mine, Gold Fever Sparks a Deadly Clash," *Globe and Mail*, June 8: A11.

2011c, "19 Villagers Dead/$155 Million Profit," *Globe and Mail: Report on Business*, October, 24–35.

Young, S. 2005, "Leading Environmental Change: The Case of the Global Mining Industry," *Review of Business* 26, 1: 34–8.

Index

institutional context, 7, 17, 71, 83,
  259, 276
at Placer Dome, 173
Barrick and, 259
Canadian, 89, 218
domestic, 83–4
importance of, 45
in developing countries, 84–6
Noranda and, 134
of headquarter countries, 39
institutionalism, 2, 43, 48
in organization theory, 13, 36, 221,
  254
institutionalization, 67
institutionalizing, process of learning, 57
integrating, process of learning, 57
Inter-American Commission on Human
  Rights, 196
internal factors, 49–52
International Copper Association
  (ICA), 134
International Council on Metals and the
  Environment (ICME), 4, 7, 8, 24,
  35, 59, 221, 222–5, 234, 269
Barrick and, 256, 265
Basel Convention and, 223
CEOs stepping out of, 231, 232
creation of, 222
Environmental Charter, 223, 224,
  225, 227, 228
member education, 224
Placer Dome and, 264
Safe Use of Metals Committee, 224
science-based approaches, 228
sustainable development and, 227, 231
Sustainable Development Charter,
  231, 265
International Council on Mining and
  Metals (ICMM), 4, 7, 8, 13, 22, 24,
  35, 58, 59, 64, 182, 210, 221, 222,
  234, 243, 251, 260
Assurance Process, 206–8, 247
Barrick and, 50, 178, 210, 216, 218,
  243, 244, 245, 256
benefits to non-members, 249
concerns with, 244
creation of, 235
CSR standards of, 274
definition of sustainable development,
  238

free-rider problem, 249
membership, 236, 252
ongoing consultation with NGOs, 236
reporting mechanisms, 238
reporting standards, 247
Resource Endowment initiative, 246
strategy of, 238
sustainable development and, 249
Sustainable Development
  Framework, 182, 211, 238, 239,
  240, 246, 252, 261
sustainable development initiatives,
  237–40
third-party assurance, 239, 252
International Cyanide Management
  Code (ICMC), 170, 182, 211, 243,
  245, 247, 256, 261
International Finance Corporation
  (IFC), 132
Policy and Performance Standards on
  Social and Environmental
  Sustainability, 64, 82, 89, 182, 214,
  237, 240, 247, 250, 268
international financial institutions
  (IFIs), 74
International Institute for Sustainable
  Development (IISD), 162
International Organization for
  Standardization (ISO), 64, 99, 108,
  134, 261, 264
14000 EMS, 98, 224, 241
14001 EMS, 17, 108, 182, 213, 214,
  240, 247
9000, 99
ICME and, 224
Noranda and, 98
Technical Committee on the
  Environment, 108
International Safety/Environmental
  Rating System (ISRS/IERS), 168
International Standard for Assurance
  Engagement (ISAE) ISAE3000
  standard, 239
*International Survey of Corporate
  Responsibility Reporting*
  (KPMG), 8
International Union for the Conservation
  of Nature (IUCN), 114, 162, 236
International Zinc Association (IZA), 134
internet, 141